AF394671

Click. Stalk. Destroy.

Click. Stalk. Destroy.

*Inside the minds of people
who stalk online*

DR JESSICA TAYLOR

CONSTABLE

CONSTABLE

A CIP catalogue record for this book
is available from the British Library.

ISBN: 978-0-34902-261-1

Typeset in Sabon by Hewer Text UK Ltd, Edinburgh
Printed and bound in Great Britain by Clays Ltd, Elcograf, S.p.A.

Papers used by Constable are from well-managed
forests and other responsible sources.

Constable
An imprint of
Little, Brown Book Group
Carmelite House
50 Victoria Embankment
London EC4Y 0DZ

The authorised representative
in the EEA is
Hachette Ireland
8 Castlecourt Centre, Dublin 15,
D15 XTP3, Ireland
(email: info@hbgi.ie)

An Hachette UK Company
www.hachette.co.uk

www.littlebrown.co.uk

Contents

Foreword

Where do I start?

Writing this book has been a strange and complicated journey. In my professional work, I often speak about the complexities of our identities. We are so many people at once. We all are.

But as I planned this book, conducted the research, and then sat down to write it up – one question plagued me.

Is it possible to take up the position of an expert psychologist teaching about stalking – whilst also being a victim of it?

It would be so much easier to be one or the other. I could write the book as Dr Jessica Taylor, the Chartered Psychologist specialising in trauma and abuse. I could maintain an image of an objective professional (whatever that means!). I could talk to you about fascinating studies, trends in data, and the theories of why people engage in such dangerous and abusive behaviours online. I could show you diagrams and tables. I could teach you about policing, prosecution, and laws.

Alternatively, I could write the book as Jess, the woman who was lied about and stalked online and in person, 24 hours a day, for years of her life. The woman who developed crippling fears and phobias. The woman who questioned whether she had slipped into the Twilight Zone. The woman who was framed as delusional and self-obsessed for trying to talk about being stalked. The woman who was a victim in multiple police investigations whilst trying to hold down mother-hood, a career and a marriage. The woman who almost lost her life.

But I am not one or the other. I am both. If I platform one part of myself, I deny the other. If I hide the trauma, the harm, and my personal experiences of being stalked, I only further stigmatise the experiences of victims around the world, who are told not to speak out. If I write a book where I prioritise my career and my professional identity, I teach the millions of women who follow me that they cannot be both capable and a victim of abuse and stalking at the same time.

And so, after much thought, I chose to write a book from both perspectives. I want to role-model our duality and our reality. This book is filled with stories, personal experiences, confessions, and thoughts – but it is also shaped by years of experience working with police and prosecution colleagues, peer-reviewed evidence, decades of theories, interesting data, academic studies, and global reports from some of the best minds in the world when it comes to these topics.

In this book, I take you through the world of online stalking – and into the minds and tactics of stalkers who are utilising the internet as a safe haven for their obsessions and crimes.

My name is Dr Jessica Taylor.

I am a psychologist specialising in trauma, abuse, and stalking.

And I am also a victim of stalking.

A new breed of stalker

Jennifer's phone lit the dark living room up again and again. It was 9:22 pm on a Thursday night.

She had been in back-to-back meetings with clients since 9 am and was exhausted. Her husband was in the kitchen finishing the clean up from dinner. The TV glowed with a frozen scene from the television programme *Bridgerton*, which had been paused now for well over an hour. She reached for her phone immediately and opened up the group chat that she had been added to earlier that evening. A rush of excitement pulsed through her. Anticipation gave her energy and then the seething resentment set back in.

She opened the chat as more notifications popped up.

Anna: *Yeah, totally agree*

Naomi: *We need to expose her for what she really is*

Anna: *She wouldn't like that now, would she?*

Samantha: *Who gives a fuck? What is she gonna do? She won't know it was us*

Jane: *She will know . . . she's not that stupid*

Samantha: *Doesn't matter. She won't be able to prove it. And she probably won't figure it out fast enough. She isn't as smart as she likes to believe*

Jane: *She will probably love the attention, knowing her*

Anna: *True! She is disgustingly self-obsessed. She had this coming for ages. I'm glad us girls are the ones to do it tbh*

Jane: *I've been waiting so long for this. I fucking hate her with a passion*

Naomi: *Girl, same*

Jennifer watched the messages pop up, one by one, with unfettered glee. She had never done anything like this before but had readily accepted the invite when Anna had added her to the new group. She only really knew Anna, but the other women seemed just as committed to this as she was.

At first, she had been worried about joining the group, but Anna had reassured her that everyone was there for the same purpose. And it seemed safe enough. Surely no one was going to expose anyone else as it would be too much of a risk. Everyone was equally implicated, after all. Everyone had jobs and lives to protect. She took another sip of the Shiraz from dinner, being careful not to get caught smirking at her phone.

She took another quick, careful glance over her shoulder. Her husband was still in the kitchen, mumbling along to a song on the radio and not paying any attention.

Anna: *I just hate her ugly face, do you know what I mean? I just want to punch her*

Samantha: *And that fucking fringe. Jesus. Looks like a bloody four-year-old cut it*

Anna: *That's offensive to four-year-olds*

Jane: *It's that face she always pulls in pictures. You can just tell by looking in her eyes what a nasty bitch she truly is behind the scenes*

Naomi: *Oh 100% – she plays this perfect role to the public, but I bet she is absolutely evil behind closed doors*

Jennifer took another sip of wine and flicked over to the Instagram app. She had been watching the profile for weeks. Silently. Carefully. Never engaging. Never commenting or liking anything. Just watching her, hating her more and more each day. She had never wanted someone to suffer so much in her life. And now, it seemed that she had found others who felt the same way.

Samantha: *She is evil. I know people who know her. I could say so much about her – and I will – I'll tell everyone everything. We just need to strategise*

Jane: *I was thinking that we should set up a website about her. If we hide our details behind a fake name, she won't be able to get it taken down*

Naomi: *Easier to just set up fake social media profiles, Jane*

Jane: *Yeah, true. We could do both?*

Samantha: *We can but it's gotta be bigger than that. We have her address, phone numbers, emails, and we know everything about*

*her. Her wife. Her kids. Her family. Her work. Who her friends
are. I know plenty of people who hate her. We could fucking ruin
her*

Jennifer giggled into her glass. Her mind buzzed with wine and exhil-
aration. This was perfect. Beautiful to witness. Finally, someone was
going to take this woman down – and she got to be right at the heart
of it all.

Anna: *I know someone who lives near her too. Sees her all the time in
Asda looking like shit, apparently*

Jane: *Trolley filled with multipacks of her beloved crisps, is it?*

Naomi: *Probably. Don't forget the chavvy Smirnoff Ice and that shitty
Jam Shed wine she drinks!*

Samantha: *No wonder she got so fucking fat and then had to use
filters on all her pictures*

Naomi: *She's gross. How is she only 32? I swear she lies about her
age. The state of her. I mean, I am not being funny but if I looked like
that, I wouldn't be prancing about on Instagram. I look better than
her and I've got 20 years on her*

Anna: *Haha! True! I could ask my friend to find out what else she
knows, actually. Do a bit of digging. She sees her all the time. She says
she goes to a restaurant called La Belle in town, too. She told me that
she walks her dogs across some fields near her house – found the road
name on Google Maps*

Jane: *Like I said, we should dig up more stuff about her and put it
online. I found her house on Rightmove – I'll send you all the link.*

You can see the purchase price and photos of the entire house – it has the room plans on there too

Anna: *Hmm. We need to think bigger. We should have a zoom call. We could plan properly then. Figure out what to do and hit her where it hurts*

Jennifer looked over her shoulder to see where her husband was. She could still hear the faint noises of glasses and plates being stacked over the soft hum of the dishwasher. He knew nothing of the plans – and nothing about the new group. The thrill of the schemes and possibilities surged through her.

She took one last sip from her wine glass, paced the living room in front of the TV that was still paused, and held down her finger to record a hurried voice note to the group.

"I am so glad we have this group, ladies. You are all such wonderful, wonderful women. I am so proud that we have all come together to do this. I have been reading all of your messages, and I am up for all of it. I hate her so much. I can't even put it into words. I say we do everything. Website. Social media. Drop leaflets all over her fucking street. Then we go to the press with stories about her. She won't know it's us, and actually, if she figures it out, I don't even fucking care . . ."

Jennifer paused briefly to catch her breath. She realised that her hushed voice had raised with every sentence and peered slightly into the kitchen to make sure that her husband hadn't heard anything.

As she finished her voice note to the other women, there were tears in her eyes. She was full of a heady mixture of overwhelming excitement and incandescent hatred for a woman she had only met the once for a few minutes.

"I, for one, cannot wait to end this cunt."

* * *

That woman they were planning to take down? That was me.

The reason I know what was said in those private groups is because months later, one day in 2023, one of those women became so concerned by what they were involved in that she chose to tell me – and then showed me everything she had. Up to that day, I had no idea what was happening to me, how it was occurring, or who was behind it all.

The moment that I heard the familiar voice say those final words of the voice note through gritted teeth is burned into my memory. The joy, the rage, the confidence, the deep-seated hatred.

When people hear the word 'stalker', they don't really picture a group of women in a dedicated WhatsApp group, do they?

More often than not, they picture something cinematic. A psychotic man in a car outside a house, watching as a woman comes home from work. A shadow at the end of a driveway, fantasising about murdering their next victim. Flowers left on a doorstep by an obsessed, socially inept weirdo. A rejected lover who cannot let go of his ex – and wants to make sure that no one else can ever have her. Even now – after decades of research, policies, legislation, and high-profile murders – stalking remains romanticised, sexualised, pathologised, minimised, and misunderstood. It is framed as obsession born of love, of madness, heartbreak, or delusion.

Worse still, 'stalking' is now becoming common parlance in the online world. People casually say, "I stalked her on Facebook", or "I still stalk my ex on Instagram all the time!"

In that way, stalking is simultaneously positioned as a common, harmless, everyday thing we all do on social media when we are being a bit nosey – and also a rare, terrifying crime by a stranger that leads to abduction and violent murder.

For me, neither of those framings were particularly helpful – or accurate.

I came to understand stalking from two directions at once. The first was familiar to the criminal justice system: I was stalked and harassed by a man who refused to relinquish control over my life.

The second was something far less visible and far less understood: the digital, obsessive surveillance, harassment, and abuse from a group of women I barely knew – resulting in months of police investigations across multiple police forces and, eventually, court orders for stalking.

These two experiences collided in my life in ways that forced me to confront a reality that our institutions have not caught up with: the nature of stalking has changed. Or perhaps more accurately, stalking has revealed itself in new forms. Obsession, entitlement and grievance have always existed, the internet didn't create them. But our digitalised world has industrialised them.

And as I will explore in this book, perhaps it has even encouraged them.

Stalking, in its simplest definition, is a pattern of unwanted, fixated and intrusive behaviours directed at a specific person that causes fear or distress. But it doesn't help that there is still so much debate and discussion about how to define stalking. Even the words are up for debate. Some call it stalking, others call it harassment. Some call it cyberstalking, others call it online stalking. Online mobbing. Group stalking. Cyberharassment. Online abuse. Trolling.

It is not easy to pull together an evidence base on a crime that appears to have ten names.

I suppose some of this issue may be because online stalking is ever evolving. Someone writes a paper back in the early 2000s about the perils of MSN messenger, and in the blink of an eye, MSN messenger is obsolete, and we are dealing with a completely new threat. Charities warn that people are setting up riots and fights via BlackBerry Messenger, and a few years later, BBM doesn't even exist. It's been taken over by something entirely new.

Academics explore the distant, conceptual dangers of smartphones, and the possibility of children having unfettered access to the internet one day, and now we all have extremely powerful smartphones in our pockets with apps that connect us instantly to millions of strangers – children and toddlers included.

I don't envy the academics attempting to keep up with this area of research. When it comes to online harassment, scholars have described this most recently as an umbrella term which covers trolling, insults, threats, stalking, aggressive communication, doxing and much more – including privacy violations, spreading false information about the victim, calls for death or physical harm, technological harms, mobbing, and coordinated attacks on reputation (Ivask & Lon, 2023; Citron, 2014; Waisbord, 2020).

Previously, the term 'cyberstalking' had been used for many of these same tactics – which was defined as the repeated pursuit to intimidate, control, monitor or harass using electronic means, usually characterised by fixation, repetition, unwanted contact, persistence and fear induction (Kavish & Naidu, 2022; Reyns et al., 2012; Dresing et al., 2014; Piotrowski & Lathrop, 2011).

As you can probably see, that's a pretty huge list of behaviours and actions that has been added to over time and which, despite being lengthy, has been criticised as being too vague and too ambiguous by others (Miller, 2023).

Personally, I am not sure that I agree that it is too vague, I think it is a rather specific list. I just think that we are used to neater and smaller definitions of crimes. The issue with online stalking though, is that the crime is so multi-faceted, varied, and immense that academics and policymakers are struggling to pin it down – especially as rapidly changing technology means that it evolves at a pace that's difficult to keep up with.

Not only is the crime evolving, but so are our populations. Different generations, cultures, education levels, sexes, backgrounds, political and religious beliefs and socioeconomic classes are all mixing together online – and they all have different relationships with the internet. Interestingly, for example, researchers have found that online stalkers tend to be younger, more educated, high performing, and more likely to be professionals than general stalkers (Kaur et al., 2020). Some research into the stalking of professionals in health and social care professions even found that professionals are much more likely to be stalked by their colleagues at work than by their clients or patients (Sheridan et al., 2019).

General stalking has more stable definitions in law, and in literature, generally harking back to Mullen's et al.'s (2001) definitions from the exploration of stalking and stalking typologies – which we will return to later in the book. Stalking is defined as a pattern of repeated and unwanted contacts experienced as intrusion, leading to distress and fear. Mullen et al. (2000) and McKeon et al. (2015) also commented that stalking is 'victim-defined' – meaning that stalking is generally determined by the impact on the victim, rather than the perpetrator's specific actions or their intent. In this way, stalking is quite a unique crime.

What they mean by this is that stalking can be made up of lots of seemingly benign, non-criminal acts – such as visiting an area repeatedly, or sending letters and gifts – none of those things are illegal, but if they are put together and if they are totally unwanted, repetitive and causing the victim psychological and emotional stress – they constitute stalking.

Stalking cannot be a singular act, and so, it is not a misunderstanding, or misplaced admiration, or an expression of romance. It is not fandom gone wrong. Stalking is defined as a course of conduct. It is repeated. It is intentional. And at its core, it is about power. Like all abuse.

Power to intrude, to monitor, to intimidate, to destabilise and sometimes, to punish.

However, one major problem with all of this is that the perceptions of professionals, police officers, friends and family must exactly match those of the victim of stalking if their concerns are to be recognised (Scott et al., 2014) – and so this presents a serious problem. If professionals do not agree, or do not perceive that the actions constitute stalking, the case goes nowhere.

The College of Policing in the UK recently introduced a mnemonic for police officers to use when identifying stalking – as so many cases are missed or wrongly categorised (Suzy Lamplugh Trust, 2022). The mnemonic is simple, effective, and useful and I use it myself in my teaching with police officers and detectives.

According to the College of Policing, stalking behaviours must be FOUR:

F – Fixated

O – Obsessive

U – Unwanted

R – Repetitive

I quite like this simple conceptualisation – it forces the officer to focus on the core of the behaviour, and not the individual incidents, which could easily be minimised or simply dismissed as coincidences. It also helps a victim to feel validated that their experience is in fact stalking, and that they are not exaggerating it, or misunderstanding it.

I guess, when we strip away the mythology and the definitions, stalking could be seen as an extension of coercive control. Coercive control, although widely recognised as domestic abuse, can occur across any domain. In the workplace, in our friendship groups, in our society, in religion, even in politics and media. We are frequently controlled, coerced, manipulated, lied to, intimidated, bullied, and monitored in many domains of our lives. As depressing as it may seem, coercive practices are part of our daily lives, and we are often groomed into decisions, experiences, desires and beliefs. This is so embedded into the fabric of our lives that we barely even notice anymore. It is no wonder that we struggle so much to recognise abuse, stalking, grooming, and violations of ourselves when it is happening all around us.

Stalking certainly bears resemblance to coercive control, which refers to a strategic pattern of behaviour designed to dominate another person by isolating them, undermining their autonomy, regulating their behaviour, and instilling fear (Stark, 2019). I had never really considered this heavy overlap before, but what I have seen and what

I experienced has taught me that coercive control does not necessarily require any intimacy. It only requires fixation, a willingness to gain and a desire to exert power over someone.

The internet has expanded the reach of that power beyond anything our legal systems were built to manage. Before the internet, how could one person possibly have so much power over the portrayal and activities of a stranger's life?

Contrary to some online criticism that calls victims 'snowflakes who can't take any criticism', online stalking is not simply 'trolling on social media'. It is not disagreement, debate or free speech. In line with traditionally defined stalking, it is a pattern of surveillance, monitoring, data harvesting, impersonation, narrative manipulation, humiliation, identity destruction, threat, intimidation, and mob activation carried out through digital platforms. It is the systematic use of the internet and other technologies to track, watch, document, distort, control, terrorise, and weaponise someone's life.

The modern landscape makes this frighteningly easy – in fact, some scholars have recently found that being stalked online is now more common than being stalked in person (Fox et al., 2024).

When it comes to in-person stalking in our general population, the patterns of victimisation match those of other forms of abuse. Women are much more likely to be stalked than men.

1 in 5 women and 1 in 20 men report being stalked in their lifetime (ONS, 2025, Smith et al., 2017). Globally, 20% of people in English-speaking nations report having been stalked in their lifetime (Spitzberg et al., 2010). Studies have found that between 26–41% of victims who are stalked in person will also be subjected to online stalking from the offender (Ahlgrim and Terrance, 2021).

The other way around, my research for parliament into online stalking victims targeted on so-called 'gossip' website Tattle Life found that out of 150 cases I analysed, 24% were covertly filmed or photographed by their online stalker, 22% were followed in person, 23% were sent letters and emails directly, and in 20% of cases, the victim's children were filmed or photographed by online stalkers who then uploaded that footage to the internet. In 16% of cases, online stalkers attended the home or work address of the victim to harass them in person (Taylor, 2025).

When it comes to the prevalence of online stalking where there is no contact offending or in-person stalking elements at all, the statistics vary greatly. Some recent academic reviews have found that in both university student and general population samples, between 5%–51% of people admit to stalking someone else online, and between 3%–41% of people say they have been stalked online (Weekes & Storey, 2025).

Interestingly, whilst some research has found that men are still the majority perpetrators of both in-person stalking and online stalking in forensic samples – more recent studies are now finding that men and women are equally likely to engage in stalking online, and that perpetration is increasing (Ahlgrim & Terrance, 2021).

My own research found that 87% of the perpetrators of online abuse, stalking and harassment were female (Taylor, 2025).

Women are more likely than men to perpetrate covert and persistent stalking behaviours over long periods of time, such as monitoring, watching, fixations on the victim's social media accounts, creating websites, and gaining access to their victim's emails and text messages (Fernandez-Cruz et al., 2021; March et al., 2020; Purcell et al., 2001; Smoker & March, 2017). This prompted me to include Chapter 3, which looks specifically at female stalkers, not least because almost all of my own stalkers were women. As a feminist psychologist, whose work centres around violence against women and girls, it was quite the confrontation to have to accept that the significant harm that I was being subjected to was being enacted by other women. When my research in 2025 found that hundreds of other victims were being targeted by women, I became interested in that emerging pattern.

With a few clicks, any person can access property records, business records and files, archived articles, cached social media posts, photographs, family members' names, friends lists, follower lists, workplace information, CV documents, videos, playlists, comments, reviews, and all manner of historical content scraped from platforms you thought you had deleted years ago. Public records are searchable. Companies sell personal data. Old usernames resurface. Tagged images reveal our locations. Even well-intentioned friends inadvertently disclose personal information through birthday posts and celebratory photographs that they tag us in. It's a minefield.

Surveillance by stalkers, once labour-intensive and risky, is now frictionless – and totally safe – for them.

People who stalk can sit in the comfort of their own living room, becoming increasingly obsessed with their victim – spending endless hours each day monitoring and harassing them – and no one around them will even notice because everyone else is on their phone.

Online stalking is invisible and hidden in plain sight.

You could be sat across from your partner in the living room whilst they obsessively stalk and traumatise their victim – and you would never even know.

Online surveillance refers to the continuous monitoring of someone's digital presence: their posts, likes, comments, professional updates, photographs, friends, and associations. It often involves screenshots taken within minutes of publication, notifications set up to alert the stalker to any activity, and the archiving of content for later use. It is an alarming level of control over the victim, who oftentimes doesn't even know they are being stalked in this way. For the stalker, it is maintenance of proximity and connection, without the need for physical presence or personal risk.

Six factors of cyberstalking – De Fazio et al., (2020)

Factor	Examples
Dissemination	Posting false information on social media; posting or sending private photos, videos and messages to networks; using email, messages and social media to spread rumours and accusations about the victim.
Threats	Physical threats to harm or kill; social threats to ruin the victim's life or career; hacking into the victim's accounts; stealing the victim's identity; creating fake social media accounts in the victim's name; sending spyware and viruses to the victim.
Harassment	Sending images, messages, voicemails, posts, comments, letters and/or any other form of communication, directly or indirectly, which can present as affectionate, romantic, hate-filled, angry, needy, suicidal, sexual, threatening, and obsessive.
Denigration	Encouraging others to contact or harass/stalk the victim; setting up defamatory websites, threads, forum topics and posts about the victim; making complaints and reports about the victim; ordering goods or items, or subscribing to services in the victim's name.
Contact/Proximity	Unwanted repeated emails and calls; spying, monitoring, using GPS or electronic devices to track the victim; checking metadata on photographs and social media posts for locations and information; following, visiting or contacting venues, workplaces, addresses.
Impersonation	Using the victim's name, photos, likeness or identity to send messages, set up accounts, post or comment on social media or forums – often pretending to be the victim whilst harming or harassing others .

In line with De Fazio et al. (2020), I identified 55 common tactics used by online stalkers, with the most common being mass dissemination of damaging lies claiming that the victim was committing crimes, abusing their children, and suffering from severe mental illnesses, or sustained ridicule, doxxing of home addresses, dissemination of personal data, public posts and doxxing of victims' children, and making malicious allegations or reports to the victim's employers (Taylor, 2025).

Social media and the rise of parasocial relationships have also changed the way that stalkers may feel entitled to access their victim, something which has been considered by scholars across several disciplines as access to the internet has spread since the turn of the millennium.

People are becoming increasingly personally and emotionally connected to acquaintances and strangers online because social media platforms allow us unprecedented access to other people's lives. They are in love with celebrities, they feel like they 'know' their favourite YouTuber, and they feel like they are best friends with the influencers they follow. They 'stalk' their old friends and exes. They obsessively watch the stories of people they used to know twenty years ago – or vaguely know through someone else.

As someone with around half a million followers at the time of writing this book, I regularly receive letters, emails, messages and even gifts from people who feel strongly that they 'know' me. They offer for me to stay in their house if I am ever in their city, they ask me out to dinner and for drinks, and they contact me to tell me about extremely personal aspects of their lives.

Don't get me wrong here – I don't think that these people are stalking me or doing anything wrong. They are often lovely, friendly people from all around the world who feel compelled and comfortable to talk to me due to the relationship and connection they have with me due to my social media or my books. I also cannot pretend that I have never done the same. I can recall writing to a woman I had never met because I felt that I strongly related to a personal story that she had posted online. I wanted to send her some support, and to offer her my help, should she ever need it.

She replied within the hour, we had a short conversation – swapped stories – and it was helpful for both of us. The online world is peculiar, and I won't pretend that I do not partake in that peculiarity! The world has changed so much in such a short space of time, and many of us now find and build friendships, connections and even significant intimate relationships online.

But a parasocial relationship is defined as a one-sided psychological attachment formed by an individual towards someone who does not know them (Brooks, 2021; Hackley and Hackley, 2016; McCutcheon et al., 2002). Originally used to describe audiences' emotional attachments to celebrities, the term has expanded in the age of influencers, activists, and public intellectuals. Parasocial attachment is not inherently harmful, and in fact, it's extremely common.

Research even shows that when news programmes were suffering from a lack of emotional connection with the viewer, TV channels realised that the more friendly, chatty, personable and attractive the newsreader, the more people would watch the news. Simply put, parasocial relationships are leveraged and utilised without us even realising.

Many of us feel very connected to public figures without crossing any boundaries. Parasocial entitlement, however, is different, as I explore across several chapters of this book.

Parasocial entitlement is the belief that access to someone's public presence creates a right to their private self. It is the conviction that reading someone's posts, listening to their podcast, following them on social media, buying their products, or watching their interviews grants intimacy and access to their personal lives, choices, thoughts, ideas and experiences. It morphs easily into resentment when that imagined intimacy is not reciprocated. The stalker feels wronged by boundaries. They feel excluded or rejected from a relationship that never existed in the first place (Brooks, 2021; Jin & Ryu, 2020).

For an online stalker, it can mean that they become increasingly angry when the person they have become obsessed with hasn't shared something personal about themselves that the stalker wants to know about. Maybe the person hasn't posted about their relationship, or their children, or maybe they have political or religious beliefs they have never shared online (McLaughlin & Wohn, 2021; Mardon et al., 2022).

Researchers exploring these reactions found ample evidence of strangers becoming fixated with influencers, media personalities and YouTubers – and then becoming disgusted, outraged and personally hurt when they felt that they were trying to keep some parts of their lives private. This is an interesting topic, highly interrelated with stalking, and so I have dedicated Chapter 11 to this phenomenon.

In my own personal experience, this parasocial element was where it got dangerous for me. People who were stalking me became alarmingly entitled, feeling like they should have access to my entire life.

When entitlement meets grievance – and 24/7 access to technology – a new breed of stalker emerges.

Grievance is a powerful psychological driver. It is the perception of injustice, humiliation or betrayal, often disproportionate or entirely fabricated. Grievance fuels revenge-seeking behaviour. Revenge justifies the endless intrusion. In some cases, the stalker constructs a false narrative in which they are the injured party and the target is morally corrupt, dangerous, fraudulent, or abusive. This moral reframing allows the stalker to see themselves not as an aggressor, but instead as a whistleblower, a protector, or a truth-teller – an approach much more common in female stalkers.

That's where I got the idea for the book you are reading today – the ponderance that the modern online stalker was not like the traditional violent male stalker we are all warned about. Thousands of people online are convincing themselves that their target is the real issue, therefore, in their minds, justifying their stalking behaviours. What's fascinating to me is how often I now see this pattern. Not just towards celebrities or people in the public eye – but towards women in the family courts, people who try to exit an abusive family, someone who owns a little shop in the centre of town, or someone who has simply left their employer for a better role.

People are working in groups to stalk and terrorise their victims online, whilst telling themselves that they are doing it for an important, justified or even moral reason. Friends do it. Families do it. Colleagues do it. Strangers do it.

This is where weaponised bureaucracy and stalking by proxy enter the story. Weaponised bureaucracy, another common tactic of online stalkers, refers to the strategic use of institutional systems to harass, intimidate, and destabilise a target. It includes repeated complaints to regulatory bodies, false reports to police or social services, vexatious legal actions, spurious safeguarding referrals and coordinated attempts to trigger investigations. From the cases I have analysed, the goal is never the pursuit of justice, rather it seems to be an attempt to exhaust and emotionally collapse the victim.

Stalking by proxy is scarily effective, too, which is something I will explore further as this book progresses.

The internet makes previously complex coordination frighteningly simple. Anonymous forums, encrypted messaging groups, and private chat channels allow individuals to organise collectively. Anonymous mobs form around a shared grievance, amplifying and exaggerating their accusations, encouraging escalating behaviours, and reinforcing each other's hostility or hatred of someone. In these spaces, rumour becomes fact through repetition – the more they all say it, the more real it becomes to them. Screenshots and Facebook posts are dissected as though they are forensic evidence in a high-profile case, and people begin to see themselves as detectives solving a mystery or proving that someone is a criminal mastermind. Ordinary human behaviour such as celebrating a job promotion or posting pictures of a sunny holiday is reinterpreted through a lens of suspicion.

The new breed of stalker often operates successfully without physical proximity. Research shows that most never approach the victim in person (Weekes & Storey, 2025; Meloy et al., 2011), making it extremely hard for victims to explain the risk to police.

These types of stalkers may never attempt to visit or stand outside their home, for example. But that is because they have found other ways to watch, to document, to obsess and speculate. They construct elaborate timelines. They attribute hidden meanings and subliminal messages to the mundane social media posts of their victims. They interpret neutral statements as coded messages directed at them. They come up with fantastical stories about why someone was cropped out of a photo or fabricate in their minds the 'real' reason why someone isn't posting about the latest political scandal.

Frankly, I have never seen anything quite like it and I am worried about where this will take us, if not discussed and then addressed. Especially because so many of us seem to be partaking in this behaviour, watching it, complicit in it, ignoring it, minimising it or have been victims of it.

Is stalking just a symptom of our toxic relationship with the internet? Or is it something much deeper?

Projection seems to play a central role. Projection is a defence mechanism in which an individual attributes their own thoughts, motives, or feelings to someone else. The stalker who is fixated and obsessed accuses the target of being obsessed with them. The stalker who monitors constantly accuses the target of monitoring them. The stalker who harbours hostility accuses the target of aggression, abuse or hatred of them or others. We do see this in general stalking cases, too – so this is not specific to online stalkers at all.

I experienced this myself. Some of the people stalking me would make posts addressed directly to me, as if I knew who they were. They would often say things like, "Hey Jess! I know you're watching me! I know you're obsessed with reading my posts!"

I was only made aware of these posts months later when police were investigating – but in the minds of my stalkers, I was watching them and reading everything they wrote about me (and to me).

As this was one of the most unsettling experiences of being stalked online, I was shocked to find that the behaviour had already been documented and analysed in academic research. Mardon et al. (2022) found many examples of online forums where the people stalking and harassing social media influencers were absolutely convinced that the victim was reading all of their posts – so much so, that they would frequently address them directly. More than this though, they would then interpret the victim's subsequent behaviour or posts as if the victim were responding directly to them.

It is quite alarming to realise that there is someone out there in the world with a parasocial attachment to you, stalking you, fixated on you, and also thinking that you are not only aware of their existence but that you are reading all of their posts in real time, and subliminally responding to them.

As the stalking that I experienced became more serious, I was presented with dozens upon dozens of my own public posts and asked whether they were 'really about' a stranger who believed I was subliminally communicating with them. The idea that my public posts – my ordinary, general commentary about psychology, abuse, VAWG, and trauma – were secret messaging for a stranger not only baffled me, but also worried me a great deal. It was in those moments I realised that the people stalking me had moved beyond disliking me or wanting to frighten me, they had come to believe I was communicating with them specifically – and this was something police struggled to comprehend.

This reveals another uncomfortable truth that will be explored in this book: our systems are woefully unprepared for this new breed of online stalker because they have been taught to cling to outdated psychological and psychiatric models.

Stalking is still frequently framed and explored in academia and practice as a manifestation of mental illness and personality disorder (Albrecht et al., 2022). Even public discourse still leans heavily on ideas of delusion, erotomania, or psychosis. Erotomania (a psychiatric term supposedly describing a delusional belief that another person, often of higher status, is in love with the individual) has been researched and theorised in stalking cases for decades – despite most stalking cases having very little to do with love or romance.

As an anti-pathology, trauma-informed psychologist myself, I reject the pathologisation of any behaviours – even the ones that harm me

– that seem totally 'delusional'. I don't think stalking is driven by mental illness or personality disorder, but I do think we need to explore what is really driving these fixations. Research has repeatedly shown that stalking is not driven by psychosis or mental illness (Albrecht et al., 2022; BPS, 2022). Instead, it is influenced by many social behaviours and it is often driven by control and grievance (even if that grievance is imagined).

By pathologising stalking as madness, we obscure its strategic nature. We render it tragic instead of dangerous and deliberate – meaning that the sympathy and support can lean towards the offender. We treat it as a helpless romantic obsession rather than coercive and abusive power – again, framing the offender as having no control. The fact is that they have all the control, whilst the victim is left to struggle. From my perspective, when we frame stalkers as sociopaths, psychopaths and people with personality disorders, we fail to see the calculated behaviours of those who are perfectly capable of planning, coordinating, evading, and manipulating systems.

In thinking so deeply about these issues as a trauma-informed psychologist, I came to realise recently that the digital environment also creates what I can only describe as a new kind of victim.

The victim of online stalking might not be afraid of being physically followed home, but she is afraid of being followed everywhere. A stalker might have knowledge of her workplace. Her children's school. Her professional regulators. Her clients. Her community. Her clubs. Her town centre. Her conversations. Her social media profiles.

She must consider not only physical safety, but another form of safety. Her privacy. Her career. Her livelihood. Her reputational survival. In our online world, her digital footprint quickly becomes one of the most dangerous and valuable assets to her stalker.

For most people, they have likely never considered how much their 'reputation' is worth. I don't just mean the reputation of a celebrity either, I mean your own reputation. As you sit there right now, reading this book – you have a reputation, do you not?

Maybe you have a reputation for being funny, caring, kind and friendly. Maybe you have a reputation for being a great parent, or a loving partner. Maybe people would say about you that you are great at your job, a person with strong morals, or someone who would go out of your way to help someone in need.

Now imagine what would happen to your life, your family, your job, and your friendships if your reputation was suddenly destroyed. You woke up tomorrow and your new reputation was that you were actually a terrible person behind closed doors, you were selfish, abusive, nasty, violent or manipulative. You neglect your children, you cheat on your partner, you steal from your workplace, you lie about your life, and you have no morals. You don't care about anyone but yourself. And now, everyone is saying it about you.

Our reputations carry incredible weight that most of us don't consider much of the time, but in a world where we present ourselves online every day, a stalker can examine, analyse, monitor and then weaponise our reputation with very little effort.

Reputational harm is not abstract. It has the power to upend our entire identity. In professional contexts, repeated allegations, even if they are unproven, can trigger investigations, suspensions, suspicion, bullying, or lost employment. In personal contexts, rumours can fracture friendships and isolate people from their families. The new kind of victim must anticipate not only violence, but narrative – something that exists about all of us, but most of us have never really thought about unless we have personal experience of having our narratives being rewritten by someone else.

Narrative control is therefore central to online stalking. The stalker seeks to define or redefine who their victim is. I have seen stalkers create dossiers filled with false allegations and lies about their victim, compile threads, set up websites, or post hundreds of 'warnings' to others. They often claim to have 'evidence' against their victim to legitimise their stalking. Most of the time they have nothing, but in some cases where the stalker is particularly invested, they curate evidence selectively. They find shreds of information, comments, conversations, hearsay or events, then they carefully strip away the context – and the job is as good as done. Screenshots are frozen in time and stripped of tone in order to make the victim look bad, abusive, deceitful, or unstable.

No matter how the victim responds – they lose. If they speak out about being stalked, they are reframed as manipulative, lying or delusional. Lots of victims who speak about being stalked are perceived as self-obsessed or self-important, as if they want the attention that comes with being stalked. If they stay silent and try not to respond, their silence is framed as guilt. If they do respond, retaliate or confront the person stalking them, it will be framed as aggression, threat or violence, and this only serves to 'confirm' to the stalker that their actions are justified – and to the observers that the victim is really the perpetrator.

It's maddening. And in short, the victim of online stalking is easily trapped.

When I was going through this, I would often say to my friends that it felt as though I was stuck in someone else's fantasy, where my persona had been carefully curated by the stalker and came to represent a dangerous villain who needed to be slain by them. They were the hero of their own story – on a gallant mission to protect people (or themselves). In their minds, I needed to be destroyed, and anything I did to try to stop their behaviour was just more proof that I deserved what they were doing to me. It was terrifying.

It was probably one of the most traumatic, oppressive, and mind-bending experiences I have ever had – and every other victim I have spoken to has felt the same way. It feels like psychological warfare.

The psychological impact of being stalked online is cumulative. Research shows that victims of online stalking suffer in every domain of their lives, and that the impact of online stalking is equal to that of in-person stalking (Hamid & Qazi, 2023; Sheridan et al., 2019; Kaur et al., 2020).

Hypervigilance, understandably, becomes constant and inescapable when being stalked. Hypervigilance is a state of heightened alertness in which an individual scans their environment for threat. In digital stalking, the environment is infinite. Notifications are no longer just your phone making that little 'ding' noise because someone has messaged you, they are potential danger – they fill you with dread.

Every new friend request must be checked. *Who are they? Are they real? Why are they adding you? Are they connected to the stalker? Is there some ulterior motive here?*

Every unknown email triggers suspicion. *Is this link real? Is it safe? Are you being monitored? Did someone guess your password?*

Our minds and bodies have no clear boundary between online and offline life because in reality, there is no difference. The online world is not a pretend world where there is no harm – it is simply an extension of the rest of the world, and the rest of our lives. When our boss sends us a shitty email, that's not any different than them being shitty with us in person. When our ex suddenly gets back in touch over Facebook, wanting to reconnect and rebuild things, we don't think that is 'less real' because it was only on Facebook Messenger. When someone sends us a death threat over WhatsApp, we don't take it less seriously because the 'online world isn't real life'.

The point I am making here is that stalking online and through technology is no less terrifying than stalking in person. If anything, I would argue that it is more absorbing and more omnipresent. Despite this, victims are frequently told that the online world is some sort of benign irritant that they can just log out of and switch off from.

Unlike traditional stalking, there is no geographical escape. Moving house does not delete our archived posts. Changing phone numbers does not protect us long-term. The stalker does not need to know our address to monitor us. All they need is our name, and they are good to go.

The law, meanwhile, often lags behind lived reality. Police officers still look for physical proximity and direct violence as evidence of seriousness. Courts struggle to understand that they are being used as a weapon of stalking and that bringing repeated cases, whether civil, family, financial, or criminal, is a convenient and legitimised way of harassing and intimidating the victim by a savvy stalker. The public still ask what the victim 'did' to provoke attention or even suggest that they like it. When victims do disclose what they are experiencing, years of stalking and digital fixation can often be minimised as 'drama', 'gossip', 'trolling' or 'online spats'.

From what I have seen across hundreds of cases, my own included, the new breed of stalker thrives in grey areas. They exploit the fact that much of what they do is technically legal when taken in isolation (Taylor, 2025). Taking screenshots is legal. Discussing public information is legal. Submitting complaints is legal. Looking at social media is legal, too. The harm lies in the pattern, the repetition, the intent and the obsession, but this is rarely understood as it should be.

When dozens or hundreds, or even thousands, of individuals participate in monitoring and dissecting one person's life, diffusion of responsibility occurs. There is no 'one' person to take responsibility if 'everyone is doing it'. Diffusion of responsibility is a psychological phenomenon in which individuals feel less personally accountable for harmful behaviour when acting as part of a group (Mardon et al., 2022). Each participant tells themselves they only commented once, only shared once, only speculated once, only posted one photo, only said that one thing. The cumulative impact is devastating on the victim, but everyone gets to convince themselves that they did nothing wrong.

And so I wonder if we are witnessing the emergence of stalking as collective behaviour. This is something entirely different to traditional understandings and theories of stalking that we have currently. Stalkers do not usually act in groups, but they do online.

Of course, it does not mean that all online criticism is stalking. It does not mean that public figures are immune from scrutiny – and unfortunately, they are definitely not immune from gossip – as harmful as that is. But it does mean that when scrutiny morphs into fixation, coordinated harassment, threats, abuse, doxxing, and vexatious reports, we are no longer in the realm of 'free speech' (which is often wheeled out as the primary defence of online stalkers).

This behaviour hasn't been caused by the internet. History shows us that it is not alien, new, or pathological. If anything, we should see this stalking behaviour as inherently human. Research since the 1990s has shown that stalking is driven by envy, grievance, entitlement, moral superiority, boredom, loneliness, anger, and the intoxicating rush of collective belonging (Albrecht et al., 2022; Kaur et al., 2020). In some cases, it is even driven by enjoyment, sadism, and righteousness. What is new is the social conditions that we are living in: the internet rewards outrage. It gamifies hostility and hatred, so that it is validated and amplified with likes and shares.

It is stalking, but you are rewarded for it. It is abuse, but you get 500 likes and 20 new followers for commenting.

The victim is left terrified and traumatised from being monitored, abused and harassed, whilst the stalker is able to close down the app for a little while, make some toast, and carry on playing with their kids on a warm Sunday morning.

Were these people always this way? Would they have become stalkers if they didn't have access to powerful technology?

No matter the answer, the internet has given the stalker unprecedented tools: perpetual access, anonymity, surveillance, scalability, power and permanence. It has given them audiences and networks that they can manipulate and activate against the victim. It has given them millions of data points to exploit – and it has given them the illusion of intimacy, connection, and a relationship with their victim.

At the same time, it has left victims navigating a landscape they don't understand, and that our legal systems can barely recognise.

CHAPTER 1

Obsession and connection

My wife, Jay, had been quiet for hours. The kind of quiet which meant something was wrong. She had a pale, frightened look on her face. She was staring at her phone screen, knees curled up to her chest, wrapped in her dressing gown.

A year ago, this silence would have been completely out of character for the extroverted, hilarious, and energetic woman I had fallen in love with, but after months of being relentlessly stalked and harassed online, weeks had gone by without hearing her laugh at one of her own infamous dad jokes.

Even though her anguished states had become the norm, I could always tell when something else had happened, or if her feelings had suddenly worsened.

"All okay, babe?" I tried gently.

Silence. No eye contact. It made me anxious.

"Babe? Has . . . something happened? You're making me nervous."

I must admit, even by this point, the stalking had taken its toll on both of us. I had made a promise to myself to never read the emails, or search for posts or comments about myself – because I knew that I wouldn't be able to cope if I could see the extent of what was being done to me. Jay had been doing the opposite. She had been watching, analysing, risk assessing, and trying to figure out who the stalkers were, and how to make it stop.

"Please. Sweetheart. You've not been right all day. What's going on?"

"I don't want to tell you," she said flatly. It wasn't an outright refusal, but she wanted it to sound like one.

"Why not?" I pressed.

"I don't want to worry you." She looked up at me from the sofa with an uncomfortable look in her eye.

"Well, that's just making me more worried, babe. What have you seen that would worry me? Please just tell me."

She sighed quietly, rubbing her face with both hands, and dropped her phone into her lap.

"There's been loads more of those posts online. Links to some weird website I've never heard of before. It's like a gossip forum of some kind, but they create a page for people they don't like, and then sort of . . . go on there . . . and target them in groups . . ."

I rolled my eyes at how desperately pathetic it all sounded and sniggered. At the beginning of being stalked online, I suppose I hadn't realised how serious it was, and I certainly hadn't thought it would be something that would impose upon my life for years. She told me about the website – something called Tattle. A site that had been set up to spread rumours, gossip and abuse. It sounded to me like the forums and chatrooms on 4Chan and Reddit that incels and abusers use to target their victims.

"Fucking hell, have these people got no life at all? First, it was fake social media accounts, then it was bombarding us with emails and messages – and now this bullshit? Why don't they get a life, have a beer, or have an orgasm or something?"

That joke didn't even raise a smile from her. She continued.

"I went on the website. Most of it is lies and horrible comments that seem to get worse the more they share them – but some of it . . . some of it is real. That's the bit that's scaring me more."

I realised that Jay was scared and stopped with the nonchalant attitude. Suddenly, I had been confronted with the fact that this weird website could actually contain real information about me.

"What do you mean . . . 'some of it is real'?"

She reluctantly handed me her phone. I took it from her, frightened of what I was about to see. I stared in disbelief at strange anonymous accounts, using my face as their profile picture and our dogs' names as their usernames. Entire conversations about where I had been that week and the commissioners I was working for.

And a conversation about my dad.

Not just speculation, not just passing comment. Someone saying they had spoken to him in real life. I froze.

I shook my head. Maybe a bit of disbelief – probably, mostly, in denial.

"Nah. This can't be real, babe. They are probably pretending to know us . . . Like how people do with celebrities . . ."

She raised her eyebrows. "Keep reading."

I didn't want to, but I flicked through some more posts until something caught my eye that I couldn't look away from. An exchange between two anonymous accounts.

Candles64: *She thinks she is so fucking important but let me tell you something, I was at her sad little wedding and spoke to her dad for a while. He clearly doesn't give a fuck about her either. Clearly didn't want to be there. I think everyone who knows her must hate her. Her own mum abandoned her. Makes me wonder what she has done to them all.*

AlabamaMama: *Doesn't surprise me. When I knew her, she was estranged from her whole family. I did my PhD with her. She made up some sob story but it was obviously lies. I used to talk to her all the time but realised she was a psychopath years ago. There was one time when she told me this story about her being on an aeroplane when the engines cut out on takeoff. Clearly utter lies. I know she lost custody of her children years ago, but she doesn't want anyone to know that!*

My throat tightened. What the fuck was this website? And who were these people?

The comments were filled with lies. My kids were sound asleep upstairs.

"Uhh. These are real people . . . No one knows my dad was at our wedding . . ."

"Except the guests, right?" Jay finished my sentence.

I sat down, feeling dizzy from the surging fear.

"But it was lockdown. Our wedding was less than thirty people . . ."

We stared at each other, both realising the same thing. One of the people stalking us had attended our wedding. The detail didn't matter so much – the horrible comments about my dad and my family were upsetting, sure, but it was more the terrifying realisation that someone around us, someone we had loved and trusted enough to invite to our tiny little COVID-approved wedding, was now part of this group of people stalking me day and night. My mind whizzed through the guest list, but no one jumped out at me, which in some ways made it feel much worse.

"But the next one . . . that Alabama account . . . what are they talking about?" Jay asked me.

I read it again – and again, my throat reacted in the same way. My hands were shaking. Suddenly, I felt incredibly unsafe.

"That incident with the plane. That really happened. It was before you and I met. I had been commissioned to go and give a series of lectures in Tennessee. It would have been my first trip to the US, and I was travelling on my own. I had done the first leg of the trip, so I was in Dublin. The plane tried to take off and as it lifted off into the air, the engine failed and we bumped back down to the ground. Everyone freaked out. I had a fucking enormous panic attack and demanded they let me off the plane. Long story, I caused absolute chaos. It was embarrassing. Never got to Tennessee. I'll tell you another time. But that's not the point . . . that story is true – which means that account is a real person, too. A real person who knows that story . . ."

"But who would know that about you?" Jay searched for answers, but I came up empty handed. I couldn't remember exactly who I had told about the plane incident. I don't remember telling anyone other than my family, and maybe a few friends.

"I definitely didn't tell anyone at university about that trip, though . . . so something isn't adding up there. In fact, I hardly knew anyone at university during my PhD because I did it part time. I did most of it remotely, the kids were young, and I was working full time. In fact, I don't know who that could possibly be . . . The story is real, but the stuff about doing a PhD with me is a lie . . ."

"So you don't know who that could be?"

"Not a fucking clue." I stared at the floor, frantically trying to piece all of this new information together.

"Well, they've posted about you 103 times in the last few days. They seem to know a lot. I noticed them saying some stuff about the kids, too. And about your old workplace. Some stuff about holidays you had been on when you were younger, which was strangely specific. Information about when you took the kids to New Zealand when you were on that contract. And that other account, the candles one, it has posted about you all hours of the day and night for about four weeks. I lost count of their posts – well over 300 . . ."

I felt my body go numb. That wasn't some passing comment. That was a full-time job.

And then there was the final post she showed me, holding her phone in her hand, right in front of my face.

CatsAndDogs78: *I still talk to her all the time. She has no idea I am on here. And she has no idea how much I fucking hate her. She thinks*

* * *

We live in a chronically online world. By that I do not simply mean that we use the internet frequently. I mean that for billions of people, the digital realm is no longer a place we visit. It is a place we inhabit. It is ambient. Constant. Portable. We wake up and reach for it. We fall asleep with it inches from our faces. It is in our pockets at dinner tables, in school playgrounds, in courtrooms, in hospital waiting rooms. It mediates our friendships, our work, our activism, our grief and our joy.

According to Statista (2025), 6 billion people have internet access, representing 74% of the global population – with the average internet user spending 33 hours per week online (ITU, 2025).

Facebook and Instagram boast 3 billion active users per month, TikTok has just under 2 billion active users per month, and X has around 580 million users (DataReportal, 2026). For clarity, this constitutes 2 in 3 people on earth, each with an average of 7 platform profiles each. Whilst the average screen time is now 7–11 hours per day, each person is spending 2–3 hours per day on social media alone (Telefonica, 2025).

Those are some serious numbers. And this chronic online existence has reshaped something fundamental: our understanding of human connection. Connection once required physical proximity (because how else would we achieve it before technology?), reciprocity, and lots of time to build rapport, trust, and relationships with people we had met in person. It required shared space – maybe a workplace, a school, a club, or a town. It also required mutual awareness – we both needed to know the other existed at the bare minimum for connection to occur.

In the digital age, none of these things are required for connection. In fact, connection can be one-sided, instantaneous, and in some cases, totally imagined.

We can witness fragments of hundreds of lives before we've even eaten breakfast.

Scroll. Scroll. Scroll. We know what someone ate. We see where they travelled. We look at their profile. We see how they vote in elections. How they parent their kids. What their living room looks like. How their voice sounds when they are tired or upset. What deodorant they wear. How long they have been married. What day their child was born.

People share so much of themselves online – me included. People can scroll through my public profiles, and I am sure they will feel that they have learned an enormous amount about me. And maybe they have. I have gone to great lengths to protect my children from my public profiles, and have private accounts for my family and closest friends, but I still talk quite openly and personally in my public-facing work. Anyone from anywhere in the world can no doubt learn a lot about me in a few clicks.

Constant access to this kind of technology in our pockets has created constant access to anyone and everyone. That constant visibility creates the illusion of constant intimacy, with anyone and everyone, even if they have no idea that you feel intimacy towards them. Or that you exist at all.

Intimacy, in psychological terms, refers to closeness built through mutual disclosure and vulnerability. It requires two people who recognise and respond to each other's interior worlds. But the internet offers something different: curated exposure without any necessary reciprocity. We see into people's lives, but they do not see into ours. We hear their stories, but they do not hear our responses beyond the metrics of likes and comments. This asymmetry is the foundation of the parasocial relationship.

My experience of this has been the way that I am approached in public spaces by people who feel they 'know' me. I have been approached whilst eating a meal in a restaurant with my wife, whilst shopping with my kids, whilst sat alone on a train to London, at a music festival with my wife, and even whilst grabbing cold and flu remedy at 1 am from the 24-hour supermarket.

Strangers light up. They might be excited, nervous, thrilled to see me – some go to hug me immediately, or burst into tears. They ask me how I am, like they are an old friend. They ask if Jay and the kids are with me, excited to see them, too. Some shake and struggle to speak, or say things like, "Oh my god, I cannot believe you are here! I absolutely love you! I have followed you for years!"

They know so much about me – and yet, I look into their eyes and feel their warmth, but they are a perfect stranger to me.

The reality of those moments means that when I hear the words, "Aren't you Dr Jessica Taylor?" I panic. I never know if I am about to be hugged or attacked.

Parasocial relationships have always been common for celebrities like television presenters, film stars and musicians. In the digital age, they extend to influencers, writers, activists, podcasters, minor celebrities, and even local community figures. A school governor with a public Facebook page. A Zumba instructor with a modest TikTok following. A campaigner who posts regularly about her work. A small business owner sharing behind-the-scenes content about her cute pet shop in the centre of the village.

Anyone can become obsessed with them. The barrier to perceived intimacy has never been lower.

When you see someone's face every day on your phone, hear their voice whilst you cook dinner, watch them laugh with their partner, talk about their childhood, cry about a loss, celebrate a success, your brain registers familiarity. Familiarity breeds a sense of knowing. Knowing breeds comfort. And comfort can breed entitlement (McCutcheon et al., 2002).

My first ever experiences of parasocial relationships came in 2020, after my first book, *Why Women are Blamed for Everything* went super viral and sold tens of thousands of copies. I was 29 years old, and I was very physically recognisable back then – I had bright silver hair, a micro-fringe (don't ask, I know lots of you loved it, but it's not coming back!), and dark blue glasses. Suddenly, my book was everywhere. I was on the news, the radio, and podcasts being interviewed all over the world. My social media grew and I was invited to public-facing events and conferences like never before.

But the hero worship terrified me. I was not prepared for any of it, and no one taught me how to cope. When I found that scholars such as Samantha Brooks and McCutcheon and colleagues had been researching 'celebrity worship' and 'fanatic' behaviour for years, I was intrigued, and also slightly terrified by their findings. I read their papers, feeling alarmed by how familiar they sounded.

Back in 2002, McCutcheon and her colleagues began to theorise a model of celebrity worship that could help us to understand the different levels of obsession and perceived connection that people have with public figures. Whilst the language used in the literature back then was that of 'celebrity worship', their framework now extends to all public figures and could even be used across any victim of online stalking and parasocial relationships, especially as our lives are now so much more digital than they were back in 2002.

This is, again, an example of a pioneering model whereby the authors would have no possible idea of how the internet and social media would develop, and how relevant and important their work would become over twenty years later especially now that online obsessions and cyberstalking are rampant and we are trying desperately to understand them.

Model of celebrity worship

Low-level celebrity worship (Entertainment/ social)	The public figure is a source of entertainment, social conversation and information. Interest is casual and does not influence or interfere with everyday life. The person watches interviews with a favourite singer or writer, for instance. They might follow their Instagram and chat about them at work, but would not feel emotionally distressed if this public figure stopped posting.
Medium-level celebrity worship (Intense personal)	The person feels a strong emotional connection to the public figure and may experience them as psychologically meaningful or personally significant. They feel like they understand them deeply, experience strong emotional reactions to their successes and failures, believe they share similarities or a special bond, and think about this public figure a lot. They may feel personally very hurt if their favourite singer or writer was criticised. They engage in obsessive monitoring and may struggle to see boundaries between them.
High-level celebrity worship (Borderline pathological)	The admiration or obsession with the public figure becomes intrusive, fixated and linked to obsessive, irrational or risk-taking behaviour. The person is willing to do something illegal or extreme to talk to or meet the public figure. They believe that they share a unique destiny. They begin to feel they are in a reciprocal relationship with the public figure and have difficulty separating reality from fantasy. They will often believe the public figure knows them or reads their posts. They may send repeated messages to the public figure, begin stalking them, follow them, or insist they have a connection. They will become extremely distressed, entitled or angry if the public figure stops posting, or does something they disagree with or dislike.

McCutcheon et al. (2002)

There were times after my public profile grew when people would come up to me and ask to touch my tattoos. Without skipping a beat, they would tell me that they had always wanted to touch my tattooed arms and then proceed to stroke me, as if that was completely acceptable behaviour.

They would ask me to pose in photos for them – or wait for me outside of toilet stalls. They would tell me that they loved me, or that they wished I was their best friend. Or their sister. One woman wrote to me to ask me to marry her several times, despite the fact that I am already married to my wife. At first, I thought she was joking, but eventually I had to block her on every platform when she started becoming upset with me for not responding to her unrelenting messages.

One of the worst versions of this for me was a woman who had followed me online for years and became extremely over-familiar with me. I had deliberately kept my distance and was only ever being polite. At an event, she came over and hugged me with one arm. Shockingly, she put her other hand up my shorts, into the back of my knickers and groped me hard whilst whispering, "Ever since I started following you online, I have always wanted to grab your arse."

I still shudder when I think of that moment. How a seemingly normal and professional woman who had read my books and followed me online thought about putting her hand inside my underwear – and then did it. Like it was nothing.

These are the experiences that have changed my life but have also forced me to confront the psychology of online stalkers. I have been wrestling with the meaning and explanations for my own experiences – and my resulting traumas – for many years now.

At one point, I even made several phone calls to A-list celebrities I knew and asked them how the hell they coped with their enormous platforms and entirely public lives. I was struggling with a relatively tiny platform but wanted insight into the bigger picture, so I made some calls and asked several famous women with tens of millions of followers for advice.

Everyone had their own stories of stalkers, threats, abuse, attacks, smear campaigns, and fears for their safety. Some were drinking and doing drugs to help them cope. Some would hide in their houses. Some had stopped going to shops, malls, events, bars, parks, and public places years ago. Some had wigs and disguises that they used to help them live a semi-normal existence. Some had hired private investigators to figure out who was stalking them, so they could report them to the police or apply for restraining orders. Some ended up with round-the-clock security. And some told me that I had to just find a way to deal with it, because it is par for the course.

Obviously, most people who follow me or others online are not stalking them, and many people follow creators, writers or activists without overstepping boundaries or ever harming them. They feel inspired, entertained, supported, or informed by us. They understand that what they see is a curated slice of a complex human being. We don't *really* bare our entire lives to the world – no matter how it looks or feels!

The problem emerges when parasocial connection becomes parasocial entitlement.

It is the quiet shift from, "Oh, I follow that Doctor online, I enjoy her work" to "I know her personally." From, "I relate to her story" to "I understand her motives better than she does". From, "I read all of her books, she is cool" to "I am invested in her choices and her personal life".

On TikTok, strangers dissect relationships in minute detail based on nine seconds of a video of a couple lip syncing to a silly song.

Are they still together? Do they even love each other anymore? Is one of them abusive? Did one of them cheat on the other? Why are they moving in together so soon? Will they have a baby? Should they even be talking about their relationship online? Why are they so loved up? Is it all an act?

Or even more minute than that: *Why did one of them smile like that when the other was talking? Did she just look to the left when he said that? Did you notice how they stood in that photo? What are they hiding? Look at their eye contact, one of them is lying . . .*

People morph into stalkers and become obsessed with micro-movements, imagined behaviours, and clothing choices. They believe there are illicit secrets to be discovered, or terrible, dark realities hidden beneath innocent pictures and videos of their victims.

Not only this, but people who experience parasocial entitlement begin to believe that they are in control of their target. Influencers are told when they should divorce, have a baby, relocate, apologise, forgive, or disappear. Minor celebrities have their facial expressions analysed frame by frame. Local activists are scrutinised as though they are characters in a long-running drama series. Comment sections become courtrooms. Threads of comments from anonymous usernames become 'evidence' (Thelwall et al., 2022; Mardon et al., 2022).

The line between commentary and surveillance blurs quickly.

Surveillance, in this context, does not always look sinister at first glance. It can look like curiosity. Like concern. Like community. But surveillance is defined by monitoring with intent. It is the systematic observation of someone's behaviour, often for the purpose of gathering information. When followers, associates, ex-partners or strangers begin archiving posts, tracking 'inconsistencies', cross-referencing timelines, and speculating about hidden meanings, they have moved beyond passive viewing. They have entered the realm of fixation.

Obsession is characterised by persistent, intrusive thoughts about a person that are difficult to control and resistant to contrary evidence. It narrows attention, amplifies resentment, and fuels rumination. In digital spaces, obsession is rewarded. Algorithms feed you more of what you linger on, whether that is for enjoyment or resentment. The algorithm doesn't care. The more you search a name, the more you see it. The more you comment, the more content is served.

Some people might begin 'hate-following' someone by deliberately watching someone they despise (Mardon et al., 2022). I have noticed this more and more lately. On the surface, it makes no sense. If someone irritates you, or triggers you – or you just straight up loathe them – why voluntarily consume all of their content? Why go on their page at all? Why not just block them?

I began to research this and found several interesting answers. The first was the concept of obsessional attachment – and the argument that hatred is still a form of attachment. Anger, envy, resentment and hatred all cause physiological and psychological activation of some sort. The attachment may be incredibly unhealthy, but it is still there, and people can become obsessed with it. They tell themselves that they cannot stand the person, but cannot look away (Mardon et al., 2022).

This led me to another thought about moral superiority. In the many cases of online stalking that I have analysed and explored, I have noted that people who stalk seem to enjoy hating their target so they can criticise their choices, appearance, or lifestyle. Comments such as "I would never wear an outfit like that!", "I would never behave like that!", "I'm more ethical than her", or "I would never bring up my kids like that!" are common – suggesting that some of this is related to a feeling of superiority over the victim. They get to compare themselves to someone they already hate and then tell themselves (and the world) a story that has very little to do with their target and much more about their own lives.

I was reminded of an example of this strange behaviour by my wife as I was writing this book. Whilst we were being stalked online, we got married. Jay wore white Dr Martens under her wedding dress, which was posted online. Several of the women became outraged that she had worn white Dr Martens, and all announced that they would be burning or throwing their pairs away because they hated her so much.

The third possibility seems to be envy. Hate-following someone can have strong links to jealousy and envy, and for some people, it is easier to convert their envy into contempt and abuse than it is to admit admiration or inspiration. If someone is successful, confident, visible, attractive, wealthy or outspoken in some way, this can activate several insecurities or desires in people who watch them. The response to this can be feelings of defensiveness or vulnerability, which in this context requires anger, hatred or aggression to shut down (Meloy et al., 2011). This creates a toxic feedback loop where the person can become angry at the target and hate them for everything they perceive them to have, but can continue to expose themselves to it to get angry in order to protect themselves from vulnerable feelings that they too want those things, and often don't know how to get them.

Cycle of envy-motivated online stalking

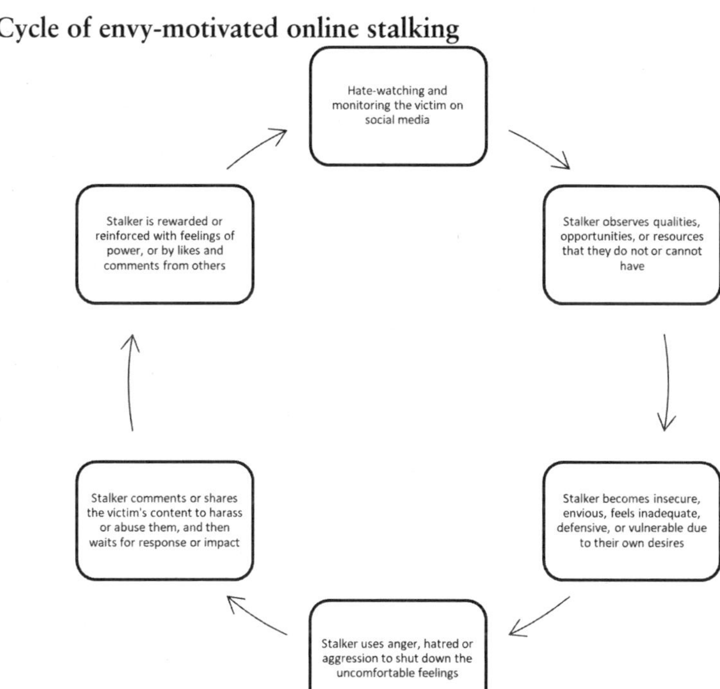

Taylor, 2026

So much of this conversation is about personal identity, something that is becoming increasingly warped in an online world. Identity, fantasy, and grievance can now merge in powerful ways.

Identity refers to our sense of who we are. Online, identity is often curated and performative. We align ourselves with causes, communities, and narratives that make us feel good about ourselves. We follow people who reflect or challenge our values. When a public figure's identity becomes symbolically linked to our own, disagreement with them can feel personal. If someone has built part of their identity around supporting a particular activist, any perceived inconsistency in his/her behaviour may feel like a betrayal of themselves (Thelwall et al., 2022).

Again, I have personal experience of this phenomenon and this is something I have battled with in the past. As a fully-fledged human being, I see myself as having thousands of complex and often contradictory views, feelings, experiences, ideas and emotions. But as a public figure, I'm supposed to be robotically consistent. I am supposed to represent an identity that others have attached to, but, of course, I didn't know this initially and it was something that I had to learn the hard way.

Still to this day, I get angry emails and messages from people who have followed me for years and agree with my work, my books and my ideas, only to find that I hold a view they dislike or disagree with. This causes people to become indescribably angry with me personally, to the point where they then feel the need to write to me to express how disgusted they were to discover that I did not align with them on a specific issue – despite them agreeing with all of my other works. Some people send offensive and abusive messages, tell me that they will never support me again and will say that I turned out to be a terrible person, but some will send me long emails demanding that I change my views immediately to align with their own, so they feel like they can continue to follow me without discomfort.

I have even had experiences of this where strangers have become very upset with me because I am friends with someone they dislike or disagree with and contact me to demand that I break all contact with my friend or they will inform me that they will never support my work again.

This perceived control over my life – way before the stalking escalated – was enough to frighten me. I felt like every connection, idea, value, or experience was being forensically analysed and then compared against their own internal identities. If something didn't line up, I was subjected to anything from a few angry emails to thousands of people engaging in weeks of online mobbing, death threats, rape threats and abuse. I hadn't realised that I had become public property.

But identities are only part of the story of obsession and connection.

Research demonstrates that fantasy has a role to play in stalking and online parasocial behaviours. Fantasy fills in the gaps left by limited information. We follow someone online who we have attached an identity to, but we do not really see their entire lives, characters, or personalities. We do not see the mundane arguments, the private doubts, the contradictions, the fatigue or illnesses, the boring errands, the family dynamics, the weekends cleaning the shed, or the days where they stay in bed eating doughnuts and wishing they could escape their lives for a while (Thelwall et al., 2022).

We see selected moments or ideas. The mind, uncomfortable with ambiguity, constructs coherence where there is none. It creates a story, even if it is fabricated. That story can be flattering or hostile. In the parasocial world, fantasy is often hostile, where neutral acts are reinterpreted as strategic or deliberate and silence is interpreted as concealment, deception, or avoidance. The person watching becomes suspicious and feels betrayed or lied to if behaviours don't align with what they want to see (Thelwall et al., 2022; Mardon et al., 2022).

Grievance then attaches to that fantasy, meaning that the person becoming fixated with the target has now become angry about an entirely imagined slight.

Grievance is the perception of having been wronged. In the digital age of parasocial relationships, people can experience grievance in response to choices that have nothing to do with them. An influencer changes her content direction. A writer blocks a commenter. An activist declines to engage in a debate. A local businessperson posts a political opinion. An old friend shares a contentious joke. A big celebrity supports a charity they don't like. These actions can trigger outrage and aggression in followers or watchers who feel personally invested.

I have experienced this convergence in deeply unsettling ways. Strangers have felt entitled to comment on my marriage, my children, my body, my motives, my childhood, and my character with the confidence of old, trusted friends. They have debated my parenting as though they were co-guardians. They have speculated about my relationship and my sexuality as though it were a television plotline. They have analysed my professional decisions as though they were shareholders in my life – and they have been outraged when they have found something (or often imagined something) that didn't align with them.

Digital culture has normalised behaviours that, a generation ago, would have been recognised as extreme.

Imagine a person sitting outside your workplace every day, taking notes on who you spoke to, what you wore, when you arrived and when you left. Imagine them discussing your marriage with strangers in the pub as though they were intimately involved. Imagine them compiling a folder of your statements and debating your personality traits at length with people who have never met you. We would recognise this as concerning, obsessive behaviour, if not outright stalking.

Online, the same behaviour is reframed as engagement, or merely as benign chatter.

The chronic online world also erodes temporal boundaries. There is no natural end point. Content is archived. Stories are saved. Old posts resurface. Past versions of you remain searchable – forever. In physical communities, towns, villages and cities – even in our own families – memory fades eventually and people move on. Online, it is preserved and retrievable. You can be accused of 'inconsistencies' when really you just changed your mind, forgot something, or grew up. This digital permanence fuels obsession because the object of fixation never fully disappears, meaning people can be fixated on someone for the rest of their lives with no barriers to the behaviour. Indeed, some scholars have argued that stalking and fixation resembles addiction (Brooks, 2021).

The normalisation of overexposure also plays a role, and I say this as someone who has spoken many times online of my personal life and my own experiences such as being raped and abused. Many creators are encouraged to share more personal stories to grow their platforms, and in fairness, I have never felt a pressure to do that. I share my stories and experiences because I naturally communicate and teach in my personal voice. I have never really had any interest in cultivating a 'professional identity' as a psychologist – I am what I am – and 'being a psychologist' is only a small part of my identity.

I am also a mother, a wife, a sister, a friend, a writer, a woman, a lesbian, a working-class person, a Stokie, a mixture of my mother and my father, an academic, a CEO, an activist, a victim of rape and abuse (and stalking . . .), a sound bath practitioner, a meditator, a business owner, an avid reader, a public speaker, a researcher, a lover of cars and driving, a hip-hop and RnB fan, a keen traveller . . . I am a thousand things, all at once. I just bring my whole self to my work, and sometimes people love it, and sometimes, not so much.

But I suppose that is just my own story. I do know that lots of people feel pressure to disclose more and more personal information in order to generate likes and views, and this is something that was researched by Thelwall et al. back in 2022. Vulnerability is commodified on the internet. Behind-the-scenes glimpses of others are rewarded with engagement. The more someone shares, the more audiences feel included. But access to slivers of personal lives is not consent to our entire existence. Public presence is not public property.

Yet in the digital age, people increasingly feel entitled to you, your life, your boundaries, your choices, and even your pain. They feel entitled to explanations. Entitled to full transparency, to moral perfection and to emotional labour. If you do not provide these things, you are framed as evasive, arrogant, evil, or manipulative. In my view, this entitlement is the seedbed of online stalking.

When entitlement is frustrated or blocked, some individuals escalate. They move to obsessive watching and monitoring. They seek out additional information beyond what is willingly shared.

Where do you go to the gym? Where do your kids go to school? How much did you pay for that house? Why did your last marriage break down? Why don't you ever mention your parents on your social media? Why won't you confirm or deny the rumours about your sexuality?

They cross-reference public records. They contact employers. They message family members. They report to authorities under the guise of 'concern'. And so, the stalking is born.

In my research on Tattle Life, I found that online stalkers frequently became invested in contacting, harassing and investigating family members, friends, employers, and even hobbies.

Obsessive and intrusive monitoring of victims of online stalking
- Partners of victims were harassed, monitored, and stalked (79%)
- Children of victims were harassed, monitored, and stalked (73%)
- Parents (40%) and siblings (31%) of victims were traced and stalked
- Colleagues at work were traced and stalked in 14% of cases

N = 150 (Taylor, 2025)

The behaviour often emerges gradually. From what I can tell from the research, and from hundreds of cases I analysed, the individual stalker does not see themselves as obsessive at all. They may frame their actions as accountability, truth-seeking, and community protection. In their internal narrative, everything they do is rational and justified. The target is just being evasive and dangerous.

Psychologically, this is reinforced by confirmation bias: the tendency to seek and interpret information in ways that confirm our pre-existing beliefs. Once a follower has decided that someone is dishonest, every post becomes evidence of that dishonesty. Contradictory information is reframed as manipulation or deliberate deceit. Entire stories and theories can be built to support their feelings (Mardon et al., 2022).

Parasocial connections to people we know

As I have written this chapter, I keep coming back to one question in my mind: how does this apply to people who are stalked online by someone they know, or used to know?

Much of the research on parasocial relationships focuses on strangers becoming obsessed with someone in the public eye – but obsession, fixation, and parasocial relationships can also occur between people who used to be connected. Ex-colleagues. Ex-partners. Ex-friends. Current partner's exes. People from our school days or someone we went on a date with two years ago.

In these examples, the parasocial, one-sided relationship and obsession is there, but the two people are not complete strangers, like in the literature. In the past, the person had a real relationship with the target. But what triggers someone to become obsessed and fixated with them in this way?

The research on ex-partner stalking is clear and robust. This is about control, power, and possession. But what about cases where someone is stalked by a contact from years ago, who they knew only very vaguely?

In my research into the identities of stalkers on Tattle Life, the results demonstrated that quite a sizeable proportion of online stalkers were in that category. Where the identity of the online stalked was revealed, 22% had met the victim once in person, usually many years prior. 18% were neighbours or people who lived locally and knew of them. 17% were ex-friends and 14% were people from the victims' childhood, most commonly people they used to go to school with, sometimes decades ago (Taylor, 2025).

These types of stalkers are neither intimates nor strangers. Whilst a parasocial relationship could be the answer here, other possibilities include a feeling of 'knowing' someone personally based on old memories of them, causing an illusion of intimacy and entitlement to them.

Secondly, Festinger (1954) proposed a theory of social comparison. He argued that people evaluate their own worth by comparing themselves to others, particularly peers from similar starting points. Usually, this will be peers from the same school or hometown. When people perceive their old classmate or someone from their upbringing to be more successful than them, happier than them, more confident, or more attractive than them, it activates envy, resentment, shame, and anger towards the person that fuels their obsession with them online. For some people, they move towards hate-following, obsessive monitoring, comparison with self, and then harassment, hatred and stalking.

Another explanation suggests that people are developing parasocial relationships with others simply by watching their content, looking at Facebook posts and watching Instagram stories online (Thelwall et al., 2022), whether they knew them or not.

The four factors involved in building strong parasocial relationships are theorised as follows:

Gaze: When friends talk it is normal to look at each other, so gaze is a logical source of parasocial interactions and relationships. This has been validated experimentally by showing that a recorded person gazing directly at the camera was more likely to elicit parasocial connections than when looking elsewhere.

Realism: Friendships are part of normal life, so parasocial relationships may form more intuitively when people see others in more naturalistic settings that mimic or show everyday life (at home, cooking, cleaning, chatting to the camera on our sofas, sharing pictures of our personal lives). There is wide evidence that the perceived realism of the media influences parasocial relationship strength.

Self-disclosure: Self-disclosure can vary from simple personal details, such as the person's real name, to information of the kind that would normally only be revealed to friends, such as relationship problems, bullying, mental health issues, physical health deterioration, and fears about the future. Self-disclosure is part of forming close friendships and can therefore cause parasocial attachments and relationships in viewers.

Time: Friendships take time to build through repeated interactions. Parasocial relationships have been hypothesised to form similarly over time. Simply put, parasocial relationships are formed when someone watches another person frequently and for long periods of time.

It is clear that we have much to learn and much to address about our online behaviour, and the way we are warping our human connections to each other.

This chapter is not a condemnation of followers, fans or communities. I have gained and learned so much from my own followers and I can honestly say that I have made lifelong friends with some of them. Some people started out as a so-called 'follower' but then became someone who I couldn't imagine life without now.

Real, powerful, healthy relationships can be built online – that much is obvious to me. But similarly, some very dangerous, abusive, and warped relationships can be built online, especially where the target isn't even aware it is happening to them. Arguably, this element is specific to the online world. Therefore, this chapter is an examination of how easily human attachment can distort when mediated through screens and technology, and it is an exploration of how the chronic online world has blurred lines that once felt obvious.

We need a new literacy and a deeper understanding of digital intimacy. We need to teach ourselves and our children the difference between knowing about someone and actually knowing them. We all need to know the difference between feeling connected and being connected. Crucially, we need to recognise that there is a significant difference between following someone online and being entitled to their personal and private lives.

CHAPTER 2

Why do people stalk?

It had taken weeks of calls to get the police to listen to us. Everyone we had spoken to had misunderstood, minimised, or totally dismissed what we were saying. However, we eventually found a police officer who listened to us.

There was one young detective named Hannah. She sat with us for hours whilst we showed her months of escalating posts, emails, phone calls, threads and the hundreds of lies being posted on Tattle Life.

First came the questions about how I knew the stalkers – to which I had to explain that I didn't know any of them for certain. We had tentatively worked out who some of them could be, but others had us stumped. The only thing we were certain of was that they had to be someone around us due to the specific information they seemed to have access to, but that meant looking at everyone. Our friends. Our colleagues. Even our own families.

We handed over the names of the people we thought we had figured out – all women.

The detective looked over them, clearly confused.

"How are you connected to these women?"

I started to explain, fully aware of how I sounded.

"Well, some of them are people I used to know many years ago. One of them is a complete stranger. One of them seems to follow me online . . ."

The detective interrupted.

"But how would they all know each other? They seem to talk as if they are friends," she queried.

I was becoming increasingly uncomfortable with the conversation, not because the detective was doing or saying anything offensive or inappropriate, but because I had started to realise that I sounded like I was describing some elaborate conspiracy every time I opened my mouth.

I took a slow, deep breath, and tried to calm my voice.

"We think they are being recruited in some way. Posts and links are being shared somewhere, and then more and more people get involved. They seem to try to find people close to us – neighbours, family members, old friends, ex-colleagues, that sort of thing – and then they target our business partners, our venues, and our workplaces. It's surprisingly organised."

I watched the detective closely. It was as if I could see the unease rising in her body. Like she wasn't sure if she was investigating a real crime or some sort of psychotic episode.

"I've never seen a case like this before . . . Why would a group of unconnected people suddenly team up to harass someone for months like this?"

And that led to the questions about motives. Hannah, the detective, was probably a little older than me. She flicked through the piles of evidence, becoming perplexed.

She had asked me why I thought this was happening to me and I had to explain that I didn't really know that either. I could see that this confused her even more, having dealt with many cases of ex-partner stalking over the years where the motive was clear. It was as if she was trying to fit our case into that mould. A square peg into a round hole, so to speak.

We had gone round in circles. Maybe they were doing this to me because they were lonely. Maybe they were bored. The detective had even suggested that they might be delusional, struggling with their mental health, or, in her words, "just not wired up right".

"Have you had any . . . intimate relationships with these people?" she asked.

I ran my fingers through my hair in despair. I knew why she was asking, of course. Through my job, I was aware that victims are normally stalked by an ex-partner or someone they knew – and to be fair to her, in those early days I was just as baffled as she was.

I shook my head.

"God, no! Well, I don't think so. I don't think any of them are my exes, if that's what you mean, and I have only had three relationships my whole life, including my current marriage . . ."

She went quiet again.

"Could any of them be people you have . . . you know . . . rejected? Or people who could be interested in you . . . or maybe people who could be interested in . . . your wife?"

I screwed my face up at the detective. The hatred and vitriol we had both endured for months had led me to strongly believe that the motive was resentment rather than romantic rejection. I hadn't considered at all that they might have some sort of attraction to one of us. From the things they were doing to us and the things they were saying about us, it seemed very unlikely that they were sexually or romantically interested in us.

"I really don't think so . . ." I dismissed.

The detective glanced at some of the messages, likes, and comments. The ones saying that they used to love me. The messages offering me gifts. Asking for tickets to my events. One saying that my book had saved their life. The posts saying that I was too unattractive to be with my wife.

"Well, you know, sometimes these stalkers only become so hate-filled and angry once they have been rejected in some way. Or once they realise that they can never have the person they want, so they set out to destroy their lives or their new relationships . . ."

Jay and I exchanged glances. The stalking had taken over our lives, but at no point had we ever considered that. I had a different theory, but I didn't have the confidence to say it out loud.

* * *

The question most people ask when confronted with stalking is deceptively simple: "Why?"

Why would someone devote hours, months, sometimes years of their life to monitoring, pursuing, or destabilising another human being? Why would they risk legal consequences, reputational damage, and social isolation? Why not simply move on?

The dominant cultural answer has long been pathology. They must be delusional. She must be unwell. They must be obsessed in a clinical sense. Psychiatry has offered many labels over the years. Media headlines have provided caricatures. The stalker is always framed as weird, unstable, irrational, or detached from reality.

As an anti-pathology psychologist who rejects psychiatric labelling, and even as a victim of stalking myself, I just cannot get behind the movement to frame stalkers as suffering from an illness. To me, stalking has a clear social and emotional purpose for the perpetrator.

When you sit across from victims for long enough, when you analyse case files, read transcripts, and observe patterns over time, another truth emerges. Most stalking is not chaotic or pointless. It is not random. It is not the by-product of some tragic or complex psychosis. It is purposeful behaviour.

People stalk because stalking serves them.

I say this all the time in my broader work. People abuse their partners because they get something out of it. People abuse their kids for the same reason. People's behaviour, no matter how terrible, terrifying or violent always has a root purpose, but oftentimes, we don't want to peak behind the curtain.

And just because the stalking serves them in some way does not make it moral. It does not make it harmless. But it does mean that if we want to understand stalking, we must be willing to examine function, opportunity, and tactics, rather than default to a psychiatric diagnosis.

The internet has become a part of every aspect of our lives, and may encourage individuals to act defiantly, which creates the increased opportunity for victimisation (Ahlgrim & Terrance, 2021). The use of technology often creates a general sense of depersonalisation and disinhibition allowing the online stalker to victimise an individual or many individuals.

So, let's explore some key theories of stalking:

To assist in understanding the motivations and psychological characteristics of stalkers, several classification systems have been developed. These typologies provide valuable insights into risk assessment, intervention strategies, and offender management, though they do not fully explain why individuals engage in their stalking behaviour.

One of the most widely used frameworks is Mullen's typology of stalkers, developed by Paul Mullen and colleagues. This classification system seeks to account for the initial motivation for the stalking, the relationship between the stalker and the victim, and the proposed 'psychopathological' characteristics of the stalker.

Mullen's typologies underpin structured professional judgment tools such as the Stalking Risk Profile (SRP) and have been instrumental in guiding policing, mental health interventions, and risk management strategies for decades. The typologies continue to be used by the National Stalking Consortium, College of Policing, police forces around the world, and academia.

It is important, however, to remember that Mullen's typologies were theorised based on in-person stalkers, largely men who had come to the attention of police and prison services.

Mullen's Five Stalker Typologies (Mullen et al., 1999)
1. **Rejected Stalker**
   - **Motivation:** Stalking occurs after the breakdown of a close, usually intimate, relationship. Initially, the stalker

may seek reconciliation, but this can shift to anger and revenge against the victim for 'rejecting' them.

- **Behavioural Patterns:** Many rejected stalkers oscillate between trying to resume the relationship and punishing the victim for leaving. In some cases, the stalking itself becomes a substitute relationship, maintaining a perceived connection.
- **Risk Factors:** This group presents a high statistical risk of violence, particularly if there was previous domestic abuse. Persistent stalking in this category is common and often associated with coercive control.

2. **Intimacy-seeking Stalker**
   - **Motivation:** Driven by loneliness and a strong desire for a relationship, intimacy-seeking stalkers develop beliefs about their connection with the victim.
   - **Victim Relationship:** The victim is typically a stranger or acquaintance, with the stalker believing they are destined to be together, despite clear rejection.
   - **Mental Health Considerations:** Some within this category are diagnosed with psychiatric disorders, usually including delusional disorders.
   - **Risk Factors:** While violence towards the victim is less common, third parties (such as the victim's actual partner) may be at risk. Stalking often persists for long periods unless legal or specialist intervention is provided.

3. **Incompetent Suitor**
   - **Motivation:** Similar to intimacy-seekers, incompetent suitors pursue a relationship but lack the social skills or emotional insight to engage appropriately. Unlike intimacy-seekers, they do not hold any delusional beliefs about an existing bond.
   - **Behavioural Patterns:** Stalking is often short-lived, stopping when the stalker is clearly rejected. However, this

group tends to repeat the pattern with lots of different victims.

- **Risk Factors:** Stalkers in this group may have developmental disorders, autistic spectrum conditions, or significant learning disabilities, which can contribute to difficulties in understanding communication, relationships, and boundaries. While the theorised risk of violence is low, persistent unwanted contact can cause significant distress to victims.

4. **Resentful Stalker**
   - **Motivation:** Stalkers in this group believe they have been mistreated or subjected to an injustice. Stalking serves as a means of seeking revenge or retribution for a grievance. Victims can be individuals known to them, professionals they have sought help from, colleagues or employers, acquaintances, strangers, organisations, celebrities, politicians and others who the stalker believes has wronged them.
   - **Behavioural Patterns:** Resentful stalkers often fixate on perceived grievances, repeatedly escalating their behaviour to force acknowledgment of their complaints.
   - **Risk Factors:** These individuals frequently collect 'evidence' to justify their claims, including emails, text messages, social media posts, letters, and official correspondence. Stalking can continue for years, with little motivation to stop unless their grievances are formally addressed. These individuals can become fixated on destroying the victim's life, relationships or career as a form of punishment or 'justice'.

5. **Predatory Stalker**
   - **Motivation:** This category includes a small but highly

dangerous group of offenders who stalk for sadistic or sexually deviant reasons.

- **Behavioural Patterns:** Stalking in this context is typically covert and involves surveillance, with the victim often unaware they are being stalked until a physical assault, murder attempt, rape, abduction, or sexual assault occurs.
- **Risk Factors:** Predatory stalkers are often found within the criminal justice system for offences such as sexual assault, rape, or sexual/domestic homicide rather than the stalking itself.

Other theories and explanations of stalking:

Behavioural theory offers a starting point. In behavioural psychology, actions are understood through reinforcement. Behaviour that produces a rewarding outcome is more likely to be repeated. The reward does not have to be material. It can be emotional. It can be social. It can be the reduction of anxiety or the feeling of perceived control. Stalking often provides precisely these reinforcements.

For the resentful grievance stalker, especially those who operate online, surveillance and intrusion reduce the discomfort of perceived injustice. Grievance stalking is driven by the belief that the victim has wronged the stalker in some way (Mullen et al., 1999). This wrong may be real, exaggerated or entirely imagined. A rejected job applicant who feels humiliated. A former partner who believes they were betrayed. A follower who thinks they have been blocked unfairly for asking a question. The internal narrative is one of moral injury.

The stalker experiences anger, humiliation, or resentment. Monitoring the victim offers emotional regulation. It keeps the grievance alive, but it also provides a sense of agency.

"I may have been wronged, but I am not powerless. I can watch. I can expose. I can pursue. I can punish . . ."

In criminological theory, this aligns with what is sometimes referred to as retaliatory or resentful stalking, as in the table of typologies above. The stalker frames their actions as justified. They are settling a score.

In my own research, this typology makes up the majority of online stalkers. In fact, some fascinating research has explored the behaviours of online communities that are set up deliberately to pursue targets in this way. Mardon et al. (2022) explored online forums where people gathered to complain, accuse and attack victims who they felt had wronged them in some way. In most cases, the victim was an influencer, or someone with a small public profile who felt aggrieved by their benign behaviour.

Here are a few real quotes from the Mardon et al. research:

Suddenly she's radio silent?! She's kept everyone updated about basically everything going on in her life these past few months and even maintained interaction through family deaths. For her to be liking and commenting [on other posts] but keeping her viewers in the dark, knowing that they're concerned about her, is pretty despicable. She could have at least posted a couple of sentences without even having to go into detail.

They act as if they don't owe their followers an explanation – they do!!!

She totally deserves to lose work and brand relationships because of this. Otherwise, there's no consequences for her behaviour. She has shown she has no respect for her followers.

As you can see here, people in these forums become angry and resentful for very minor reasons (not posting frequently enough whilst commenting on another post elsewhere), which leads them to become obsessed and write that she is 'despicable'. In the third quote, the users had coordinated mass harassment campaigns against the woman, even writing up templates for hundreds of people to use to send to her employers and business contacts.

I have seen this countless times now in cases where individuals dedicate extraordinary amounts of time to documenting perceived inconsistencies in their victim's public statements or private social media profiles. They create timelines and archive posts. They write long analyses of character flaws. The stated aim is often some form of 'accountability'. The psychological function for the stalker though, is vengeance.

Revenge-based stalking is closely related but often more explicitly punitive. This form of stalking seeks to harm the target's reputation, relationships, or livelihood. It may involve coordinated complaints, spreading rumours, contacting employers, friends, families, or regulators. It is strategic – and very common in online stalking tactics. From a sociological perspective, revenge stalking can be understood through the lens of power and status. When someone feels that their social standing has been diminished or their authority challenged, stalking becomes a means of restoring dominance. It is a power struggle enacted through persistence.

Identity-seeking stalking, as we have begun to explore in the previous chapter, operates differently. Here, the act of stalking provides structure, purpose and belonging. In a world where identity is increasingly constructed through online communities, fixation can become a central organising principle of the self. An identity-seeking stalker may begin as a follower, a friend, a customer or an acquaintance

(Thelwall et al., 2022). They consume content, feel connected, and feel seen. Over time, the target becomes symbolic. Monitoring them becomes a routine. Participation in group discussions about them becomes a social anchor (Mardon et al., 2022). The stalker's sense of self becomes intertwined with the pursuit.

In these cases, stalking is not only about the target. It is about the stalker's internal emptiness, boredom, or lack of direction. Surveillance fills time. Analysis creates meaning in their life. Group outrage provides belonging and friendship. The behaviour is reinforced socially through likes, agreement, and shared narratives.

Entitlement stalking is perhaps the most pervasive in the digital age. It is rooted in the belief that access equals ownership. A former partner who cannot accept the end of a relationship. A follower who believes public presence requires total transparency. A colleague who feels they are owed recognition. Entitlement stalkers experience boundaries as rejection. Psychologically, entitlement is linked to narcissistic injury, not in the diagnostic sense but in the descriptive sense of wounded pride. When someone's self-concept relies on being acknowledged, admired or prioritised, boundaries feel like humiliation. Stalking becomes an attempt to reassert relevance (Meloy et al., 2011; Weekes & Storey, 2025).

Jealousy and control also remain powerful motivators, especially for female stalkers (Meloy et al., 2011). In intimate contexts, stalking frequently emerges after separation. The stalker cannot tolerate the loss of proximity or influence. Monitoring offers an illusion of continued connection. Even negative contact is preferable to none. In these cases, stalking is an extension of coercive control. It is an attempt to re-establish dominance after formal relationship structures have ended.

My own life has shown me how these motivations can overlap. A former partner may stalk to maintain control and punish autonomy. A stranger may stalk to pursue grievance and construct their own identity. The behaviours look very different on the surface, but the function is similar: stalking provides psychological reward.

Criminological theories, such as Cornish & Clarke's Rational Choice Theory from 1986, suggest that individuals weigh perceived costs and benefits before acting. In stalking, the perceived benefits often outweigh the perceived risks, particularly in digital contexts. The benefits include emotional discharge, attention, validation, control, power, revenge, and sometimes financial gain through content creation or monetised gossip.

The risks or costs are generally related to being discovered, arrested, or punished. However, when it comes to online stalking, the risks feel distant – because they are. Legal consequences range from non-existent to inconsistent. Platforms rarely ever intervene when victims report to them. Social circles may validate or minimise the behaviour rather than condemn it or support the victims. Rational Choice Theory could be applied here too to explain that the perceived costs to the stalker are lowered by anonymity online. They are able to use pseudonyms and access private forums. This, partnered with slow policing response, cross-jurisdiction barriers and issues with cross-force working means that there's a lack of any real consequences.

Sociological perspectives remind us that stalking and obsessions never occur in a vacuum – because ultimately, nothing does. Stalking is shaped by cultural norms around entitlement, gender, status and power. In patriarchal contexts, men are often socialised to view women as relational assets. When those assets assert independence, control strategies will intensify. In digital cultures, audiences of female professionals and influencers are socialised to expect access. When access is restricted, the backlash follows, which is demonstrated very clearly in Mardon et al. (2022).

We must also consider the role of fantasy across all forms of stalking. Fantasy in stalking is not necessarily delusion, but it is narrative construction. The stalker creates a story about themselves and the target. Maybe they tell people that their victim is a liar, that they are dangerous, or did something terrible, so are deserving of consequences. Ex-partners who stalk their victims will often concoct stories and fantasies about them – very often about betrayal, affairs, and lies – and will even claim that their victim is mentally ill.

In identity-seeking stalking, the fantasy may cast the stalker as a protector or truth-teller. In grievance stalking, the fantasy casts them as a victim-hero exposing corruption. In jealous stalking, the fantasy may involve imagined betrayals or conspiracies. These narratives are important because they sustain the stalker's behaviour. They provide coherence to the stalker, and they justify escalation of tactics and impact on the victim.

Digital factors amplify all of this.

Anonymity reduces inhibitions of the stalker. The online disinhibition effect, theorised by Suler in 2004, refers to the phenomenon whereby individuals behave more aggressively or intimately online than they would face-to-face. Screens create distance. Distance reduces empathy. When people cannot see the immediate emotional impact of their behaviour, it is easier to rationalise it.

Suler (2004) found that people would very often behave online in ways that they would never behave in person. They were more likely to engage in harassment, bullying, abuse, threats and stalking online – due to disinhibition. Research on this has since found that people dehumanise their victims online and depersonalise themselves, so they do not have to hold themselves responsible for their online behaviours – as if they are not real – or that the behaviour they engage in online is not carried out by their 'true' offline self (Alimu et al., 2025).

Anonymity also fragments accountability. Pseudonyms, multiple accounts, private forums and encrypted messaging create layers between action and consequence. The stalker can test boundaries incrementally and escalate gradually. Each act feels small in isolation. Surveillance capacity has expanded beyond anything previous generations could imagine: location tags, searchable records, archived posts, image metadata, and shared networks. The collapse of physical barriers means that distance no longer protects the victim.

In the past, stalking required effort, time and physical proximity. Now, it requires a device and an internet connection. This does not create stalkers from nothing, but it lowers the threshold for behaviour that might once have remained fantasy – or a passing thought.

I am sure many people have had passing thoughts of stalking their ex, following them somewhere, and finding out who they are with. Some people will have even contemplated stalking a celebrity, or trying to find out where they live, or what bar they might go to. I am sure that people have had revenge fantasies of attacking or harming someone who wronged them, too. But did they act on these fantasies? Probably not.

Would they be more likely to do it now that they have an anonymous digital avenue?

The research in this space, both old and new, suggests that they would.

One of the most common questions is whether stalking is a mental illness.

Stalkers take so many different forms that people often try to theorise one overarching reason why people behave in particular ways. There is the resentful former employee who sends dozens of emails to regulators claiming malpractice after being dismissed. The anonymous forum user who spends years dissecting a public figure's personal life under the banner of accountability. The ex-partner who repeatedly reports false allegations to police to trigger investigations. The self-described crusader who frames relentless monitoring as activism.

In each case, the stalker often describes their actions as necessary. They emphasise the victim's supposed wrongdoing. They deny their own investment in the behaviour and they cast themselves as the rational one merely raising concerns. They create fantasies and justifications. They see themselves as heroes or warriors.

But if we examine the behavioural patterns, common threads appear long before systems intervene. Escalation. Increased frequency of contact or monitoring. Boundary violations framed as concern. Attempts to recruit others into the narrative. Use of institutional mechanisms to pursue the target. Persistence despite clear requests to stop.

These patterns are clearly not symptoms of mental illness. For me at least, they are signs of someone pursuing power and control over their victim, not someone struggling with their mental wellbeing – but researchers have been debating and exploring this for decades. Very often they conclude that stalkers are suffering from personality disorders, psychoses and mental illnesses.

Albrecht et al. (2022) found that 67% of stalkers had lifetime use of mental health services and over 70% of stalkers in prison or probation services had at least one diagnosed psychiatric disorder. They also reported studies by Nijdam-Jones and colleagues which had assessed and then diagnosed people who were stalking their ex-partners. In a sample of 137 stalkers, they diagnosed 30% with mood disorders, 10% with psychotic disorders, 46% with substance use disorders, and 50% with personality disorders. In 44% of the cases, they diagnosed multiple disorders, but interestingly, in 28% of stalkers they diagnosed nothing.

When it comes to types of stalking versus psychiatric diagnoses, people who stalk strangers and acquaintances are 3–5 times more likely to be diagnosed with a psychotic disorder than people who stalk their ex-partners (Albrecht et al., 2022).

Despite this, the general consensus as I write this book is that whilst the diagnosis of mental disorders is clearly extremely common in stalkers, they are not the reason people stalk others, online or offline. Generally, stalking is now thought to be caused by many different factors including situational, social and vulnerability factors. Contrary to popular portrayals, stalking is not caused by psychopathy and is actually very rarely diagnosed, even in convicted stalkers (McKeon et al., 2015).

Mental disorders have always been explored in relation to stalking, especially where professionals felt that stalkers had developed 'delusions' about their victims. This is because where untrue beliefs were found to be held by stalkers about their victims, the stalking would usually last longer, and be more intense (Albrecht et al., 2022). Further, it seems easier for us as a society, and as groups of professionals, to suggest that someone is mentally ill, or suffering from some sort of illness, than to address much larger structures which normalise stalking behaviour, control, abuse and violence.

One possible explanation for this overlap not being causal is that there is no pathway (for example, mental disorders do not cause stalking, and stalking does not cause mental disorders) – but that both issues share a common root cause. As an anti-pathology psychologist, I reject the concept of a mental disorder entirely, but I do recognise that the two factors could share this common root.

For example, someone could begin to stalk and begin to struggle with their mental health due to the very same thing. A person could go through the sudden breakdown of a relationship and simultaneously begin stalking, obsessing, monitoring and threatening their ex-partner, whilst also developing psychological responses such as self-harming or becoming very anxious that are then cast as symptoms of a mental disorder or personality disorder.

In this case, a psychologist or psychiatrist might assess the stalker, see the collection of those behaviours as connected and go on to conclude that the stalker has a psychiatric disorder that is causing them to engage in stalking. They might even think that because the stalking and the mental health problems began at the same time, they must be one and the same thing.

Like rational choice theory, I would argue that instead of mental illnesses and personality disorders, stalking behaviours are strategies. Strategies that serve many purposes to the stalker.

To say that stalkers stalk because it serves them is not to absolve them or excuse them at all. They need to be held fully accountable, and they need to be stopped. It is to refuse the comforting fiction that stalking is inexplicable, or some mental disorder that they cannot control. When we treat stalking as incomprehensible madness, we avoid examining the social structures that enable it. Stalking serves emotional regulation of perpetrators that require swift intervention. It channels their anger and entitlement – whether imagined or not. It reduces anxiety about loss of control – again, whether imagined or not. It transforms their sense of vulnerability and humiliation into action they take that satisfies them in some way.

Stalking therefore serves psychological needs. It provides identity and purpose to the stalker. It creates narrative coherence in lives that may otherwise feel empty and fragmented.

Online stalking in particular serves social goals. It builds community among the like-minded. It earns validation. It generates attention – and this is something that is very specific to online stalkers. As discussed, in-person stalkers rarely want attention or validation in the same way. Ex-partner stalkers may want the attention and control of their victim, but they generally do not want the attention of everyone in the town, or thousands of people online. Stalking can even serve political aims. When surveillance and harassment are directed at activists, journalists or campaigners, the behaviour functions as intimidation (Ivask, 2025). It is a tool of silencing – but it is always framed as righteous. In recent research, academics found that 98–90% of politicians were victims of stalking (Sheridan et al., 2019).

Online and in-person stalkers: similarities and differences in offending

Domain	Online stalker	In-person-only stalker
Geography	Global – no geographical boundaries or barriers	Local and specific physical locations
Anonymity	Often anonymous	Rarely anonymous
Audience	Potential for mass audiences of thousands of people; Can involve thousands of allies or third parties to support the stalking	Usually secret or private behaviours; Avoids being seen or witnessed
Evidence	Digital trails of behaviours; Enormous levels of digital evidence; Likely to be minimised; Extremely low likelihood of prosecution or arrest	Physical sightings, such as CCTV or witnesses; Likely to be taken more seriously; Higher likelihood of prosecution or arrest, but still very low

Violence risk	Highly variable, may escalate to in-person stalking in some cases; Less likely to use physical violence	Often higher immediate physical risk, and higher risk of homicide or sexual assault
Reputational harm	Central tactic	Less common tactic
Scale	Can target many victims at once, or over a period of time; Can stalk 24/7 with no barriers	Usually one victim at a time, or one focus at a time; Stalking is at specific times and places
Demographics	Equally likely to be male or female; Likely to be younger (18–35); Likely to be more educated; Likely to be a professional; Likely to have good IT skills	Majority male; Average age is 30–55 years old; Likely to have history of committing domestic abuse
Typology	More likely to act in groups	More likely to act alone
Tactics	Monitoring social media; Screenshotting; Posting threats and tagging publicly; Doxxing; Large online smear campaigns; Searching for public records, databases, trawling digital footprints; Recruiting online groups to stalk victim collectively; Mass complaints and reports online; Viral posts; Sharing victim to forums and groups; Setting up websites about victim; Hacking emails, messages, phones	Physical following and monitoring; Turning up at work/home; Local smear campaigns Talking to neighbours and contacts; Harassing local friends and family; Contacting employers; Leaving physical objects and gifts; Sending physical letters and threats; Physical assaults of the victim; Damaging victim's property; Breaking into homes and property; Going through bins and waste; Adding trackers to cars and items
Goal	Reputation and life destruction; Punishment of victim	Physical proximity; Control, fear and power
Victim	More likely to be female; More likely to be journalists, academics, professionals, activists, influencers, politicians, business owners, public figures	More likely to be male; More likely to be ex-partners, colleagues, former acquaintances, neighbours, family members

Motive	Fixation, obsession and entitlement; Control and power over ex-partners; Desire for control, punishment or retaliation; Rejection and resentment; Grievance-based thinking; Seeking punishment; Romantic pursuit is less common	Seeking physical proximity; Control and power over ex-partners; Fixation, obsession and entitlement; Desire for control, punishment or retaliation; Rejection and resentment; Grievance-based thinking; Seeking punishment; Romantic pursuit is more common
Psychology	Believes they are in moral pursuit of justice; Justify behaviour as 'free speech'; Use a community identity of 'seeking accountability'; Believes they are a righteous warrior or hero; Believes that they are a victim of their target	Escalates after relationship and romantic rejection; Exhibit territorial or ownership thinking; Believes they are a victim of their target (usually interpersonal such as betrayal or loss)

The table above is built from many different studies cited throughout this book. However, there is a very important overlap between online and in-person stalkers: the hybrid stalker. As mentioned in the introduction, large proportions of stalkers use both online and offline stalking, whereby in-person stalkers regularly use online stalking tactics, or less frequently, online stalkers move to in-person stalking.

This is similar to the evidence base on online and contact child sex offenders (Elliott et al., 2009; Mandeville-Norden et al., 2008; Beech et al., 2008). Online child sex offenders will very often see themselves as more righteous, more sophisticated and less culpable than contact sex offenders. According to forensic research, while contact sex offenders will often use online sex offending alongside sexually abusing children in person, online sex offenders rarely move into contact offending (Elliot et al., 2009). One of the obvious reasons for this is risk to the offender themselves. Academics found that contact offenders were better manipulators, better communicators, felt less empathy for their child victims when they abused and harmed them, and were generally better equipped to carry out their offences psychologically. Online sex offenders preferred to sexually abuse children online, groom them, talk to them, and exploit them from behind anonymous accounts or pseudonyms, and reported feeling more empathy for their victims.

Interestingly, according to CEOP and the NCA (2013), online child sex offenders were more likely to be professionals, in stable relationships, highly educated and have good IT skills. CEOP (2013) also reported that online child sex offenders were found to be teachers, healthcare professionals, IT professionals, youth workers and clergy. This is the same pattern emerging in online stalkers – and probably an overlap we should do more research into.

In my own research into the Tattle Life stalking cases, where victims knew the identity of their stalkers, they reported them as being:

- Mental health nurses
- Teachers at their children's school
- Therapists and counsellors
- Academics
- Lawyers
- Social workers
- Police officers
- Healthcare professionals
- Doctors
- Charity workers
- NHS managers and leadership

The evidence base consistently shows that stalking is patterned behaviour, which often escalates when unchallenged. Yet professional systems frequently dismiss early warning signs as trivial. A few messages. A few posts. A few complaints. It is only when physical harm occurs that the seriousness is recognised. By then, the behavioural rehearsal has often been underway for months or years.

There is a motivation for professionals to deny the seriousness of the stalking, especially if they were aware of it for long periods of time where the victim was ignored or dismissed. In cases where victims were being stalked, harassed and threatened, it is common for systems to deny their accountability or their failure to protect. Admitting that they could have acted earlier or that they could have identified the stalking sooner, opens up questions, investigations and weaknesses in both the system and the individual professional who overlooked the stalking patterns.

If we want to prevent stalking properly, we must look earlier. There is a saying I often use in my teaching which is: "At some point, we need to stop pulling the bodies out of the river, and instead go upstream to figure out why (and if) they keep falling in."

Preventing stalking works in the same way. We cannot keep waiting for stalkers to escalate and harm their victims to do some retrospective research into why they did it. We must examine how entitlement is socialised. How grievance is amplified online. How anonymity shields escalation. How institutions can be manipulated through repeated complaints.

And we must be honest about the rewards that stalking offers to those who engage in it.

As long as stalking provides emotional relief, social validation or political leverage with minimal consequence, it will continue.

In my opinion, there is plenty of research out there being funded and undertaken that is a giant waste of time and money (see the studies exploring whether men are more sexually attracted to women who are struggling with endometriosis or not, or whether the viral satirical concept of the 'hot-crazy matrix' has any clinical applications. . . don't get me started).

Understanding why people stalk is not one of these useless navel-gazing academic exercises. It is a vital and necessary step in dismantling the myths that protect them. It allows us to finally move on from asking, "What is wrong with these people who stalk?" to asking, "What are they gaining, and how can we disrupt that reinforcement to protect victims?"

Stalkers stalk because it works for them – so how do we stop it from working for them?

CHAPTER 3

The female stalker

I had one of my worst experiences of disassociation at the launch for my book *Sexy But Psycho* back in 2022. Three private close protection officers were dotted around the room. An event designed to celebrate my new book had turned into the stuff of nightmares.

I was terrified, but I didn't even know who I was supposed to be terrified of.

I don't remember any of that night. I don't remember the words I said, the reading I did, the book signings, the hour-long Q&A, or the huge sea of faces. There are photos from the night that I have no recollection of. I felt completely detached from reality, and so I have no memory of the actual event.

The last thing I remember is the plain-clothes private security officer putting his hand on my shoulder and saying quietly to me, "We have checked all exits, corridors, and toilets. Everything looks good for now. We are positioned here, there, and over there if anything happens."

Another thread had appeared online, just a few days prior.

This should have been one of the most exciting days of my life, my first official *Sunday Times* bestselling book, the 'pinch-me moment' for thousands of authors, coupled with a sold-out book launch to boot.

Instead, I had endured an entirely silent taxi drive to the venue and I was exhausted in every way possible. Solid sleep would have been something I could have only dreamt of, if I was sleeping enough to even achieve dream-state. I had piled weight on and I looked positive swollen. My skin was pale. My hair was lifeless. My nails were brittle, and in any case, I had bitten them down to the skin. In the days approaching the book launch event, I felt as though I would vomit at any moment. I wasn't myself.

I was still refusing to read anything about myself online, and again, it was Jay who brought it to my attention. Whilst the threads, the posts, the comments, and the anonymous accounts had certainly increased – I kept telling myself that online trolls and weirdos were not going to jump out of the screen and hurt me. I had relied on that reassurance for months.

Until the moment I read the exchange below, just three days before the event.

Handbasket32: *Anyone else got tickets to her book launch? I wanted to go just to be in the room near her, but I refuse to give her any of my money.*

Traveltime89: *Oh gosh, I wish I had thought to get some! Then again, I am not sure I could cope with listening to her droning on for an hour about her pathetic book.*

OrangeDoor67: *I got some and I will definitely be going. Couldn't help myself. There's a few of us who managed to get tickets from someone who works for her. Self-obsessed bitch probably thinks it's a room full of her adoring 'fans'. She makes me cringe so bad.*

Handbasket32: *Ahh! Now you're making me want to come. Are you going to do anything? So many possibilities . . .*

Traveltime89: *You should just heckle her all night. Or ask her questions she can't answer to expose how stupid she really is. Is she doing a Q&A or is it just a book signing? Have you remembered to give fake names? Make sure you protect yourselves, I've heard she is extremely dangerous behind the scenes.*

OrangeDoor67: *Oh, we've got our ideas! Yeah – all in fake names, she won't know anything. Will be sure to report back everything for those of you who can't make it. She won't notice we are there, too busy obsessing over herself.*

Handbasket32: *Perfect. Have a 'great' night. And by that I mean – drink plenty of wine so you don't have to listen to her grating accent.*

OrangeDoor67: *Hahaha! I don't know how I will cope!*

Traveltime89: *Good point. Glad I'm not coming – I would not be able to help myself. But you know, there is more than one way to skin a cat. Plenty of other ways to bring her down.*

My heart was thumping in my chest, my throat, and my jaw. A wave of nausea ran through me. I was already nervous, but knowing that these people had deliberately got tickets to my event purely to stalk me (and ridicule me) was beyond frightening.

"I can't do it," I whispered to Jay in disbelief.

"It's sold out babe, you are going to have to do it . . ." She put her arm around me gently.

"But . . . how am I supposed to know who these people are – or how many of them are coming? What if they try to ruin my event? Why are they even coming? They clearly hate me . . . why come to the book launch and sit there for two hours?"

We looked at each other, shifting uncomfortably – both of us imagining how this might play out. We went back and forth. We questioned whether we were catastrophising slightly, and whether we needed to just treat these people like harmless weirdos. We anxiously discussed how far these people were willing to go – but eventually concluded that they were only brave on the internet.

That was until the very next day, when my phone rang at 9:00 am sharp.

"Is this Dr Jessica Taylor?"

The voice was quiet and serious.

"Uhh, yes. Who is speaking, please?"

"This is Anne, the event manager at the venue for your book launch on Friday night. Do you have a minute to talk? It's quite urgent, I'm afraid."

"Umm. Yeah . . ."

I panicked, which caused Jay to silently signal for me to put my phone on loudspeaker. The woman was hesitant but clearly disturbed by something.

"Unfortunately, we've received several emails and phone calls in the last few days. They are from people raising very serious concerns about . . . well . . . you."

We frowned at each other, still sat in bed, wrapped in our duvet.

"Me?"

"Yes. The emails contain quite a bit of information, stating that you are currently under police investigation for . . . well . . . some very serious crimes, truth be told. And that you are running some sort of illegal pyramid scheme that you will be promoting at the launch . . ."

"What?" I laughed, unsure whether I was horrified, enraged, or genuinely amused by this latest development. Jay had her head in her hands.

"Well, I am sorry to have to ask you this Dr Taylor, but is there any basis for these emails?"

I gasped at the ridiculousness.

"Of course there isn't! I have never been investigated by police in my life and I definitely do not run a pyramid scheme! This is a book launch for a nationally published book – both my publishers and my agents are attending on Friday. I am sure they can confirm anything you need."

The woman went quiet.

"I must tell you, there are emails urging us to cancel your event. Some of the people are threatening to boycott our venue if we go ahead . . ."

"You're not actually taking these emails seriously, are you?"

"Well, umm. I am not saying we believe them Dr Taylor, but the emails do claim that you are being investigated for human trafficking and exploitation of women. You must understand our position. We will have to get our own legal advice, especially as our venue would be targeted if we made the wrong decision here . . ."

***

For decades, stalking has been narrated as a male-only crime – and as a psychologist who specialises in male violence, and in supporting female victims of trauma and abuse, I accepted that narrative. I saw the cases of women being stalked and even murdered by their exes. I worked on police data which clearly showed that the majority of cases being referred to them were from women being stalked by men who they dated, married, divorced, or had children with.

The archetype is familiar and uncontroversial in the sector: the violent ex-partner, the rejected lover, the coercively controlling man who refuses to relinquish ownership of a woman he once dated or married. The research literature has, understandably, focused heavily on this pattern. Intimate partner stalking is common. It is dangerous. It is frequently lethal. It demands serious attention (Monckton-Smith, 2019).

The Suzy Lamplugh Trust reported that in over 90% of domestic homicides, it was stalking and coercive control that preceded the murder and in over 80% of those murders, there was prior police contact, reporting the perpetrator for stalking, harassment or domestic abuse.

When it comes to male stalkers of female victims, Monckton-Smith's vital work on the theorised Homicide Timeline (2019) has demonstrated clearly that there is a reliable pattern of behaviour and tactics of intimate partner stalkers before they escalate towards the homicide of their victim. Monckton Smith's eight-stage model outlines a gradual process of escalation, moving from fixation and coercive control to an eventual crisis point that triggers a lethal event. Each stage provides opportunities for intervention, particularly in stalking cases, where persistent fixation and surveillance indicate significant risk.

The eight stage homicide timeline – Monckton-Smith (2019)

Homicide timeline stage	Stalker behaviour
Stage 1: Pre-relationship or pre-occupation	• Persistent attempts to initiate a relationship (whether romantic, professional, or acquaintance-based). • Unwanted attention, gifts, or excessive communication. • A growing obsession with the victim, including surveillance and research into their life.
Stage 2: Early relationship or early fixation	• Rapid involvement and intensity in the relationship (if applicable). • Attempts to control aspects of the victim's life, including their movements, friendships, and online activity. • Testing boundaries, such as unexpected visits or tracking behaviour.
Stage 3: Coercive control and monitoring	• Surveillance of the victim through tracking devices, hidden cameras, or online monitoring. • Repeated unwanted contact, such as excessive messaging, showing up at workplaces, or appearing at social events. • Using legal systems (e.g. vexatious litigation or family court proceedings) to exert power over the victim.
Stage 4: Triggers for escalation	• The victim attempting to leave a relationship or sever contact. • Legal actions taken against the stalker, such as restraining orders or arrests. • A perceived humiliation or rejection.
Stage 5: Escalation	• Increase physical surveillance and intrusion into the victim's life. • Threaten violence, harm, or suicide. • Engage in property damage, cyberstalking, or reputational harm.
Stage 6: Crisis Point	• A sense of desperation or perceived loss of control. • Increased reckless behaviour, substance abuse, or detachment from reality. • Attempts to force confrontation with the victim.
Stage 7: Planning	• Collecting weapons or making logistical preparations. • Communicating their intent to third parties (which is often ignored or dismissed). • A final 'grand gesture' of control, such as a forced meeting.
Stage 8: Homicide	• Carries out homicide. • 85% of murders occur in victim's home.

The homicide timeline is extremely important work for anyone concerned with ex-partner stalking committed by violent men – and my research has shown me that it is frighteningly accurate.

But online something else has been happening. While institutions, academics, and policymakers concentrated on the violent male stalker, a different form of stalking was proliferating in the digital world. It did not always involve physical proximity. It did not always involve romantic rejection. It did not fit the cinematic script. And increasingly, it was being perpetrated by women.

This chapter is going to be uncomfortable for some. Hell, this was an uncomfortable realisation even for me. Having previously only been abused, attacked, harassed, threated and assaulted by men, it was quite the twist in the old tale when I was then stalked relentlessly for years by a group of women.

At first, I made excuses for them, tried to understand them, even tried to reason with some of them. I tried to reach out to explain the impact their behaviour was having on me, all of which are approaches I would never have attempted with male stalkers.

And herein lies my interest. If men were behaving in this way towards me, I would have recognised the risk immediately. In fact, when men have stalked me, I have realised straight away and reported it. Maybe that is because I know the risk of violence and the connection to lethality, but maybe that is also because those cases fit the stereotype of a stalker and so my mind and my nervous system recognised it as a familiar threat.

When women did it to me, I didn't assess the risk of harm in the same way.

Even when the woman who had become obsessed with me online put her hand inside my underwear at a professional event and told me she had always wanted to do it, I didn't know what to call it. Was that sexual assault? Yes. I suppose it was.

Why have I never called it that until this day? Because she was a woman.

Would I have recognised her weird, fixated online behaviour and then the sexual assault as dangerous if she had been a man? Honestly? Yes, I think I would have done.

And my responses mirror those I found in the academic literature. When tested with scenarios of stalking and harassment, participants were more likely to view scenarios as crimes when the stalker or perpetrator was male, and the scenario was perceived as more severe when the perpetrator was male (Ahlgrim & Terrance, 2021).

Yeesh. We have a lot of unpacking to do here.

This chapter is also uncomfortable because it disrupts the widely recognised narrative that many of us rely on: that women are over-whelmingly victims, whilst men are overwhelmingly perpetrators. In the context of domestic abuse and homicide that pattern remains statistically dominant. Men still represent the majority of in-person stalkers (Lambert et al., 2013; Ahlgrim & Terrance, 2021). But when we shift our focus to digital stalking, harassment campaigns, covert stalking, coordinated surveillance and reputational attacks, a differ-ent gender pattern begins to emerge.

In the Tattle Life scandal, the overwhelming majority of accounts that were engaging in sustained surveillance, analysis, character assassination and coordinated harassment were female. In fact, the majority of daily users of the site and members of the site are women (Taylor, 2025). The same pattern appears in other online spaces dominated by women, including large parenting forums and community platforms. Women stalking women is not a marginal phenomenon. It is central to the modern digital landscape. In fact, more and more studies are being published which now find that women are just as likely to stalk online as men (Ahlgrim & Terrance, 2021).

Profiles of female stalkers:
- More persistent than male stalkers
- More likely to stalk strangers and public figures than male stalkers
- Around 60% are white women
- Generally well educated, most graduated high school and most had bachelor's degrees
- Around half are single
- Around 60% are heterosexual
- More likely to stalk online
- More likely to develop obsessions with people they found through public visibility or internet
- Around 20% of female stalkers pursue secondary targets – usually friends, family, partners and co-workers of the victim
- More likely to use written communication to stalk and harass victims
- Less likely to seek proximity to their victims
- Less likely to use physical violence to assault their victims
- More likely to be motivated by envy and jealousy, especially towards other women who they deem to be attractive, glamorous, or successful

(Santos et al., 2024; Meloy et al., 2011; Jin & Ryu, 2020).

Some studies even find that women are more likely than men to stalk online (Smoker & March, 2017) – and that they are much more likely to engage in covert, persistent stalking behaviours. Large US population studies of over 65,000 people have shown that 24% of female victims and 43% of male victims were stalked by a woman.

My own case sits within this pattern, but it is not unique at all. It is illustrative.

When thousands of posts are written dissecting your marriage, your children, your body, your motives, your facial expressions and your tone of voice, you begin to notice something about the authors. The language. The cultural references. The jokes. The shared assumptions. The internal hierarchies. We knew instinctively that the tactics were not those utilised by men. The perpetrators were clearly women.

This does not make the behaviour softer. It just makes it differently expressed. Where a male stalker often has the physical presence and increased potential for violence and intimidation, a female stalker is more likely to use covert, manipulative, long-term tactics that cause different kinds of harm (Meloy et al., 2011).

The evidence base on stalking has historically skewed towards violent male perpetrators. Female perpetrators are often treated as anomalies, curiosities, or lower-risk outliers. In much of the published literature, female stalkers are simply seen as a bit mad, disordered, mentally ill and maybe even psychotic. It's as if there can be no other reason why women would engage in stalking, so they *must* be crazy (Santos et al., 2024; Meloy et al., 2011).

I can hardly say I'm surprised. After all, I did write an entire book on the pathologisation of women and girls. Let's not forget the now famous caricature of the 'bunny boiler ex', a portrayal from the 1987 film *Fatal Attraction*. The woman is so 'psychotic' and vengeful towards her lover that she literally boils his pet rabbit on the stove whilst stalking him.

But the digital environment has expanded the scope of stalking beyond intimate relationships. When stalking is defined accurately, as a pattern of unwanted, fixated and intrusive behaviour causing fear or distress, women are clearly present within the perpetrator population online. In fact, research demonstrates that in large samples of female stalkers, they are much more likely to stalk public figures, strangers, and celebrities than men (Santos et al., 2024; Meloy et al., 2011).

Traits associated with male and female cyberstalkers

Trait	Explanation
Male stalkers	
Machiavellianism	**What it means:** A personality tendency characterised by manipulation, strategic thinking, emotional detachment, and a willingness to exploit others to achieve personal goals. Stalking behaviours may be deliberate, calculated, and instrumental rather than purely emotional. The person may plan tactics to maintain access, control, or intimidation. **Example:** A man carefully times messages, uses mutual contacts to gather information, or engineers 'chance' encounters to maintain influence over an ex-partner.
Narcissism	**What it means:** An inflated sense of self-importance combined with entitlement, hypersensitivity to rejection, and a need for admiration. Rejection may be experienced as humiliation or injustice, triggering persistent attempts to regain attention, status, or control. **Example:** After a relationship ends, a man insists she 'owes' him closure and repeatedly contacts her because he cannot tolerate being ignored.

Problematic attachment styles	**What it means:** Insecure patterns of relating to others, often described as anxious (fear of abandonment) or avoidant (fear of intimacy but desire for control). Anxious attachment may drive repeated contact to reduce abandonment anxiety. Avoidant styles may lead to controlling or intrusive monitoring without emotional closeness. **Example:** A man repeatedly checks her social media and messages constantly, feeling panicked when she does not respond immediately.
Anger	**What it means:** Chronic or poorly regulated anger, especially in response to perceived rejection, disrespect, or loss. Stalking can function as retaliation or punishment following perceived wrongdoing. **Example:** After being blocked, he begins sending hostile emails and publicly posts accusations to 'teach her a lesson'.
Control strategies	**What it means:** Behavioural patterns aimed at dominating, restricting, or influencing another person's actions. Stalking becomes an extension of coercive control, particularly post-separation. **Example:** Tracking her whereabouts, contacting her employer, or using children or legal processes to maintain power over her life.
Physical aggression	**What it means:** A history of using or threatening physical force. Where stalking co-occurs with physical aggression, risk of escalation and fatality is higher. **Example:** A man who has previously assaulted a partner begins turning up at her home and workplace uninvited.
Female Stalkers	
Narcissism	**What it means:** Entitlement, need for validation, and hypersensitivity to perceived slights. May manifest as persistent attention-seeking, reputation attacks on others, or retaliatory behaviours when feeling rejected or excluded. **Example:** After a friendship breakdown, she creates multiple accounts to monitor and comment on the other woman's posts.

Envy	**What it means:** Distress or resentment triggered by another person's perceived advantages, success, relationships, or status. Stalking may involve monitoring, undermining, or attempting to damage the envied person. **Example:** A woman obsessively tracks a colleague's achievements online and spreads rumours that she has slept with the boss to diminish her success.
Interpersonal jealousy	**What it means:** Fear or resentment regarding a rival for affection, status, or belonging. Behaviours may focus on monitoring romantic rivals or interfering in relationships. **Example:** Repeatedly checking a former partner's new partner's social media and sending messages warning them about him.
Sadism	**What it means:** Deriving satisfaction from causing psychological or emotional harm to others. Online harassment, humiliation campaigns, or coordinated targeting may provide emotional gratification. **Example:** Participating in group harassment threads where the distress of the target is mocked and celebrated.

Santos et al. (2024) and Meloy et al. (2011)

The Tattle research offers a data set rarely examined with seriousness. Thousands upon thousands of posts written by women about other women. Threads spanning years. Coordinated efforts to monitor pregnancies, break down marriages, investigate and publish finances, disrupt and explore friendships and mock parenting decisions. Repeated reporting to employers, regulators, police, social care, and authorities. Archive-building. Screenshotting within minutes of posts going live.

Physically following victims around town centres to covertly film them on their phones. Standing outside of children's schools to watch their victim pick their kids up. Finding their address and house price data on Rightmove and sharing the floorplan on to the threads. Deliberately finding ways to access their personal social media and restricted Instagram stories in order to screenshot them and post them publicly to humiliate or monitor the victim.

Make no mistake, this is stalking behaviour.

Women stalking women online is often fuelled by resentment, envy and projection (Santos et al., 2024; Meloy et al., 2011). Resentment can arise when one woman perceives another as possessing something she lacks: visibility, success, beauty, confidence, influence, love, autonomy. Envy is a painful emotion. It threatens our sense of self. It destabilises identity. One way that people try to regulate envy is to devalue or completely destroy their target.

Projection plays a significant role here too. The insecure woman accuses the confident woman of arrogance. The deceitful accuse the authentic of manipulation. The resentful accuse the successful of fraudulent activity or theft. In online spaces, projection like this is rewarded. A woman who frames another woman as dangerous, narcissistic, fraudulent, unethical or abusive may receive social validation from a group of insecure or emotionally vulnerable women who are primed to believe it. But beyond envy and projection lies something more structural: internalised misogyny.

Internalised misogyny refers to the unconscious absorption and reproduction of patriarchal beliefs about women by women themselves. It manifests as harsh judgment of female behaviour, policing of other women's bodies and choices, suspicion of female success, and the perpetuation of narratives that women are manipulative, hysterical, attention-seeking or deceitful.

When women stalk women, they often do so through these scripts:

The successful woman must be a fraud. The confident woman must be hiding something. The ambitious woman must be neglecting her children. The outspoken woman must be unstable. These narratives are not new. They are centuries old. Digital platforms have simply given them amplification.

In my case, it was all of the above as well as a very strange obsession with my marriage and my sexuality. The stalking escalated around the time I married Jay. We were young and very open about how loved up we were. We would go to events together, post pictures and videos, we even recorded podcasts and webinars together. For some reason, this was transformed into something disgusting. Hundreds of posts appeared online which claimed I was lying about being gay. That my relationship was being faked for content.

Once that passed, the rumours moved to our sex life, our mental health and our personal relationship. Women we had never met posted online that they could 'imagine them having sex' and that they wondered 'if their tits got in the way when they talked'. Others claimed that we were both clearly suffering from borderline personality disorder, and that we needed psychiatric intervention. Some questioned why my wife was attracted to me, posting publicly that I was too fat and too ugly to be found attractive, and therefore I must be financially motivating or exploiting my wife. Some women posted online that my wife was a 'sugar baby', and that my marriage was a disgusting form of sexual exploitation – that I was paying for sex and intimacy.

Throughout the years of being stalked, our marriage and our relationship have been attacked, mocked and recast as an illicit affair, a form of exploitation, as two mentally ill attention-seekers, or as completely fake.

But of course, the women doing this to us would post online that they were doing it out of concern, from their fantasy ethical vantage point.

Research demonstrates that the female stalker frequently casts herself as morally superior to her victims (Meloy et al., 2011). This is where the 'justice seeker' or 'moral crusader' identity emerges. In the thousands of posts written about me and other women just like me, a recurring theme appeared: we were not simply disliked. It was more than that. We always had to be dangerous. Harmful. Abusive. Fraudulent. In their minds, these women who were posting online were not gossiping or stalking. Rather, they were protecting the public. The justice seeker believes, or pretends, that she is saving others by attacking and cancelling her victim.

This mindset is psychologically coherent for women. It reframes their hatred and aggression as altruism. It transforms stalking into activism. It allows the perpetrator to experience herself as heroic rather than hostile. In this way, she is a warrior for others – not a stalker at all.

In criminological terms, this aligns with what has been described as the 'resentful' or 'crusader' stalker (Mullen et al., 2000). But in female-dominated digital spaces, the crusade is often couched in the language of safeguarding, activism, politics, ethics, accountability or feminism. The target is framed as a bad mother, a bad wife, a bad professional, a bad woman, a bad human. They need to be taken down.

This is not incidental. It is highly gendered.

Most research finds that women are not likely to use physical violence against each other – we are not socialised to behave this way (Santos et al., 2024; Meloy et al., 2011). From birth, our aggression and violent potential is shamed, punished, and repressed until we never show it; whilst boys are taught that fighting is cool, that violence is power, that we attack people when we are angry. Boys see their favourite cartoon characters kill people who do bad things or who make them feel bad. Boys will be boys, they are told. Violent behaviour is made permissible.

The same is not generally true for girls.

Women are socialised to politely police each other. To compete subtly. To measure worth relationally. To take down the other woman using passive aggression, covert abuse, bullying, rumours, lies and character assassination. They are not encouraged to use violence, and so violence doesn't usually show up very often in their criminality or in their stalking of others.

In an interesting finding I came across from Meloy et al. (2011), male and female stalkers were compared for their use of violence and threats against their victims. I have pulled the findings together, along with the prevalence of stalking typology, so it is easy to see the similarities and differences between men and women who stalk.

Use of violence and threats against victims of stalking

Type of stalker		Female stalkers	Male stalkers
Ex-partner stalker	Prevalence	22%	55%
	Threats used	74%	83%
	Violence used	68%	74%
Acquaintance stalker	Prevalence	18%	12%
	Threats used	58%	68%
	Violence used	39%	51%
Public figure stalker	Prevalence	50%	23%
	Threats used	10%	20%
	Violence used	3%	1%
Private stranger stalker	Prevalence	10%	10%
	Threats used	53%	49%
	Violence used	47%	28%

As we can see from this table, men were likely to fixate on, threaten, and physically harm their ex-partners. But female stalkers present with a completely different profile. They were most likely to stalk a public figure, but their use of violence and threats in that category, combined, was the lowest of all groups. They were much less likely to stalk other types of victims, but when they did, they would use threats and violence against them more often.

The female stalker may experience her target as a threat to the fragile hierarchy she inhabits. Surveillance becomes a way of containing that threat and then public dissection becomes a way of diminishing it.

There is also an identity function. In large online communities, particularly those centred around motherhood, lifestyle, fashion, homemaking, or local gossip, belonging is built through shared narratives. Participating in the critique of a particular woman becomes a bonding exercise. Agreement signals alignment. Escalation signals loyalty. The group constructs a collective identity around opposition to the target. In this context, online stalking is socially reinforced. It earns status within the group. It provides belonging. It creates purpose.

Unlike the archetypal male stalker, who is usually isolated and acting alone, the female online stalker often operates within a network. Diffusion of responsibility reduces individual accountability (Suler, 2004). Each participant tells herself she is only contributing a small piece.

Why, then, are female stalkers so rarely recognised?

In my own experience, everyone from friends through to the police found it strange, or rather ridiculous, that we were being stalked by women – but not at all serious. People around us struggled to understand why a group of (predominantly professional) women would behave in this way, not just for a few hours, but all hours of the day and night, for several years. They expected that these women would stop, get bored, apologise or explain eventually – however, that day never arrived.

Partly, it was because stalking is still imagined as physically threatening male behaviour. When harm is reputational, relational, coercive, or psychological rather than immediately violent, it is often minimised. Partly because women are stereotyped as less dangerous, their aggression is reframed as cattiness, gossip or drama. Research backs this up, too. When scenarios of male and female stalking are presented to participants, they generally perceive female-perpetrated stalking to be less serious, less criminal, and less harmful (Ahlgrim & Terrance, 2022).

Even victims themselves struggle to name it. When I was working with the hundreds of victims of Tattle Life, many of them had never actually called their experience 'stalking'. Usually they would use language such as 'trolling' or 'harassment', but for many of them, they had never considered that what the perpetrators were engaging in was actually stalking.

There is a particular disbelief that accompanies being stalked by women. It does not fit cultural scripts. It feels petty to outsiders. "Just ignore it," people say. "It's only online," or "she's just jealous of you!" The absence of physical violence is often misread as the absence of harm – even by police, who, in many cases, told victims that nothing they were experiencing was criminal. In my research, I found that victims were frequently told to delete their social media to solve the stalking, told that it was a civil matter, and that stalkers were entitled to 'free speech'. One third of victims were blamed for being stalked by the police and half of victims of stalking were told that it was not a crime at all (Taylor, 2025).

Law enforcement may dismiss female perpetrators as low risk. Systems trained to identify coercive male ex-partners on the pathway to homicide may fail to recognise coordinated female harassment campaigns as stalking at all. This dismissal is itself gendered. It reflects an assumption that women lack the capacity for sustained, strategic aggression. Academic studies from around the world, and the Tattle data contradicts that assumption (Meloy et al., 2011; Taylor, 2025).

Female stalking is not a softer, pinker version of male stalking. It is differently motivated and differently expressed. It often centres around reputation rather than physical proximity. It weaponises moral narratives rather than overt threats. It operates collectively rather than individually. It is embedded in communities rather than enacted from isolation.

But its impact is profound and should not be underestimated. The psychological toll of thousands of posts, emails, comments and accusations designed to dissect or destroy your life is not lighter because the perpetrators are female. If anything, the gender dynamic can intensify the harm. Women do not suspect other women. They underestimate each other or expect kindness and support from each other. Despite this, women know how to wound other women. They know the cultural fault lines to exploit and attack: motherhood, body image, relationships, competence, popularity, confidence, sexuality.

Internalised patriarchal scripts are deployed with precision – women engage in abuse, stalking and harassment of women that they would not be able to cope with themselves. The female stalker may believe she is dismantling power, when in fact she is reinforcing it. By attacking other women through misogynistic tropes, she strengthens the very hierarchies she may claim to oppose.

Linking the personal with the political is essential here. Online female stalking does not occur in a vacuum. It exists within broader cultural narratives about women's worth. It is shaped by media economies that reward outrage. It is facilitated by platforms that monetise engagement regardless of harm. It is fuelled by internalised misogyny and envy.

Fascinating then, that whilst the majority of Tattle Life users are female and the majority of their victims are also female, the owner of Tattle Life who is profiting from the comments, threads, and traffic – is a man. A man who posed as a woman for years, no less.

The online world profits from and encourages polarisation – divide and conquer. The justice seeker identity thrives in polarised cultures. When moral certainty is valued over nuance, casting someone as irredeemable becomes socially rewarded. This works well for female stalkers who often position themselves as righteous whistleblowers exposing hidden wrongdoing (Santos et al., 2024; Meloy et al., 2011). The target is stripped of complexity and reduced to a villain. This moral framing is powerful. It allows the stalker to bypass empathy. If the target is dangerous, harassment becomes justified. If the target is fraudulent, exposure becomes noble. If the target is abusive, destruction becomes protection.

If the victim can be reframed as evil, then nothing is too far, and they deserve everything that happens to them.

The Tattle Life scandal exposed not only the scale of female online stalking, but also the narratives sustaining it. Women described themselves as watchdogs. As investigators. As guardians of truth. Meanwhile, the targets experienced sustained fear, distress, and reputational harm.

Even after targets on the website died, sometimes from cancer and illnesses, and in one case by suicide, the women on Tattle continued to obsess, stalk, mock and ridicule. Some wrote that they were immensely saddened by the deaths, and in one case they claimed that they (the stalkers) were the only ones who ever truly cared about the victim, and only targeted them for accountability and ethical pursuit.

This is the paradox of the female stalker: she often sees herself as the hero of her own story. Understanding this is crucial. It moves us beyond caricature. It forces us to examine how ordinary emotions like envy, resentment, and insecurity can fuse with moral certainty and digital tools to produce sustained harm.

It also challenges feminism to confront uncomfortable truths. If we refuse to acknowledge female perpetration because it complicates gendered narratives of harm, we leave victims unprotected. If we dismiss female stalking as trivial because it is non-physical, we fail to grasp the evolution of coercive behaviour in digital spaces. Feminist narratives of female perpetrators are often accompanied by assumptions that women do not and will not offend of their own volition. They must have been pushed to it, they must have been forced to do it by a man, or they must be mentally ill.

As a feminist psychologist, this is a narrative I have always rejected. When women commit murder, I see them as a person who chose to kill someone – just the same way I see a man. I don't see that murder as any less violent because it was committed by a woman. When women abuse their children – I see them as a person who chose to harm and traumatise innocent children – just the same as a man. I don't think the impact on children who are abused is lessened because their mother abused them instead of their father.

Within feminism, I found myself at a crossroads many times, usually around cases where women have killed their male partners. The narrative I was asked to support was often that the woman was not responsible for the murder due to male violence, patriarchal abuse of power, previous history of abuse, trauma or distressing circumstances, or mental illness – but even before I was stalked, assaulted, and abused by women, I could never support those campaigns.

I didn't feel that it made sense for us as feminists to begin protecting and defending the lethal use of violence. I also made it clear to several organisations and feminist activists that they could not criticise male violence, or the excuses often used for male violence (mental illness, previous history of abuse, trauma or distressing circumstances), if they were going to deploy them when it suited them to defend female perpetrators.

As you can imagine, that went down exceptionally well.

But the fact is, women are not helpless. Women can commit as much violence and abuse as men – they just don't. We are not socialised to behave in those ways, and socialisation is extremely powerful. Men have been socialised and excused in that way and therefore make up between 90–98% of all violent offenders across the world (FBI, 2011; ONS, 2026; Pew Research Centre, 2024). They commit the majority of all homicides, abuse crimes, sexual crimes, assault crimes, child abuse crimes, in-person stalking crimes, and domestic abuse crimes.

However, a crucial point is that these are all violent contact offences.

What happens when women have access to anonymity and online platforms which give them power that they do not have in real life? What happens when they can victimise people from a distance, with no threat of comeback or physical risk to themselves? What happens when they can work together in groups to cause maximum damage, whilst telling themselves that they are doing it for a greater good? What happens when their aggression and abusive behaviour is rewarded by their carefully selected peers and allies on forums and social media?

Are women more abusive in the digital world because it disinhibits their socialisation or because it removes their physical identity? Women may not feel powerful or violent enough to stalk someone in person, but they know they can do it online.

And none of us have been socialised to believe that we cannot abuse people online because the gender roles, stereotypes and tropes do not yet include online behaviour. It is too new to have sets of tropes. In that way, we could argue that online behaviour is evolving and developing without influence of parenting, governance or moderation telling us what is right and wrong, or what is socially acceptable for our gender role.

Nothing is stopping female stalkers from expressing their hatred and abusive natures online – no physical, psychological, social or emotional barriers exist. The things that confine women and girls to their gender roles in the real world (physical threat, bodily risk, lack of socioeconomic status) do not exist in the same way online. Women can create named or anonymous identities through which they can become threatening, intimidating, powerful, and aggressive.

There is a reason why the majority of users of sites such as Tattle Life are women. Men are not interested in engaging in that kind of behaviour in the same way, especially when they can meet their stalking or abusive needs elsewhere in the real world, in a society where they already have power and status – both as ordinary people and as perpetrators of abuse.

Conversely, men could lack the emotional intelligence, communication skills, covert tactics, cognitive constructions, and patience to stalk, harass and abuse online over months and years – something that women appear to be adept at (Meloy et al., 2011; Taylor, 2025). On the other hand, women lack the physical power, threat, socialisation, and utilisation of violence to stalk in person.

Female stalking is not new, scholars have been looking at this for decades. It has simply evolved for the digital age. It is socially acceptable in ways male stalking is not. A woman would likely recoil from the possibility of physically stalking someone down a dark street, sitting outside of their house, or threatening them on their way home from work. But online, they can stalk, threaten and intimidate in different ways. It can be hidden under the language of concern, accountability, and community. It is minimised by systems that do not expect women to be perpetrators and refuses to see them that way.

But when we examine the behaviours rather than the gender of the actor, the pattern is unmistakable. A clear course of conduct. Fixation. Obsession. Repetition. Intrusion. Harm.

The female stalker exists. She is not a myth. She is not a psychotic anomaly. She is not a footnote at the bottom of a piece of research. She is a central figure in the modern landscape of online stalking and abuse. If we are serious about understanding stalking in all its forms, we must be willing to look at her clearly.

Not as a monster. Not as a joke. But as a willing, active participant in a cultural and psychological phenomenon that we can no longer afford to ignore.

My lived experience anchors this chapter, but the analysis is universal. Across professions, communities, and platforms, women are engaging in sustained surveillance and harassment of other women at scale. Naming it is not betrayal of my feminism or the women I love, serve, support and mentor. Many women I work with have been abused and stalked by other women – they just can't talk about it.

Naming it like this is accountability.

CHAPTER 4

Stalking: trauma like no other

Jennifer's husband was out for the evening. Some curry night with his workmates or something. She hadn't really listened. The good news was there was no need to worry that he would overhear the meeting that evening. She had curled up on the sofa and balanced her phone on the bookcase so her arm wouldn't ache forty minutes into the meeting, like last time.

Everyone was supposed to be joining the Zoom. They'd become a frequent thing over the months. A place to talk, offload, gossip, laugh, share new information, and crucially, to plan. Jennifer had never been involved in anything like this before, but it felt so right. So good. That woman was going to get what was coming to her, and everyone on the Zoom agreed.

Jennifer knew that her husband would never understand. She felt that if he knew what they were doing, he would overreact, or demand that she stopped completely. The main concern, of course, was not her husband, but work. Jennifer had worked as a therapist for the last six years for a national domestic violence charity, and she was uncertain how it would look if she was ever discovered. Sometimes that played on her mind, but most of the time, she would find a way to rationalise it away or convince herself that what they were doing was for a greater good. Sure, it could look pretty bad from the outside, but they all knew she deserved everything that was being done to her.

And truth be told, the greater good was this: that woman needed to be destroyed. For her own good. For the good of everyone. She was too big for her boots. She was disgusting, dangerous, vile, and self-centred. They say that justice comes in different forms, and unluckily for her, this was the way her justice was to be served. Publicly and without reservation.

Jennifer beamed and waved to everyone as the Zoom meeting began and everyone joined. Anna was wandering around her kitchen with the baby on her hip whilst she was making the older kids some snacks. Naomi was in her car on the way home from work and had put the phone in the holder whilst she sat in traffic on the M6. Jane was in her office, still at work due to a huge deadline that was looming, and Samantha was in her pyjamas and dressing gown, looking rather unwell.

"Oh dear, Samantha, are you still sick?" Jennifer asked.

"I thought I was getting better and then Jacob came home from school with some virus, and its completely wiped me out. I cannot believe how terrible I feel. That pharmacist must be sick of me by now!"

"It's really going around, isn't it? All three of mine have had it, Sam. I am praying I don't come down with it next," Anna chimed in, the sound of her chopping some cucumber echoing in the background.

"Well, I've got something to cheer you all up! Are you ready for this?" Jane grinned. Jennifer was intrigued as she also had something to tell the group, but Jane seemed to have something big.

Everyone laughed excitedly and encouraged Jane to spill everything.

"So," Jane started, "Don't ask me how I got them, but I have screenshots of an entire conversation between her and a woman I know. And let me tell you, we can do so much with these!"

"Whaaat? How? Oh my god, you legend! How the hell do you have those?" Jennifer replied to the news, barely letting Jane finish her final word.

The thrill was obvious. Everyone jumped in, begging Jane to reveal her source. And it didn't take much. Jane had been desperate to share her scoop for days.

"I told her a bit about what we were doing and how fucking awful that bitch is. I got her to befriend her and chat to her to see if she would talk, and she fucking did. I mean, of course she did. She cannot fucking help herself. But you should see the shit she said. I've got it all in a zipped folder, ready to go!"

Jennifer gasped, not knowing what Jane could possibly have gotten her hands on. Her mind whirred with the possibilities. Were the messages incriminating? Had she flirted with the other woman? Had she confessed horrible things she had done to people? Outed herself as the nasty piece of work she really was?

Anything could be possible.

There was a tense wait as Jane waited for the hubbub to die down.

"She tried to kill herself. She fucking tried to kill herself!"

Everyone gasped and clapped their hands to their mouths. This was perfect. Better than perfect.

"Nooooo! You have that in actual screenshots? She told her that she tried to kill herself?"

"Yep," Jane laughed.

"No way! Did she say how?" Anna shouted over her car engine.

For a moment, the Zoom meeting was chaos. Everyone was talking over each other, asking questions, laughing, speculating, and trying to get to the bottom of this revelation.

"Okay, okay. One minute. Let me just read the messages out to you. It's easier. I have them right here. They are fucking gold, let me tell you! She's fucking pathetic!"

Jennifer listened intently as Jane read out the conversation.

"Okay, so in one message she goes, 'I can't cope anymore. I don't understand what is happening to me. They seem to know everything I do, everyone I talk to, everywhere I go. They target my work, my colleagues, my venues, my lectures. I've asked around and everyone pretends not to know. People must know. They must be lying to me. I can't get it to stop. It is going to ruin my entire life . . .' "

Samantha screeched with laughter. "Yes it is, bitch! Yes it is!"

"At least she got something right!" Anna cried.

"Wait, wait, I haven't even got to the good part yet." Jane tried to calm the giggling women down so she could continue. "Then she says, right, 'I feel like I can't escape them. They've turned me into this monster. I'm losing friends and family all over the place, and I don't think I will live to see this through. My hair is falling out, I can't sleep,

I'm so ill. Some days I can't even get out of bed. I have never ever been suicidal in my life until recently. I can't believe I'm gonna say this, but I actually tried to end it last week. Jay walked in on me and had to physically stop me. I don't know what came over me, I just couldn't handle it anymore. There was this really sharp pair of scissors in the drawer and I just wanted to die so badly . . .'" Jane paused, trying to contain herself from bursting into fits of giggles. "I mean . . . I'm sorry, I shouldn't laugh but . . . she's clearly a fucking loon . . ."

The whole meeting laughed, whooped and giggled.

"No Jane, laugh as much as you like! She deserves it all. And she's probably fucking lying anyway!" Naomi shook her head in disbelief, shouting over the other women. "She's too much of a coward to kill herself."

The women were all nodding in agreement until Anna jumped in, then they hushed.

"I reckon she would do it you know, but only for the attention. She would probably be one of those people who does a pathetic non-attempt at it, so she could be hospitalised and pretend she tried to kill herself . . . and then write a blog about it or something!"

"Or another shit book!" Samantha cried.

Everyone fell about laughing again.

"So, listen. Listen. I will share the folder in the group chat in a minute, and then I think we leak it online. Let's put the link to it everywhere, and send it to key people who will want to see it." Jane became serious about the strategy. "It makes her look unstable, and it makes her look absolutely pathetic . . ."

Anna agreed. "Yes, but mostly, it will really mess with her to know that someone shared her private messages. That's when she'll realise how fucked she truly is and that no one around her cares about her. Even when she wants to 'die' . . ."

Anna said the word 'die' whilst sarcastically signalling quotation marks in the air with her hands.

The women nodded again.

"Oh god, true. She is going to fucking lose it when she sees these!" Samantha laughed as Jane beamed with pride at her work.

"Well, with any luck, she will do us all a favour and follow through with it next time!" Anna snapped, seeming genuinely annoyed at the interrupted suicide.

And speaking of dying, Jennifer was simply dying to tell everyone what she had found out, too. Although she thought it wouldn't be as big as what Jane had, which took a bit of the fun out of it, truth be told.

Jennifer waved to everyone on the camera to get their attention, whilst they were joking about the pathetic methods of suicide she would probably use.

"Okay, so I have something too. Not as important as Jane's discovery by any means but . . . I'm in this Facebook group, right, and a few of us had all met up for drinks on Saturday. There was this woman there called Heather, and she works for her. She actually works for her. Anyway, I told Heather everything . . . and she was shocked. She said she really liked her and was always nice to her . . ."

Jennifer watched as some of the other women shifted uncomfortably at this. No one wanted their cover blown. Heather was a risk. Jennifer realised and immediately reassured the group.

"Don't worry, don't worry! I made her realise what she really is. And I managed to get her number. She said that she has access to all of her files. Her usernames and passwords. Accounts. Finances. She even has a list of everyone she is working with and the contract values. I think we work on her, get her into this group, and we go from there . . ."

The group was momentarily quiet. This was huge. The suicide thing was big, but access to her passwords? Her finances? Her private documents? Nobody was expecting that.

The group burst into awe and loud excited chatter, congratulating and thanking Jennifer profusely for such an important development.

* * *

The trauma of being hunted in a world that never switches off is unlike anything else I have ever experienced. For all victims, online stalking is a particular kind of trauma that does not explode into your life in a single catastrophic moment, like a car crash or a random attack. It seeps slowly, whilst you are still trying to figure out whether you are overreacting or exaggerating the whole thing.

It hums in the background. It vibrates through your phone at midnight. It sits in your inbox at 6 am, waiting for you to wake up. It lurks in the comments beneath your work. It lives in screenshots you will never see but know are being taken somewhere by someone. In the people who are watching you day and night, the ones you will never know about. In the cars that drive slowly past your house. In the anonymous threats sent to your social media. In the allegations of child abuse sent to social care, and the allegations of serious crime sent to the police. It is not episodic. It is relentless.

This is the trauma of being stalked in a digital world that never switches off. Traditional trauma models were built around discrete events: an assault, a car crash, a natural disaster. Previously (and technically, still to this day), PTSD could only be diagnosed where there had been a specific, recognised traumatic event. According to the DSM-III, those events were originally listed as sexual assault, combat, physical assault, natural disasters and serious accidents. As the years went on, the American Psychiatric Association added to the list, which eventually included witnessing a traumatic event, being seriously injured, and exposure to actual or threatened death of another person.

As of today, being stalked in person (or online) where there was no direct threat to life and no serious physical injury doesn't meet the criteria for PTSD diagnosis, which is ridiculous.

As an anti-pathology, trauma-informed psychologist, I understand that when women and girls are stalked online, their responses are not signs of disorder but signs of danger. When someone is repeatedly watched, discussed, misrepresented, lied about, stalked, harassed, abused and targeted, their nervous system does exactly what it is designed to do under threat: it becomes vigilant, defensive, and protective. No matter how others may frame that, I believe that they are adaptive responses to sustained interpersonal harm.

What harms women and girls further is the reflex to pathologise them instead of addressing the stalking. Telling them to log off, ignore it, or toughen up compounds the trauma and shifts responsibility away from the perpetrator. Telling her that she is mentally ill or to just go to her doctor only stigmatises and gaslights her when she is being stalked like prey in the wild.

The trauma of online stalking has no ending and no barriers. Even in cases of repeated domestic abuse, there are some possible physical boundaries. A victim might leave the house. Go to work. Stay with a friend. See their mum for a few hours. There are moments of distance, however fragile.

Digital stalking removes the last refuge of safety.

When the stalking is online and enacted through technology, there is no closing the door. There is no geographical escape. There is no guarantee that sleep will bring respite. The intrusion travels with you in your pocket. It waits on your bedside table. It follows you on holiday. It accompanies you into work meetings, into classrooms, into birthday parties, parents' evenings and hospital waiting rooms.

The 24/7 nature of digital stalking reshapes trauma itself. Hundreds of people abusing you online, all hours of the day and night, for months or years of your life. There is nothing else quite like that.

Trauma, at its core, is the experience of overwhelming threat coupled with helplessness. It disrupts the nervous system. It alters perception. It embeds fear responses. In stalking, the threat is not always immediate physical violence. It is the collapse of safety and predictability. The knowledge that someone or that many people are watching us, discussing us, speculating, waiting, and planning the next attack.

At some point, we realise that we have lost control of our lives. It is reported by the UK National Stalking Helpline that 67% of cyberstalking victims suffered from post-traumatic stress responses, and that 35% had a full PTSD diagnosis due to being stalked online (Alhaboby et al., 2019).

But trauma is not a mental disorder of any kind. Trauma is our body and mind trying to respond to distressing and harmful experiences. I would expect most people who have been stalked to become very traumatised indeed. Hypervigilance becomes your baseline. You scan constantly for threat. Every notification becomes a potential attack. Every unknown number feels like danger. Every police knock at the door sends adrenaline through your veins that lasts days or weeks. Regulation of your nervous system is nearly impossible.

Physical and psychological trauma impacts on stalking victims

Impact on victim	Workplace stalking	Ex-partner stalking
Psychological		
Feeling anxious	84%	84%
Feeling depressed	67%	61%
Difficulty sleeping	63%	70%
Difficulty concentrating	61%	56.5%
Loss of confidence	59%	70%
Feeling isolated and lonely	59%	62%
Frightened to be alone	43%	59%
Panic attacks	43%	55%
Problems with trust and difficulties with intimacy	43%	55%
Suicidal thoughts and/or made attempts at suicide	24.5%	29%
Self-medicating using alcohol, drugs, medications	18%	22%
Developed an eating disorder	2%	15%
It has not affected my psychological wellbeing	2%	6%
Physical		
Headaches	55%	71%
Heart palpitations and sweating	47%	51%
Stomach and digestive problems	33%	31.5%
Dizziness and shortness of breath	33%	40%
Worsening of existing illnesses	20%	20%
Loss of libido and sexual dysfunction	18%	23%
It has not affected my physical health	12%	13%

N = 191 Sheridan et al. (2019)

The impact on our mind and body when being stalked is immense, and it is no wonder that some victims have described it as 'slow murder'. I have lived this crushing feeling of overwhelm and it made me very unwell.

I have opened my phone to see hundreds of posts analysing my marriage. I have been presented with pages of my own public words and screenshots taken within minutes of publication, as though I were under surveillance by an intelligence agency. I have had police arrive at my home following false allegations triggered by individuals watching my life online. I have watched my children's faces change when they realise that strangers are discussing them. I have watched my wife cry for hours, asking me why this is happening to us. I have tried to explain to my colleagues and my business partners that I am doing all I can do to stop the stalking. I have begged police to help us.

Sleep becomes fractured. Even when exhausted, your body and mind remain on high alert. Cortisol levels remain elevated. You wake repeatedly. You check your phone before your feet even hit the floor. You scroll to see what happened while you were sleeping. You check your emails for threats, abuse, and further allegations that you need to respond to.

Work is contaminated – it is no longer a job. Instead of focusing on tasks and deadlines, most of your cognitive bandwidth is scanning for fallout. Will a client receive an email today? Will a regulator receive a complaint? Will a colleague stumble across a thread filled with lies? Will I be removed from a conference? Will my emails be hacked again this week? Will my colleagues receive messages from the stalker threatening them to stop working with me? The mind rehearses possible scenarios endlessly, and oftentimes, they come true. This isn't a form of paranoia.

Parenting shifts, too. You monitor your children's online presence with heightened anxiety. I banned my children from all platforms when they were much younger, but as the stalking intensified and shifted to an obsession about my children, and why I don't post them online, I became even more strict about their online footprint. As they are now much older, and one is almost an adult as I write this, I have had to teach them how to hide themselves from my stalkers online, how to use pseudonyms, turn off location settings, protect their friends lists, restrict their visibility, and never accept follow requests or messages from people they do not know personally.

But parenting is much bigger than social media. You end up second-guessing school communications. You prepare them for potential rumours that could go around at school. You try to shield your kids from information you know exists but cannot fully control. You worry what will be sent to them as adults, or what will be shown to them as teenagers. You do regular searches for their names and photographs online to ensure that nothing has been leaked or posted. You are forced to ask the schools to exclude them from sports team photographs, newsletters, and local press releases, even if they won a big tournament or did something exceptional. You realise that your children are an extension of you, and so they are an extension of the stalker's obsession with you. And that truly is traumatic.

With time, identity itself begins to erode – and you begin to question who you are.

One of the most insidious aspects of digital stalking is narrative take-over. When hundreds of people are writing about you, defining you, diagnosing you, and accusing you, a strange dissociation can occur. You begin to see yourself through their words. You question if they are right about you. Shame creeps in, even when you know deep down that the allegations and rumours are false.

My personal experience of this was utterly crushing. As someone who has always been so sure of herself, I became a shell. Everything I had inside me had been violently ripped out – and I was left with nothing. I realised that I was having my identity reconstructed right in front of me, without my consent, and there was nothing I could do about it.

I noticed people's behaviour towards me changed. Whether they meant to or not, they were treating me as a risk or a liability instead of a colleague or friend. I would find myself rehearsing explanations for the lies and rumours that were being circulated and steeling myself for pain and rejection whenever I was invited to do anything. I had no confidence left to hold myself with. I walked into a room and expected everyone to have been sent the emails and the links – the ones that said I was abusing my wife, committing crime, lying about being raped, and embezzling funds into illegal schemes. I didn't know who I was anymore. The years I had spent building my life into a safe space after experiencing violence, abuse and poverty in my earlier life had been collapsed within weeks by anonymous users of a forum I had never even heard of.

Humiliation attaches itself to your name. Humiliation is a powerful trauma trigger. It involves exposure, degradation, and the collapse of social standing. In evolutionary terms, social exclusion was dangerous – we would die if our tribe isolated us. There are hundreds of possible ways to be harmed and then isolated. Like one police officer said to me once, "Attacking the credibility of someone is like shooting fish in a barrel."

Your employer can be contacted. Your children's school can be emailed. Your clients can be warned. Your professional regulators can receive complaints. Your neighbours can be approached. Your extended family can be messaged. Old posts can be resurfaced. Your businesses can be destroyed. Your colleagues can be sent links to unsubstantiated and fabricated allegations. Images can be manipulated or completely doctored online. Private information can be stolen and published. Your floor plans of your house can be shared online. Your friends can unwittingly become a part of it, sharing your deepest, darkest fears with stalkers who love every tiny morsel of information.

The multiplicity of threat vectors means the nervous system never settles. Nothing is safe. No one is safe. Nowhere is safe. Fear conditioning begins to occur. Fear conditioning is a process by which neutral stimuli become associated with threat. If police have arrived at your door following false reports, a knock on the door becomes a trigger. You jump out of your skin every time the doorbell rings. If a particular notification sound preceded a wave of abuse, that sound on your phone becomes loaded. If certain phrases were used in defamatory posts, seeing those phrases elsewhere can provoke a surge of anxiety and shame.

The triggers are constant and everywhere. Over time, the threat and trauma make the world feel smaller. Or, maybe more accurately, your world does actually become smaller. You try a thousand things to cope with being stalked, and ultimately many of them fail.

I found this pattern across many other cases of online stalking, including an interesting study by Begotti et al. (2022), which compared the coping strategies of victims who knew who their online stalker was versus those who didn't.

Coping strategies of online stalking victims

Coping strategy used by victim	Unknown cyberstalker	Known cyberstalker
Collect evidence	35%	35%
Decrease all internet use	15%	21%
Have a safety plan	0	2%
Increase social contact	30%	25%
Increase alcohol use	3%	11%
Increase drug use	0	4%
Decrease social contact	1%	8%
Increase psychiatric medications	1%	4%
Buy a weapon	0	4%
Try to reason with the stalker	13%	27%
Block the online contact	71%	60%
Ask for intervention from social media platform	34%	10%
Ask for intervention from mobile provider	3.5%	3%
Change identities and profiles online	4%	4%
Contact the police	4%	3%

N = 242 Begotti et al. (2022)

You avoid posting. You avoid attending events. You hesitate before speaking publicly. You withdraw from platforms that once felt like community. You stop telling people what is happening to you because no one understands. You watch your back in public places. You are too scared to go to conferences, parties or lunches. But even withdrawal does not guarantee safety. Silence can be reinterpreted. Absence can be filled with speculation.

Why is she no longer here? Why has she stopped attending events? Why has she stopped speaking about things online? She is obviously hiding something. She must be what everyone says she is. She's been exposed for who she really is.

This is where digital stalking diverges sharply from older models of harassment. There is no off switch. There is no clear boundary between public and private. The home, once considered a sanctuary, is penetrated through screens.

For many victims I have worked with, the most distressing aspect is the impossibility of closure. In physical violence, there is at least the theoretical possibility of prosecution, sentencing, and containment. In digital stalking, justice is non-existent. Stalking laws and practice guidance exist, they are just not applied to, or designed for, the online world. Legal thresholds are difficult to meet when police officers believe that behaviours are individually lawful and do not see them as a course of conduct.

Helplessness compounds the trauma.

When every attempt to stop the stalking fails, like reporting posts, blocking accounts, seeking legal advice, contacting authorities, then a sense of futility can set in. The victim may begin to doubt her own perceptions. Am I overreacting? Is this really that bad? Gaslighting often accompanies digital stalking. The victim is told she is dramatic, paranoid, and attention-seeking. The very responses produced by the trauma – anxiety, vigilance, emotional reactivity – are used as evidence that she is mentally unstable. The more she tries to show people how much the stalking is affecting her, which ironically, is required in order for cases to be prosecuted, the more she can be recast as mentally ill.

This secondary invalidation deepens the wound.

I have spoken to women who describe feeling as though they are living in a psychological war zone. As I've already stated, some women describe being stalked as a form of 'slow murder'. Not because they are physically attacked daily, but because they are psychologically surrounded. Every corner of the digital world contains a potential threat. Every attempt to rebuild is shadowed by the possibility of renewed attack.

Some have told me that the trauma of digital stalking felt worse than any physical assault.

This is a difficult statement to make publicly. It risks comparison that can be misinterpreted. But when survivors say this, they are not minimising physical violence. They are describing the particular horror of omnipresence. Physical violence, horrific as it is, often has an identifiable perpetrator and a temporal boundary. Digital stalking can involve hundreds of anonymous participants over years – there is not one person to be scared of.

The scale alone is traumatising.

When one person harms you, you can sometimes locate the threat and process the trauma by humanisation. When thousands participate in dissecting your life, and when most of them are anonymous or ambiguous, the threat becomes diffuse and everywhere. Diffuse threat is especially destabilising because it cannot be contained cognitively. There is no single face. No single narrative. No single endpoint.

Research shows that one of the coping strategies for online harassment is to research the opponent or attacker on the internet, as it helps to rationalise the attacks (Riives et al., 2022). In Ivask (2025), the study explored the stalking of journalists. Sometimes, an individual who attacks a journalist may have a personal connection to someone or something the journalist has covered. Such connections can offer insight into the motivation behind the attack. This leads them to research and try to uncover their stalker.

This is an interesting coping mechanism, but one that is not specific to journalists at all. Almost every victim I have spoken to has engaged in this behaviour, mainly out of fear. For some, fighting an invisible, anonymous threat is much harder than fighting one with a real name, a real face and a real identity. Humanising the stalker and finding out as much about them as possible becomes a way to cope with the abuse. Whilst I would argue that this researching and trying to unmask the stalker is completely rational and understandable, I have also come across cases where the victim has been punished for this, reported to the police, or recast as the stalker themselves. This means that their only coping mechanism, the only thing that gave them some sense of control again, resulted in them being harmed further.

Ivask went on to report that some journalists prefer to deal with harassment by ignoring or downplaying it (Binns, 2017; Chen et al., 2020), which again bears resemblance to the way many other people try to cope with online stalking. In fact, lots of victims are given explicit advice to ignore it or downplay it – with the assumption that this will make it stop. Several studies exploring the coping mechanisms of people subjected to stalking and harassment mention 'growing thicker skin' (e.g. Chen et al., 2020) as a coping mechanism, with public figures and journalists claiming that online harassment and stalking had forced them to silence their emotions, minimise their reactions, and just learn to accept it.

Trauma compounds into helplessness and hopelessness when there is no light at the end of the tunnel, which is something that certainly caused immense harm in my own life. I couldn't see a way out – because there wasn't one.

Shame, humiliation and public exposure add extra layers rarely addressed in traditional trauma models. Public trauma involves harm that unfolds in front of an audience. The victim is not only hurt; they are displayed. Their pain becomes content. Their responses are scrutinised. Even their attempts to defend themselves can be clipped, reframed and circulated. This level of scrutiny can fracture self-trust. You question your memory. You question your tone. You question your motives. You know that every word you say can be used against you – every shred of information you share can be used to trace you. Trauma researchers have long noted that chronic threat can alter cognitive patterns, increasing rumination and intrusive thoughts. In digital stalking, rumination and daily checking is almost unavoidable because new material appears constantly, and often, you are advised by authorities to collate it and monitor it.

Finally, I wanted to ensure that this chapter included a discussion of suicide and self-harm, caused by being stalked online.

Across the literature, it is common for researchers to find that victims of stalking have become suicidal or have attempted suicide. Sheridan et al. (2019) found that 24.5% of people stalked by their work colleagues and 29% of people stalked by their ex-partner had become suicidal and/or made attempts to end their lives.

In the research I conducted with 150 people who were targeted on Tattle Life, 43% of victims felt suicidal or considered ending their lives, 11% of the victims went on to attempt suicide, and 9% self-harmed.

The trauma impacts of being stalked cannot be overstated, and they appear to mirror the developing conversation around suicide in domestic abuse and coercive control. In the last several years, academics and professionals have begun to collate evidence of the number of women who end their lives as a result of being subjected to domestic abuse and stalking, and the findings so far are deeply concerning. The most recent statistics released by the NPCC in February 2026 showed that the team had found at least 98 suicides of women which followed reports of domestic abuse and ex-partner stalking in England and Wales in 2024. This is a higher number than the 80 femicides in the same period.

In my research, victims of online stalking reported a wide range of trauma responses and impacts, including becoming withdrawn (77%), becoming too frightened to leave the house (63%), losing friendships (43%), being diagnosed with a psychiatric disorder due to the stalking (25%), and their marriage breaking down due to the stalking (19%).

Yet, within this devastation something else often emerges, through utter desperation. Survival. Many victims of online stalking I spoke to had been stalked for years and in some extreme cases for over ten years of their lives. This was shocking even for me, and I have now been a victim of stalking for nearly five years. The simple fact is that most of us have to find a way to carry on, even if it is breaking us. Many of us have children and other responsibilities which mean that no matter how bad the stalking gets, we must find a way through.

I rebuilt myself while still the victim of active stalking. That sentence sounds strong, but it was messy, difficult, and uneven. It involved therapy, meditation, alternative practices, sound therapy, research, music, extreme anger, the lowest lows I have ever felt, and years of indescribable exhaustion. It involved learning how to cope with something I could not control. It involved reclaiming narrative where possible and accepting the limits of my power.

I had never had to do that before. I am a resilient and resourceful person, and whilst my life has been complex, I have never felt like I cannot solve a problem that presented itself to me. I have walked through many a storm, knowing full well that I would eventually come out the other side. I left abuse as a teenager, ran away with my baby as a single teenage mum, put myself through university whilst raising two babies, lived in poverty, recovered from a stroke, and had a very premature baby. I'm well acquainted with having the kitchen sink thrown at me.

I knew I was strong, but being stalked tested me like nothing else and has given me immense and lifelong empathy for other victims of stalking.

Online stalking eroded my power, my identity, my confidence, and my self-esteem. I had no way of making it stop. I couldn't run away with my wife and my kids. The threat was everywhere – there was no escape. Their monitoring of me never stopped. The stalking never slowed. Around two years into the ordeal, I realised that I would have to try to process the trauma whilst still being actively traumatised, and whilst still having no solutions to the harm.

Sort of like trying to heal from a stab wound whilst still actively being stabbed. It was torture and it presented a new form of trauma that I didn't have the tools to process or cope with.

Rebuilding yourself whilst still under surveillance is a unique psychological task. Most people begin processing trauma once the initial trauma is over. But when stalking is spanning years, you cannot wait for safety to begin healing because safety may never fully arrive. You must construct pockets of refuge within an environment that offers none. You must teach your nervous system to stand down even while acknowledging that the risk continues. This, by far, was one of the most twisted and toxic forms of trauma processing I have ever engaged in.

I am not accustomed to relinquishing power over my life and my identity, but I realised that I had to let go and stop fighting back in order to try to move forward. I had to let go of everyone who had abandoned me. I had to stop explaining myself, stop defending myself, and stop trying to correct the narrative. I had to find a way to live healthily and happily, whilst knowing that my life was being destroyed, piece by minute piece. And not only was it being destroyed, but people were using it as a form of entertainment. People believed anything and everything that was being circulated about me online, and I had no power to stop it.

This required new trauma models. Models I didn't have. Models that didn't exist. Even therapists I worked with had no advice for me. They would have been brilliant if the stalking had ended, and they were helping me to process it, but they didn't know how to support me whilst I was being actively stalked.

We need frameworks that reflect relentless organised, abusive intrusion rather than episodic events. We need to recognise that digital stalking produces cumulative harm. That it alters sleep, work, parenting, relationships and identity simultaneously. That it collapses the distinction between private and public trauma.

No previous generation has faced this exact configuration of trauma. The tactics are new. The tools are new. The scale is new. The permanence is new.

And in my opinion, this calls for new forms of support for traumatised victims and their families.

CHAPTER 5

She was asking for it

Angry tears had filled my eyes and were threatening to pour down my face. I blinked them back as I stared out of the window, one hand on my hip, the other holding my overheating phone to my ear.

Outside, the sun shone and the hydrangeas around my office swayed in the breeze. Quite beautiful, if you were not consumed with terror from an unidentifiable threat that never took a day off.

I had already been arguing with Graham for half an hour and I was getting nowhere. If anything, he was enjoying it. I had never spoken to Graham before, but when my phone had unexpectedly rung at work and I answered, he had introduced himself as the police sergeant who was closing our case.

No further action. No more help from Hannah, the sympathetic young officer. This was the end of the road.

Whilst our detective had done everything she could, it was her sergeant who had decided to make the call – both figuratively and literally. I couldn't believe what I was hearing. Our lives had become one never-ending misery and now it felt like the only people who could intervene to protect us were turning their backs on us.

I had already begged him not to close our case, but now I was going around in circles trying to get him to understand the extent of what we were being subjected to.

"What you need to understand, Miss, is that you are choosing to use the internet and you are choosing to have a public profile." He paused for a moment, clearly losing his temper. "If you really wanted this to stop, you could just delete all your social media profiles and stop posting online."

I ignored his deliberate choice to switch to calling me 'Miss' instead of 'Doctor' once he had become annoyed with me. I felt that he was smirking ever so slightly as he said it. I could hear his lips curl up at the side as he took satisfaction in speaking down to me.

"I cannot delete my entire social media presence and stop using the internet, I need it for my work . . ."

Inside, I was raging. Life is probably 90% online these days, but what do I know? It wasn't as if I hadn't thought about it. If I could unplug my router and drop kick it into orbit to stop the stalking, I would have done it there and then.

"Well, that's your choice then, isn't it?" he quipped back.

"Yes, it's my choice to keep my social media but it isn't my choice to be stalked 24/7 for six months. I don't think you . . ."

I didn't even get to finish that time.

"Miss. Miss. Let me stop you there . . ."

I gritted my teeth and took a deep breath. Do not rise to the condescension, Jessica.

He started up again, intent on teaching me a lesson in his own logic.

"Let's use an example, okay? If a celebrity chooses to go down to Asda and then someone in Asda follows them around the shop, comes up to them, and starts being unpleasant to them, or follows them back to their car, whose fault is that, really?"

My mouth fell open. He must have been joking.

"What!? It's the perpetrator's fault! Harassment is illegal!"

I was moments away from slamming my head on a wall.

"No, Miss. No. That celebrity knew what they were doing when they chose to go to the supermarket . . ."

"That is ridiculous! This is victim blaming!" I exclaimed.

"No, it is not!" He kicked back immediately, but I was all in and if he wanted a lesson in logic, he could have one with pleasure.

"Yes, it is. The scenario you just gave – it's bullshit. It is not illegal for the celebrity to go to Asda, but it is illegal for someone to harass them and follow them, or to become abusive to them. Only one of those people is breaking the law . . . and it isn't the celebrity!"

"That's your opinion, Miss."

"No, it isn't! That's literally the law!"

I felt like I had slipped into the Twilight Zone.

"Again, that's your opinion. And I think we will have to agree to disagree on this one," he concluded, insincerely.

"I am not 'agreeing to disagree' when you are blatantly wrong. We have given you hundreds of pages of stalking evidence. We have had emails and phone calls to all the universities I lecture at. My publishers have been targeted. My agents. My producers. My friends and family. Someone even threatened the office building of my colleagues. Your detective has seen all the posts containing information about where we live, even the registration plate of my wife's car has been posted online. There are hundreds of disgusting lies and rumours being spread that I am being investigated for human trafficking and sexual offences . . . people are somehow finding out where I am going to be, and then harassing the organisation or the venue I speak at . . . if this carries on, I am going to end up losing everything . . . We have so much evidence and . . ."

He cut me off again.

"And how did you gather that evidence, hmm?"

This pivot took me back.

"I don't know what you mean . . ." I mumbled, feeling confused.

"Well, you claim that you are being stalked. But how did you find out all this information? It seems to me that you are the one going looking for this stuff. Have you considered that?"

Considering I had been running on empty for months, I filled with defensive rage in an instant.

"Are you fucking joking me? You lot, the police, asked me, the victim, to gather this fucking evidence to help you to investigate . . . and now you're suggesting that I am 'going looking for it'?"

"Well, you could just stop looking at it, couldn't you?"

"This conversation is over."

I put the phone down, tears streaming down my face.

* * *

"She was asking for it."

The wording changes. The tone softens. The language becomes more respectable. But the message remains the same. When someone is stalked, especially a woman, the scrutiny often turns not towards the perpetrator's behaviour but instead towards the victim's visibility, personality, choices and, tone.

Why was she online? Why did she share that?

Why didn't she just ignore it? Why did she respond?

Why didn't she stay quiet? Why doesn't she just delete her accounts?

Victim blaming is one of the key mechanisms that allows stalking to continue. The myths are predictable. The impact is devastating.

This chapter is a full-circle moment for me, especially considering that the reason I began to be targeted and stalked online was because my book on the psychology of victim blaming went viral, and that's how my public profile grew in the first place. How strange to now be exactly six years on, writing a chapter in a book about the stalking that almost took my life and explaining in a new context how the psychology of victim blaming works.

If that isn't motivation to never give up on your dreams, reader, I don't know what is.

It reminds me of that satirical social media quote about ambition: "Every dead body on Mount Everest was once a highly motivated person with a big dream, so maybe calm down."

I nearly printed that for my office wall.

Anyway. Moving swiftly on.

The concept of victim blaming spans many different social issues, harms, and crimes. Whilst it is mostly associated with sexual and domestic violence, victim blaming occurs frequently in everything from bullying to robbery, and from war to tsunamis. There are even studies which look at victim blaming in disability and cancer. Frankly, humans quite like to blame the victims of traumas, violence, crimes, oppression, war, and abuses.

Humans, sure. Women? Absolutely.

The concept of 'blaming the victim' did not originate from feminism or from violence against women and girls. Most people associate it with those topics, but it was said to have been coined initially by William Ryan in 1971, when he responded to the US government-commissioned 'Moynihan Report'. In 1965, the Moynihan Report examined racism and violence towards Black communities, and concluded that the poverty, harm, violence, oppression and daily racism was actually being caused by Black people themselves. The report spoke of Black communities being filled with single mothers, absent fathers, low levels of education, high levels of criminality and drug use. Moynihan argued that Black communities were essentially bringing racism upon themselves by the way they acted, and lived.

In response, Ryan argued that this report was 'blaming the victim', and ignoring the actions, choices and attitudes of White people and White leadership who were perpetrating the harm, oppression, segregation and discrimination.

Theory of victim blaming	Brief description
Belief in a Just World (Lerner, 1970)	The belief that the world is fair leads people to assume that stalking victims must have done something to cause or invite it. If someone is being persistently monitored or targeted online, observers may conclude she 'provoked' it because accepting random harm threatens their sense of safety and order.
Attribution Bias (Kelley, 1967; Ross, 1977)	Observers tend to attribute stalking to the victim's character ('attention-seeking', 'dramatic') rather than the perpetrator's choices. Situational factors such as coercive control, obsession, or misogyny are minimised, while the woman's behaviour is over-scrutinised.
Defensive Attribution Hypothesis (Shaver, 1970)	People distance themselves from stalking victims to feel safer. By blaming her decisions, visibility, or online presence, they reassure themselves that they would avoid stalking by behaving differently.
Myth Acceptance	Cultural myths about stalking, such as 'it's just trolling' or 'if it was serious, she'd go offline', minimise harm and shift responsibility. Acceptance of these myths increases the likelihood of blaming the victim rather than recognising patterned abuse.
Sexism and Misogyny	Women who are visible, outspoken, or successful are more likely to be blamed. Misogynistic beliefs frame women as attention-seeking or manipulative, making their victimisation seem deserved or exaggerated.
Perceived Control and Counterfactual Thinking (Roese, 1997; Rotter, 1966)	Observers focus on what the victim 'could have done differently' ('she shouldn't have posted', 'she should block them'). This creates an illusion of control for the observer, while implying the stalking was preventable by the victim.

Integrated Theory of Victim Blaming (Taylor, 2020)	Victim blaming in stalking emerges from overlapping forces: gendered stereotypes, just-world beliefs, institutional bias, and the need to maintain faith in systems. Together, these dynamics protect perpetrators and social structures while pathologising or scrutinising the victim.
The Perfect Victim (Christie, 1986)	Stalking victims are only fully believed if they fit the 'ideal' image: passive, vulnerable, and blameless. Women who are confident, public-facing, or assertive are seen as less credible and more responsible for the stalking they experience.

Taken from Taylor (2020)

Victims of online abuse and stalking typically report receiving little or no support from friends or authorities. This may be because observers attribute some of the blame for abuse incidents to victims (Scott et al., 2020). Online stalking and abuse is often perceived as fair or acceptable when it can be explained by the victim's initial behaviour (Scott et al., 2020).

In cases of online abuse, research demonstrates that victim blaming increases as more personal information is disclosed by the victim (Weber et al., 2013), putting those who are more active on social media at an increased risk of being blamed when they are subjected to abuse and stalking. This means that the more the person talks personally about their lives, experiences, ideas or thoughts on social media, the more likely they are to be subjected to victim blaming – not dissimilar to how the police officer treated me on the phone.

There are so many possible ways to blame a victim of stalking. Let's break some of them down below.

She's attention seeking.

This narrative reframes fear of stalking as performance. When a woman speaks publicly about being stalked, she is accused of enjoying the drama and as wanting the attention. Her trauma is trivialised into theatre. Her distress becomes content to scrutinise and share. Her attempts to warn others are cast as narcissism or delusion. The psychological function of this myth is simple: it neutralises empathy. If she wants attention, then the stalking is not harm, it is supply. The perpetrator is recast as someone giving her what she craves. The violence disappears behind a smirk. She is, after all, bringing it upon herself.

She provoked it.

This is the oldest script in the book. It has been applied to rape, domestic abuse and sexual harassment for centuries. It rests on the assumption that women's behaviour causes men's aggression. In the digital age, the provocation shifts from clothing and location to content and opinion. She shouldn't have posted that if she didn't want comments. She shouldn't have said that, if she didn't want people to scrutinise it. She shouldn't have built a platform, if she can't handle the heat. The burden shifts seamlessly. The stalker's decision to fixate, monitor, harass and threaten is reframed as an understandable, benign reaction to her presence. If she wasn't sharing herself online, none of this would be happening to her, so this is all her own fault. No one has empathy for someone who 'causes herself' to be stalked.

She loves the drama.

Drama implies exaggeration. It suggests that the conflict is mutual and performative. It erases the power imbalance. It positions the victim as co-author of the chaos. In my own experience, I was repeatedly told that if I spoke about it, I would be fuelling it. By discussing what was happening, I was told that I was amplifying it. That my silence would make it disappear. The stalking itself was minimised into catty gossip, and my response or decision to speak about being stalked was cast as the real problem.

Just ignore it.

This phrase is often delivered as advice, even kindness. It was said to me hundreds of times. It suggests that the solution lies entirely within the victim's behaviour. If she stops reacting, the stalker will lose interest. This advice misunderstands stalking at a fundamental level. Stalking is not sustained by polite engagement. It is sustained by fixation, entitlement, and grievance – feelings that lie within the stalker, not the victim. Ignoring someone who feels entitled can escalate their behaviour. Silence can be interpreted as arrogance, guilt or provocation. In digital spaces, ignoring does not prevent monitoring. It simply removes the victim's voice from the narrative. I learned this one the hard way! The more I retreated out of fear, the more I was framed as 'hiding' or 'guilty'.

You brought this on yourself by being online.

This is perhaps the most modern myth, and unfortunately, the one I heard most from police.

In a world where work, community, communication, research, teaching, and activism are increasingly digital, being online is not a frivolous hobby for me – or for most of us. It is participation in public life. Most business owners and professionals have to be online, even if they loathe it. Yet women who build platforms, share expertise or advocate for change are routinely told that visibility equals consent to abuse. The idea that women create their own harm by existing publicly is a deeply misogynistic script. It positions women's ambition, voice and visibility as inherently provocative. It suggests that safety can only be achieved through smallness.

Many victims of online stalking, myself included, encountered victim blaming at every level. Strangers online insisted that if I stopped speaking publicly, the posts would stop. Members of the public suggested I enjoyed the attention. Even professionals, at times, implied that my platform was the real magnet. This kind of framing always protects perpetrators, who can continue to abuse and stalk, whilst everyone points the finger at the victim and asks "What could you be doing differently?"

If the victim is the cause, the stalker becomes reactive rather than responsible. His or her behaviour is contextualised as understandable. The narrative shifts from "Why is this person stalking her?" to "Why does she keep attracting this?" or even "Why does she keep going on about it?"

Misogynistic disbelief cultures sustain this shift. Disbelief culture refers to the tendency to doubt, minimise or reinterpret women's accounts of harm. Women are routinely scrutinised for inconsistencies, emotional tone, and perceived exaggeration. When stalking is reported, the victim's credibility is assessed more harshly than the perpetrator's behaviour.

Is she paranoid? Is she dramatic? Is she misreading it? Is she lying? Is she mentally ill?

Ironically, the symptoms of trauma (hypervigilance, panic, fear) are used as evidence that she is unstable. The harm becomes proof of weakness and disorder. As my work has always shown, this is not accidental. It is structural.

When we blame victims, we preserve the comfort of believing that harm is controllable. If she caused it, then we can avoid it by behaving differently. If she was careless, then we can be careful. If she was provocative, then we can be quiet. Acknowledging that stalking can happen to someone who has done nothing wrong is much more frightening. It means that control lies with the perpetrator, not the target.

Victim blaming also operates horizontally among women. Other women may distance themselves from a stalking victim by subtly implying poor judgment. She shared too much. She engaged too publicly. She antagonised the wrong people. These narratives reinforce internalised patriarchal scripts that hold women responsible for managing male and female aggression alike.

In online spaces, victim blaming can become communal. Threads may emerge dissecting the victim's response. Screenshots of her distress are circulated as evidence of instability. Her attempts to defend herself are reframed as aggression.

I had this happen to me several times before I had learned the rules of this new game. I tried to tell people what was happening, and I tried to explain the impact it was having on my wife and I, only to be framed as manipulative, abusive, attention seeking, delusional, a conspiracy theorist, and mentally unstable. I thought that people would see how much it was terrifying me, but instead it was evidence that their tactics were working, and so they escalated immediately. It was at this point that I realised my trauma was entertainment and positive reinforcement to sadistic stalkers and observers, and that I must stop showing the impact their behaviour was having if I was to conserve my energy and wellbeing.

The result of that is silencing.

Victims learn quickly that speaking out invites further scrutiny. They weigh the cost of disclosure against the inevitability of doubt. Many choose silence, not because the harm has stopped, but because the secondary harm of disbelief feels unbearable. This is one of the reasons why all the victims of Tattle Life had stayed quiet for years.

The myth that women create their own obsession is particularly insidious in online stalking. It suggests that by sharing online, building community, and expressing opinion, a woman is inviting fixation. It implies that stalking is a choice. By shifting focus to the victim's behaviour, we obscure the choice that the stalker made to terrorise and fixate on someone else. The perpetrator fades into the background of their own crime.

There is also a class and power dimension. Women with platforms, influence or professional authority are often framed as too powerful to be victims. The logic goes: if she is visible, if she has a following, if she speaks confidently, or if she has money and resources, then she cannot be vulnerable. Harm against her is reframed as accountability. A rite of passage. An obligation.

This binary – powerful or victim – is false.

A woman can have a platform, money, success and resources and still be terrified when police arrive at her home due to false reports. She can speak publicly and still lie awake wondering what has been written overnight. She can advocate for others and still feel humiliated by anonymous threads stalking and obsessing over her children.

Victim blaming ensures that stalking remains underreported and under-prosecuted. We know from decades of academic research that if victims anticipate disbelief, they are less likely to seek help (Taylor, 2020). If professionals are primed to question rather than protect, early warning signs are easily missed and if the public normalises harassment and stalking as the cost of visibility or success, perpetrators operate with impunity.

The cultural script of 'she was asking for it' is a very effective mechanism of control. There is no winning within a victim-blaming framework. The only way to dismantle it is to return responsibility to its rightful place. Stalkers stalk because they choose to.

And they are enabled by a culture that would rather interrogate a woman's existence, instead of a perpetrator's persistence.

CHAPTER 6

Destroy her

"So why are you selling?" I asked the man as the three of us looked out over the balcony.

"Oh, we are downsizing, you know. The kids all went off to university and settled down. Our daughter got married and went to live in Cornwall. We don't need to be rattling around in this big old place anymore," he replied, stroking his friendly dogs, who had followed us around the entire house as if they were leading the viewing.

I watched the tall bamboo sway in the sunshine.

"Why are you moving?" he replied politely, just trying to make conversation.

Jay gripped my hand tighter, but the warm faked smile on her face never faltered.

"Oh, just to be closer to family. Lots of them live around here, and it would be nice to see them more," I lied.

The truth wasn't the sort of thing you discussed with a vendor.

How do you explain to someone that you are being relentlessly stalked online, and that details about your house, your address and your car registration plates were being shared with thousands of people?

How do you explain that your beloved home, the one you swore you would never sell, was becoming a target of terrifying rumours and lies online?

How do you tell someone that you are certain your neighbours are in on it without sounding like you need psychiatric assessment?

The man kindly let us wander around his house for a while before we left. It was an interesting house. It was spread over four floors, with a huge multi-level garden and a very large balcony to the first floor with outdoor seating and beautiful views across the valley. The top floor had been converted into a penthouse suite, which we loved. The cellar had been turned into a games room, complete with a billiards table and a cinema. It was very different to our house, which was an extended old doctor's surgery built at the end of the 1800s.

We were stood on the lawn at the rear of the house, looking up at the balcony and the huge chimney stacks when my phone buzzed.

An email from a national magazine asking for a comment.

Media outlets would contact me frequently for comments and interviews on cases or current affairs, so it wasn't out of the ordinary to get an email like that, but something about it caught my eye. Jay carried on chatting to me about the house, oblivious for a moment that I had zoned out. My blood pressure surged in my ears as I read the email in horror.

The comment that the magazine was seeking was not about some case in the press, or some interesting feature they were exploring. It wasn't a comment at all, it was a right to reply to a story they were printing about me. I scanned the email. It was bad. It was really bad.

"Are you listening? What's happening? What's that email?" Jay had stopped talking about the house and was now looking at my phone screen.

I couldn't speak. I just had no words. The magazine were planning to print a story about me that would end my career. Allegations that I was dangerous, that I was putting women at risk, and even an allegation that my work had caused a woman to be sectioned. All from an anonymous source, all taken from Tattle Life. None of it was true, but when had that ever stopped the magazines?

I was given until the end of the day to respond to the allegations in writing, and it was already 2 pm.

We made our excuses, thanked the lovely man for the viewing and got in the car, where I burst into tears.

"What the fuck am I going to do? What do I do?"

"You need to call your agent. This cannot be real. Surely, they can't just print a story about you that someone made up? I mean, they could be sued!"

"I don't think they care about nobodies like me trying to sue them, Jay. I don't understand why they are doing this to me. Who would do this?"

"Who is the email from? Is it a journalist?"

I handed my phone over to her, feeling my stomach knot and my blood pressure rise.

"I dunno. I skimmed it and then had to conceal a fucking panic attack to get out of that house before I passed out in front of the man . . ."

Jay scanned the email again before whispering the name of the journalist. "Maria Vasko . . . why do I know that name?"

"Dunno . . ." I mumbled through tears, slumping into my seat.

But suddenly, the name slotted into place and I sat up straight.

She was right. We did know that name. My mind cleared.

"Hang on a fucking minute. Maria Vasko? She's . . . the journalist Blanche uses when she needs to attack someone but doesn't want her name on the article! Remember when she had too much to drink, and she told us about how her and Maria swap articles to protect each other, so they can write hit pieces to put into the press?"

Jay gasped, jaw open. "Oh my fucking god, you're right, she did say that. But that means . . ."

"Blanche is involved in all of this," I realised, suddenly piecing together the network of women who had been hounding me for months.

"But why would she do this to you? Why would she become part of this?"

I sat in the car, tears streaming down my face, wracking my brain for a memory, a reason, a rationale. A woman I barely knew ordering hit pieces for *a huge magazine* right at the peak of the stalking.

Suddenly, it hit me.

"The last time I spoke to her it was when I refused to speak at that event for her. Do you remember? When she sent me all of those horrible messages whilst I was at work? If I remember, she threatened me with . . . something about outing me publicly . . ."

I reached for my phone and quickly searched for her name. The conversation popped up immediately.

I scrolled through it, reliving the strange and unexpected argument that had seemingly occurred out of the blue one day. After a friendly few minutes of messages in which she had casually asked me to become the keynote speaker at the event she was running, my polite refusals had been interrogated.

When I had refused to engage any further, she had messaged again to say that she didn't believe my 'stories' about being raped as a child anyway, or the way I was treated by police, and she had set about proving that I was a liar. She had said people were talking about me, and that everyone agreed with her. The conversation had shocked and devastated me at the time, but I hadn't ever considered that it could be related to what had been unfolding.

I scrolled my phone, looking for the old message.

"Aha! I found it . . . So . . . she wrote in the message, 'You're lucky I am not doing this to you publicly.' Wow. If that's the case, it seems like my luck just ran out . . ."

* * *

There is a moment in many stalking cases when something shifts. It is no longer about contact or proximity. The stalker's behaviour is escalating. It is now about total destruction of the victim.

The modern online stalker does not always want or need proximity. They do not necessarily want a relationship, a reply, a romance, or a reconciliation. What they want is domination. Not intimacy really, but obliteration. Punishment – the more public, the better. The sabotage mentality is central to understanding this evolution.

Sabotage is deliberate interference designed to damage, disrupt or collapse something of value. In stalking, sabotage becomes multi-directional. It targets reputation, employment, finances, relationships, friendships, parenting, and psychological stability simultaneously. Once a stalker (or group of stalkers) has decided that this is the aim, the message is simple: if I cannot control you, I will destroy you.

Reputational sabotage is often the first frontier. The goal is not debate. It is contamination. When enough doubt is seeded, even those who do not believe the allegations may hesitate to support the victim, privately or publicly. Friends cut contact. Family members back off. Clients pause the work. Colleagues withdraw. Invitations dry up. The social circle disappears. The victim becomes isolated and pre-emptively defensive, constantly anticipating the next rumour or loss.

Emotional sabotage runs parallel and leaves victims in extremely frightening situations, without a support network. False reports to authorities trigger life-changing investigations. Police arrive at your door following anonymous allegations. Social services contact you to raise concerns about your children. Regulatory bodies initiate inquiries into your career or your qualifications. Even when allegations are baseless, the processes that these claims trigger are traumatising.

Very often, the process is the punishment and the stalker learns quickly that systems can be weaponised to great effect. Freedom of Information requests, Subject Data Access Requests, formal complaints, safeguarding referrals, police complaints, and Crimestoppers reports. Individually, these mechanisms exist to promote vital transparency, safeguarding, and accountability. In the hands of a determined stalker though, they become powerful tools of harassment. The stalker stays just within the law, exploiting procedural rights to generate chaos.

Every victim I have met who has been abused in this way has spoken of how this particular part of the stalking drained every ounce of energy and hope they had left. Financial sabotage often follows reputational damage. If clients are warned away and employers start investigations, income drops, contracts are delayed, promotions disappear, and cash flow tightens. If legal advice becomes necessary, costs escalate exponentially. I was quoted £100,000 by legal firms to help me stop the online stalking, money I simply didn't have.

Relational sabotage is also life-altering and corrosive. Stalkers contact friends, family members, colleagues, collaborators – everyone they can think of. They may present themselves as concerned whistleblowers, or as someone who is contacting them to warn them. They may imply danger, instability, secrets, or hidden wrongdoing. The aim, like in most forms of interpersonal abuse, is to isolate the victim. To seed doubt in intimate circles. To fracture support networks. Isolation increases vulnerability.

However, relational sabotage rarely stops at friends and family. In cases of online stalking that I analysed, over 70% of the victims said that the stalker targeted or contacted their partner and 40% said that the stalker targeted their parents (Taylor, 2020). In some cases, this caused the breakdown of their marriage or relationship. In one particular case I analysed in 2025, the partner was so ashamed by what had been written by an online stalker about the victim that he left her.

Professional sabotage can be relentless and extremely embarrassing. The stalker positions themselves as a protector of standards, sending legitimate-sounding emails that 'raise concerns' about suitability, qualifications, experience, ethics, or personal lifestyle.

In my own life, I have seen how quickly this escalates. Emails sent to institutions containing pages of curated allegations, attempts to frame me as a risk to myself and others, efforts to trigger investigations that would stain my record regardless of outcome. Each action carefully constructed to appear serious and real. In almost all of my own experiences of this, the damage was done the second my colleagues or contacts read the email. They believed some, if not all of it, and by the time I was meeting with them or talking to them about it, they had already changed the way they treated me. It was heartbreaking and probably some of the most embarrassing moments of my adult life.

And I say that as someone who was casually offered a slice of toast by catering staff whilst my legs were in stirrups having episiotomy stitches. I would sooner experience that a thousand times than have to sit through one meeting whilst someone read out the wild stories, accusations and lies about my life, my sexuality, my children and my relationship, before going on to ask me to defend myself in front of people. Truly horrifying.

Impersonation and defamation intensify the attacks. Fake accounts can be created within seconds. Emails can even be sent out in your own name. Statements can be attributed to you that you never made. The digital environment allows identity to be manipulated with ease. Even when impersonation is eventually uncovered, the initial damage may linger. When the stalking really ramped up for me, one of my stalkers impersonated a police officer and sent emails to my TV producers, claiming that I was under police investigation. When the producers showed me the emails, I instantly knew that the person was not a real police officer by the way they communicated, but by then it was already too late, and the stalker's actions were enough to frighten my colleagues into believing them.

More recently, a woman had been posing as me on lesbian dating sites, using my full name, stolen pictures, my work, books, blogs and likeness to groom women. I was horrified to receive multiple emails from victims of the account, saying that the person who was impersonating me had convinced them to disclose years of abuse and trauma to them, thinking it was me.

A few years back, someone else used my holiday photos and my full name to create a sugar baby account, where the person was talking sexually with men and then having them pay for my bikini photos. Again, I was only made aware of this when a very embarrassed man contacted me to double-check if he had been talking to me for months. When I explained it was not me (and that I was a married lesbian), he realised that I was telling the truth and showed me the transactions of money he had sent to the account. I genuinely didn't know how to respond. Here was a man who thought it was acceptable to pay a woman to send him images of herself, but also, here was a man who had been a victim of catfishing and who felt emotionally and psychologically connected to me, having believed that he had been speaking to me for months. I had to resort to blocking him because it was clear to me that he couldn't separate the real me from the fake me.

Being stalked online truly is something else. As if stalkers didn't have enough tools, doxxing (the publication of private information) is another common and powerful tactic that stalkers use to intimidate their victims. Addresses, family details, school names, travel plans, car registration plates, hotels and phone numbers can all be shared deliberately online with ease. The release of such information may not always be explicitly illegal (especially if sourced from public records), but its intent is clear: to increase fear. And children are not exempt.

In some cases that I have encountered, children have been doxxed, discussed, photographed, and speculated about. School environments and uniforms have been identified and posted online. Children have been bullied by groups of grown adults about their appearance, their behaviour and their hobbies. The cruelty of this cannot be overstated. Targeting children serves two functions: it amplifies fear, and it signals total disregard for boundaries. The line between legal and criminal behaviour is deliberately tested.

Very often, stalkers engaging in doxxing are seeking total collapse and intimidation of their victim. If the victim cannot cope and withdraws from public life out of fear, the stalker may experience this as victory. If their life is destroyed, they live in fear. Like me, they may even have to move house. The victim's life is completely upended and so the domination is complete even without direct interaction. This is why modern stalking can be so psychologically devastating. The victim is not only afraid of being watched. She is forced to watch her own life shrink. She becomes aware that she is being defined in rooms she cannot enter. The sabotage mentality thrives in online communities that validate it (Mardon et al., 2022). Within certain digital spaces, the destruction of a target becomes a shared project. Participants trade information, encourage escalation, and celebrate their perceived wins. The language shifts from criticism to elimination.

She needs to be stopped. She needs to be exposed. She needs to be destroyed.

The rhetoric of protection masks the reality of persecution. In my research on Tattle Life, this pattern was unmistakable. Threads evolved quickly. And yet, because much of it existed in digital space, it was dismissed by police as gossip (Taylor, 2025). We must be clear about the stakes. Victims describe feeling as though they are fighting on multiple fronts simultaneously. Defending against allegations, reassuring clients, protecting their children, managing fear and panic, documenting evidence daily, and seeking legal advice. All while trying to maintain normality.

It's a wonder any victim survives. The exhaustion is strategic. A drained person is much easier to dominate, especially once they have no energy left to fight back. A silenced person is easier to control. A financially strained person is a lot more vulnerable.

Examples of the financial and professional impact of being stalked

Impact	Workplace stalking	Ex-partner stalking
Professional		
Work performance deteriorated	47%	41%
Had to take sick leave	31%	29%
Had to resign and change job	20%	17%
It has not affected my professional life	10%	25%
Financial		
Had to pay for home security or personal security	39%	34%
Lost income from wages, leaving or losing work	31%	34%
Had to pay for psychological therapies	22%	22%
Had to pay to repair property damage	18%	24%
Had to relocate	16%	30%
Had to get a lawyer and pay legal costs	10%	16%
My finances were not affected	12%	11%

N = 191 Sheridan et al. (2019)

Modern stalkers seem to understand the impacts they can have. They may never explicitly threaten violence. They may never demand contact. They may present themselves as concerned citizens. But their trajectory reveals intent: to destabilise every pillar of the victim's life until she collapses or retreats. This is a targeted, relentless campaign.

In my case, several of my stalkers wrote on the internet, some in their full names, that they were aware of the financial and professional impacts they were having on me and that they were glad they were doing it. They never made much of a secret of their tactics. It was clear that one of their main goals was complete financial and professional ruin.

Destroy her. That is the unspoken (and as it turns out, sometimes spoken) objective behind many modern stalking campaigns. Not win her back. Not talk to her. Not reconcile with her. End her influence. End her credibility. End her safety. End her.

Until systems learn to recognise sabotage as stalking – even when it is dressed up in formal complaints and polite emails – victims will remain exposed to a form of domination that thrives in the gaps between legal definitions whilst destroying them.

And it tells us something vital about modern stalking: it is no longer merely about access and proximity. It is about erasure.

CHAPTER 7

Does gang stalking really exist?

One thing I learned about being stalked for years is that life goes on around you.

Whilst you become wrapped up in a web of terror, your friends get married, your siblings have children, your job demands your attention, your kids have their birthdays and parent's evenings, and your relationship ages and changes.

Stalking takes over every corner of your life – and by extension, it takes over your relationships too.

Jay and I had clung to each other for dear life during the turmoil. No matter what was being said about us online, we knew that our marriage was sacred to us and that it was the only stable thing we had left. When the world felt hostile, our bedroom was our oasis. We realised fairly early on that the pressure and the trauma of being stalked could easily end our relationship if we did not commit to protecting it. We saw the tactics quickly, the bets on our marriage ending. We chose to prioritise our love, and our connection, over everything else.

As I have always taught, coping mechanisms come in all shapes and sizes during trauma. I am often thankful that neither of us were into taking drugs or heavy drinking during the stalking because one, or both of us, would definitely be dead by now. Instead, rightly or wrongly, we were each other's coping mechanism. Remaining connected whilst feeling like we were being battered by a hurricane was complex, but looking back, it was probably the only thing keeping us going.

Sometimes that connection would be sharing a bottle of wine in a hot bath together. Sometimes it would be ignoring our responsibilities and binge-watching trashy series that made us forget about what was happening to us. Sometimes it would be booking flights and disappearing for a break from reality. Other times, it would be reading books to each other or trying to master increasingly difficult recipes, but sometimes connection looked like a long weekend of sex and intimacy, only ever emerging for snack breaks.

It had been one of those weekends in late 2023 and we were lazing in bed on a Sunday evening sharing a box of grapes, when I noticed an email pop up on my phone. Jay was lying across my stomach as I started to screw up my face at the strange message. Crunching another grape, she asked if I was okay, and what I had seen.

I put my finger to my lip, silently asking her to hold her questions until I had finished reading one of the most disturbing emails I had ever read in my life.

"Jess, you're scaring me. What are you reading?" She sat up, searching my face for a clue. I tried to respond, but I couldn't find the words. My throat dried up and my heart pounded in my chest. I suddenly felt extremely unsafe.

"Are the doors locked?" I whispered to her, grabbing some clothes from the floor.

Jay jumped up from the bed, raising her voice. "Why? Why are you asking me that? I don't know!"

I dropped my phone on to the duvet and stood up, confused and frightened.

"Let's just check all the doors, first. Okay?" I whispered firmly again, signalling to my wife to lower her own voice.

In less than 30 seconds, the mysterious email had transformed our safe haven into an extension of the danger outside and all I could think about was the doors and windows downstairs. Shaking, I quickly checked every lock and alarm system in the house, testing them all one by one before returning to our bedroom.

"I think you need to tell me what the fuck you just read, Jessica," Jay demanded in the hushed tone I had requested.

But just as I opened my mouth to speak to her, I remembered a line of the email and reached for the notebook on my bedside table. I always keep a notebook near my bed, as I often journal my dreams, or wake up from revelations or ideas that I note down. I flicked to the back and pulled out my fountain pen with the deep purple ink.

'Turn your phone off and don't speak – communicate here instead,' I wrote, half terrified, half worried that I had finally cracked under the pressure.

We both turned our phones off.

'What the hell is going on?' She scribbled underneath.

'I just got an email from a dodgy Proton Mail account saying I was being watched and I was going to be killed.'

She read the sentence, looking up at me in panic.

'Do you think it's real?' she scrawled, passing me the pen.

'Fuck knows. But fuck risking it.'

She nodded and wrote back.

'Yeah, fair. What else did it say?'

We passed the pen back and forth, the way my little sister and I would do as teenagers many years ago when we needed to talk to each other about something that no one else could overhear.

'It said that they needed to inform me that there were plans to kill me, that I was being targeted and stalked by a group. It said the group were watching me.'

Chills ran through me as I looked out of the bedroom window.

'Was it a threat?'

I shook my head as I took the pen from Jay.

'No, it was a warning. The person is warning me to try to protect me, not to threaten me.'

'What if it is fake?' she wrote back quickly.

'Then it's someone playing with me. But what if it's not?'

She looked at me, her eyes filling with tears. She was pale, shaking, and tired. Every week, something new cropped up, pushing us further and further into a state of alarm. I hated to see her so traumatised by everything that was happening to me, but I was powerless. I was trapped in this nightmare alongside her, and I had no idea how to get us both out of it. I breathed for a few moments while I thought. I kept hold of the pen and wrote something to her that I had been secretly worrying about for weeks.

'The email also says my phone is hacked. And yours is, too. Maybe that's what's wrong with them?'

We both stared at each other. Admittedly, our phones had been playing up for a couple of months. We would be on the phone to each other when weird noises would break through the call. Both of us would be able to hear it at times, a strange background noise, as if there was a third person on the call in a busy atmosphere. One time, we were having a sensitive conversation about work when we suddenly heard someone else on our call. We had both heard it, asked each other to confirm, and then put the phone down.

Another time, we were on a facetime to a colleague who was chatting away, completely unaware, whilst both Jay and I could hear a loud, strange, high-pitched static noise through the phone. It was so loud and unnerving that we couldn't concentrate on the conversation with our colleague, who couldn't hear it at all. Other times, it would be weird clicking noises or beeps.

'I think we need to get rid of them. Something is wrong. How would the sender know about our phones being weird?'

'But who would want to hack our phones? And how would they do it?'

I hesitated. I had no idea. I knew nothing about phone tapping, beyond the fact that it existed. The newspapers had been doing it to politicians and celebrities for years, so there must have been a way to do it, I reasoned.

'I feel like I am going crazy. Are we being toyed with, or am I going to end up dead?'

Disassociating from the panic, I looked at my own flowing cursive in my favourite purple ink. The way my letters joined to each other. The smooth, deep purple ink on the cream page of my notebook. I imagined what it would be like to shrink into tiny form and slide into the paper along my letters.

I stared at the silent question to my wife: am I going to die?

She sat in silence for a while, tapping the pen on the page, deep in thought.

'Do you remember when the guys contacted you last year to warn you that your name was coming up on the dark web a lot?'

I raised my eyebrows at her. I had totally forgotten about that.

'Yeah . . .' I wrote back.

'You think we could ask them for help? Do they still do covert work?'

Jay was referring to a group of guys I had done some work with years back, who had unexpectedly texted me to warn me that whilst they were on an undercover operation, they had coincidentally found a group of people who had been watching and discussing my work and my social media posts at length. The text didn't go into detail, but it told me that my name was coming up in places that were extremely dangerous, and that I should be careful. When I had replied to ask for more information, they had told me that they couldn't give me further detail, but they would tell me if I was ever at imminent risk.

'Yeah … but they are all on jobs, god knows where. I never know where they are when they are on jobs.'

'I don't think we should go to the police over this,' Jay wrote back. I exhaled slowly. She only wrote what I was already thinking, but there was something unnerving about us both realising that the police were not the right people for this, and that they would likely think we were going crazy.

Maybe we were?

* * *

Few phrases shut down a conversation as quickly as 'gang stalking'. Say it out loud and watch the reaction. Eyebrows lift. Tone shifts. The word 'paranoid' is bounced around.

Online, the term is often associated with conspiracy forums and psychiatric case studies. It is routinely framed as evidence of delusion: the belief that a coordinated group is monitoring, harassing or targeting an individual without basis in reality.

But what happens when a coordinated group really is monitoring, harassing, and targeting someone?

I couldn't write a book on online stalking without exploring this topic. The binary we have created says that either you are experiencing a rational fear of one perpetrator, or you are mentally ill and imagining a group of them. This is dangerously simplistic. It collapses complex digital stalking behaviours into psychiatric shorthand and means that when victims are being stalked by a group, no one believes them.

Whilst researching this book, I came across a study in which the academics deliberately excluded a case of an Instagram influencer who said they had been targeted, harassed and stalked online by over 1000 accounts that they had to block. The authors said that the average number of stalkers that Instagram influencers had been targeted by was between 1 and 10, according to their findings. Because this influencer claimed that she had been targeted by such a comparatively high number of accounts, over 1000, the researchers said that they removed her case from their study as it "didn't seem realistic when compared with the others" (Fox et al., 2024).

I was appalled to read this blatant dismissal of her experience in an academic paper. Additionally, I find this disbelief perplexing, especially as forums and websites are clear evidence of stalkers working together in a group. If anything, I have noticed that coordinated harassment is very real and appears to be the norm online.

Level with me here. It is not exactly rare for someone to be stalked by their ex or for their entire family and friendship network to get involved. Many people know of someone who split up with a partner, only to be harassed, stalked, abused and bullied online for months or years by their associates.

The term 'gang stalking' appears to have emerged in the early 2000s within online communities of individuals who stated that they were being systematically targeted by groups. In many discussions, the reports involved covert government surveillance, implanted devices or orchestrated stranger behaviour in public spaces. These narratives were quickly absorbed into psychiatric frameworks of paranoia or delusional disorder.

And the label stuck.

Over time, 'gang stalking' became shorthand for imagined persecution, whereby victims' experiences were put down to delusions or psychosis. To claim you were being gang stalked was to invite immediate diagnostic speculation. The cultural association hardened: multiple perpetrators equals mental illness. After all, stalkers don't work in groups, do they?

Maybe not in person, but the digital age has altered the landscape entirely.

Today, it is possible for hundreds or thousands of individuals to participate in sustained, coordinated harassment of a single target. No implanted devices. No secret agencies. No elaborate groups of police officers or military. Just forums, group chats, algorithms and shared grievances.

And as much as it would probably be easier for me to avoid this topic, I cannot dismiss the reality that some stalkers are police officers. Some are military or ex-military. Some are working for the government in one capacity or another. Some are nurses, doctors, lawyers, social workers, psychologists and psychiatrists.

The evidence I gathered from analysing the Tattle Life stalking cases demonstrated that, where the victims knew the identity of their stalkers, many of them were professionals. Some examples included teachers, social workers, nurses, academics, lawyers, doctors, therapists and counsellors.

In at least one case, the online stalker was a serving police officer.

In my mentoring service, I have also supported at least five women whose stalkers were very senior police or government officials, usually ex-partners. In all of those cases, perpetrators enlisted the help of those around them to stalk, monitor, and target their victim. In my own case, one of the women who shared the links to Tattle Life was a female judge who was actively sitting on criminal trials.

Once I had been exposed to these cases, some of which resulted in criminal investigations and criminal trials, I started to wonder about the framing of group and gang stalking victims as mentally ill. In almost all verified cases I know of where the victim was being stalked by a group, a gang, or a collective of professionals and officials, the victim was diagnosed with multiple mental disorders, was publicly and privately framed as delusional, and would often tell me that no one believed them for years.

And I know what that feels like.

When I was being targeted by hundreds of users simultaneously, there were moments where the scale felt surreal. Threads updated in real time. Screenshots appeared within minutes of posts going live. Narratives were built collectively. They knew where I was at all times. Emails were sent to institutions. Complaints were coordinated. False reports were filed. I couldn't work out how so much was happening to me so quickly. Some days, it felt like I was being deliberately tortured. If I had described this to someone unfamiliar with online culture twenty years ago, it might have sounded implausible.

Hell, when I described this to people two years ago, I was still chalked up as losing grip on reality. Even when I googled group and gang stalking so I could seek help and understand what was happening to me, I was met with hundreds of pages of search results about psychosis, persecutory delusions, and mental health. It was as if being stalked by a group was globally portrayed as utterly impossible. I may as well have been googling for help with my flying pigs.

It was only through collecting the cases of 150 victims of online stalking that I realised that group stalking online was the norm rather than the exception.

The psychiatric dismissal of 'gang stalking' has created a chilling effect. I certainly have never used that language to describe what I was subjected to, despite it being true. I was stalked by a coordinated group. Startlingly, that group included professionals, highly networked people, and those with the power to cause immense damage to my life, whilst managing, for the most part, to keep their hands clean. What happened to me and hundreds of other victims was completely real, but victims of coordinated harassment hesitate to describe the scale of what is happening for fear of being labelled paranoid. They downplay numbers. They sanitise language. They speak of 'a few people' when in reality the online group could easily be hundreds.

It is said that the difference between conspiracy delusion and genuine coordinated harassment and stalking lies not in the number of perpetrators, but in the evidence and structure of behaviour.

In many of the documented persecutory 'delusions', the alleged coordination is often vast, argued by professionals to be implausible and lacking corroboration. Strangers in cars are believed to be part of a network. Random events are interpreted as signals.

The trouble with this, and where the line blurs, is that this can all be true of genuine stalking and harassment. In the digital world, the coordination can be vast thanks to group chats, threads, websites, social media and forums. When victims explain what is happening to them, professionals very often believe their stories to be implausible. And victims often do struggle to corroborate or demonstrate that what is happening is true, mainly because the targeted stalking and harassment is happening in small, connected, deliberate ways that only the victim can understand.

In lots of cases of group stalking and coordinated harassment, there are visible networks that someone could verify, but even then, so much of this is perception. A police officer could go and look at the forums, threads, group chats, archived posts and shared hashtags. All of this is publicly accessible documentation of discussion and planning. They could read through it all, and still roll their eyes and conclude that it is not stalking because it is not high risk enough, and therefore nothing more than trolling. In some cases, including my own, police have incorrectly applied the law and told victims that if they are not named in full in all of the posts, then the behaviour does not amount to harassment or stalking. This leaves victims with no advice or protection for months or years because their stalkers refer to them by nickname, a slur, or their initials.

Digital platforms enable what sociologists might describe as distributed networks of action. Individuals do not need to meet physically. They do not even need to know each other personally in order to work together to stalk. Toxic online disinhibition (Suler, 2004) can amplify individual aggression and increase the propensity for online stalking in groups. Under such conditions, individuals are more likely to disregard the consequences of perpetration, reduce self-monitoring, and shift from passive observers to active contributors in bullying, stalking and abuse (Alimu et al., 2025).

They gather around a shared narrative or a collective hatred of someone, whether it be in a forum, on a subreddit, in a private Facebook group, or on a gossip site. They enter an echo chamber of people who support their thoughts and feelings. Echo chambers amplify intensity in those spaces. An echo chamber is an environment in which beliefs, narratives and feelings are reinforced through repetition and reinforcement within a closed community. Dissent is minimised and alternative interpretations are excluded or ignored. Within such spaces, suspicion escalates rapidly. Users add their speculation and accusations, one after the other, until minor grievances become moral panics or total outrage.

This interests me as I recently learned that many of the online stalkers have family and friends who are oblivious to their online behaviour.

In one case I was exploring, the professional woman (a prolific and obsessive online stalker of several unconnected male and female victims) had colleagues and friends in real life who had never heard her mention any of her targets. On her private and personal Facebook page and Instagram, she appeared completely normal. She shared photos of her walking her dogs, meeting up with friends, travelling, and doing everyday things. There was no mention of the celebrities and influencers that she abused every day for years. No posts about her grievances against them, false claims she was taking them to court, or evidence of her long posts explaining why she hated them so much.

On her accounts that she used to stalk her victims, she posted aggressive, abusive, and obsessive content hundreds of times each week. She threatened suicide if they didn't respond to her. She wrote messages, emails, and posts to her victims, claiming that she was reporting them to the police, that she was taking them to court, that she was never going to stop until she brought them down.

She found a community online that supported and encouraged her behaviour. She had teamed up with several others in forums and on social media who felt the same way and was becoming increasingly emboldened. She would write posts thanking her fellow online stalkers for supporting her, helping her, and validating her 'concerns'.

Yet, she never shared these feelings, thoughts, concerns, or behaviours with anyone around her. Her family knew nothing about it. Nor did her friends or colleagues. Until one day, she began to stalk her friend's ex-partner, and the two worlds collided, leading to her friend finding out about all of her other online profiles where she stalked and harassed strangers.

For years, she had managed to maintain two separate identities and networks. She had engaged in targeted and coordinated behaviour with a large group of other stalkers and had been celebrated, thanked, and supported in doing so.

In my Tattle Life research, I observed clear patterns of coordinated behaviour just like this. Users would share screenshots, speculate collectively, identify employers, encourage reporting, celebrate perceived victories when institutions responded or when victims were harmed or upset. The language of protection and justice was deployed repeatedly. The target was framed as dangerous. The group framed themselves as vigilant.

Online, some might call that a 'pile-on': the sudden influx of attention, criticism, doxxing or harassment directed at a target by multiple individuals simultaneously. It may be triggered by a viral post, a call-out thread, or a shared accusation. Participants may not see themselves as coordinated, yet the cumulative effect is synchronised aggression and harm.

A pile-on feels like gang stalking because, in effect, it is.

Loveluck (2020) wrote an interesting paper on digital vigilantism and stalking, in which he sets out four common strategies of groups who stalk online. He argues that it usually involves large groups of people working together on the internet to cause coordinated public denunciations and harassment, sometimes to inflict direct harm and damage, but more often to humiliate, destroy and disgrace their victim.

Four strategies of digital vigilantism

Flagging	This usually takes the form of public shaming, often by circulating pictures of a behaviour deemed to be objectionable. The actions are generally loosely coordinated, although they can be aggregated and coordinated via specific hashtags, webpages, forums, or social media pages.
Investigating	Investigating aims at naming a person. Here, a collective effort is made to identify individuals suspected of wrongdoings, which can range from minor disagreements to crimes and terrorist activities. It usually involves finding personal digital traces and records (such as pictures of a victim, screenshots from social media accounts, or contributions on forums and chats) being collected as evidence. The material is then shared directly via dedicated platforms or on social media in order to leverage 'collective intelligence'. The aim is to solve a puzzle, but also to identify the persons involved and expose them. 'Web-sleuthing' is common, which involves 'varying levels of amateur detective work, including but not limited to searching for information, uploading documents, images and videos, commenting, debating, theorising, analysing, identifying people around the victim.
Hounding	This involves naming and shaming victims and then sharing personal information about someone accused of wrongdoing in order to punish them by presenting them in a negative light. The aim here is no longer to denounce a behaviour, to solve a puzzle or identify a suspect, but to accuse a person publicly and discredit or humiliate them by providing incriminating evidence. In its most extreme form, it manifests as mass online bullying, harassment, staking and digital sabotage which are wielded in the name of justice, order or safety (rather than individual malice or revenge). One of its main tactics is doxxing.
Organised leaking	Organised leaking is primarily directed at institutions or organisations and involves a higher degree of structure through setting up specific processes and tools intended to encourage and manage the documentation of problematic situations or the disclosure of confidential information. It is different from one-off whistleblowing initiatives on the part of 'insider' witness to unethical practices and can be understood as an architecture of denunciation, which usually include protecting sources.

Loveluck (2020)

For the victim, the experience is overwhelming emotionally and physically. Notifications suddenly flood in and because those notifications pop up on our phones, it can feel extremely intrusive and dangerous. Messages multiply. Comments escalate. The scale can feel incomprehensible. The nervous system registers threat from multiple directions.

The first time this happened to me was in 2018 when I was delivering a lecture on the psychology of trauma in children who had been sexually abused. On my break, I picked up my phone to check the time and saw that every single possible way of contacting me had been overwhelmed. My emails were full of abuse, death and rape threats, and disgusting harassment, updating with new messages every few seconds. My social media accounts were bombarded with thousands of notifications and DMs – the apps were freezing, not able to cope with the activity. I stood in the lecture hall, silent and panicking.

I had no idea what was happening to me, and I was terrified. It turned out that whilst I had been busy at work, a man who had disagreed with one of my social media posts had done some digging, found my email addresses, workplace, all of my social media handles, private information about me, and some photographs, and then posted them across every digital platform that he could. He had over 2 million followers, but he had also posted them across Reddit and several other closed community platforms for the Far Right.

I had never seen anything like it before, and I wish I could say that I hadn't seen anything like that since, but this was the first time of many more to come. And those networks were relentless – they didn't just bombard me for a few hours, or even a day. This went on, 24 hours a day, for three weeks. I was stalked, harassed, threatened, doxxed, and abused endlessly by groups of coordinated people, culminating in one of them managing to hack my laptop and take over the desktop right in front of me. I screamed and ran to unplug the Wi-Fi router as I watched the cursor move, the person searching through my files and folders. I couldn't understand or explain what was happening to me, but I felt under siege.

This is where the language gap becomes dangerous.

Victims struggling to articulate what is happening may reach for the term 'gang stalking' because it captures the feeling of collective pursuit. They do not mean secret government agents. They often mean hundreds of usernames dissecting their life daily. They mean groups of coordinated people stalking them, harassing them, threatening them, and monitoring them.

If professionals respond reflexively with psychiatric suspicion, the harm only deepens. Disbelief compounds trauma. The victim then not only faces the coordinated harassment alone, but also the insinuation that their perception is distorted or imagined. The stigma attached to 'gang stalking' silences legitimate reports of networked abuse. Separating myth from reality requires nuance.

Yes, some individuals do experience beliefs involving imagined networks. Some people who are traumatised and distressed can develop coping mechanisms and trauma responses which lead them to believe that they are being monitored, stalked, or watched when there is no evidence that it is occurring. That is a reality. But it does not follow that all claims of group targeting are 'delusional'. In a hyperconnected digital environment, collective harassment is structurally possible and increasingly common. The architecture of tech platforms makes it easy, and so we need a major shift in recognition of these possibilities and tactics.

Forum culture fosters shared identity around targets. From what I can see from my research, group stalking online does not require a central leader issuing instructions, as some might assume. It can emerge organically through shared grievance and reinforcement. Individuals observe each other's actions and comments and escalate in response. A complaint posted publicly prompts others to file similar complaints. A rumour repeated often enough becomes assumed truth.

On Tattle Life, this rolling, iterative behaviour is common across all threads. One person may make an unkind comment, which triggers another person to make a similar comment. Other people like it, share it, and add their own comment. Then someone ups the ante and says something much more abusive. That gets some likes too, so others feel compelled to follow suit. The abusive behaviour escalates. Someone suggests that action needs to be taken against the victim – and people agree with that, too. Then someone floats their suspicion or accusation, and people speculate and agree with it. They collectively decide that the victim needs to be punished, exposed, reported, and destroyed. Someone shares their address, their social media handles, photos of the victim, or information about their children. Within minutes, the conversation has moved organically from someone making an unkind comment to plans to destroy the victim's life and target their children.

Group stalking then commences and in some cases it can last for years, whilst the stalkers validate and support each other in their endeavours.

Very often, we find ourselves talking about trolling, pile-ons, even smear campaigns. But these terms often minimise the sustained, fixated, intrusive and criminal nature of the behaviour. When a group monitors one individual over months or years, tracks her movements, contacts institutions, sends threats and abuse, archives her posts and coordinates action, we are certainly in stalking territory.

The fact that it is a collective of people, rather than a singular stalker, does not make it imaginary.

And so, the real question is not "Does gang stalking exist?" as a monolithic phenomenon. The better question is: "Can groups coordinate to harass, monitor, abuse and target an individual persistently online?"

The answer is unequivocally yes. Sometimes that group of people will be a family, or a group of friends. Sometimes it will be a forum. Sometimes it will be a group of professionals, or officials. For some victims, the group of stalkers may even include private investigators hired by abusive ex-partners. This crime is much broader than people realise.

The psychiatric dismissal of the term has obscured this reality. By conflating all reports of multiple perpetrators with delusion, we have left genuine victims without credible language. The digital age has created forms of collective aggression that previous generations could not easily imagine or define. Victims are now having to describe forms of abuse to police, authorities and therapists that simply did not, and could not, exist before now. We must update our frameworks accordingly.

Otherwise, we risk doing something profoundly unjust: telling people who are genuinely surrounded by coordinated hostility that the problem exists only in their minds. And in doing so, we continue to protect the mob, whilst gaslighting the victim.

CHAPTER 8

Stalked, or just paranoid?

"I'm glad today went well," I said to Jay, relieved that the cohort we'd just trained had been so nice and engaged.

They were the penultimate team we had left to train on that contract – a mixture of high-ranking officers from CID and the RASSO unit.

"Me too," she smiled "Sometimes I feel like we're really getting somewhere with this work."

It had been about two years since the murder of Sarah Everard, but eight years since I'd started training police and detectives in this area. The enhanced public scrutiny had made even good officers defensive at best, and combative at times. We'd worked hard to build rapport with our forces, and even harder on building the reputation we had.

We walked across the car park of the venue and got into the car together. I rubbed my forehead and the sides of my face with my hands.

"One more left, babe." Jay smiled, trying to reassure me. I smiled at her, but I could feel my cheeks and lips were tense as I did. My eyes were sore and my body didn't relax.

"What's up, babe?" Jay frowned at me, sensing that something was wrong.

"I'm just worried," I sighed. "We're just not getting the amount of work in that we used to, or that we need to be able to pay everyone's salaries."

Jay tried to interrupt with more reassurance, but I continued.

"This is usually our busiest time of year . . . and . . . I'm just worried." As I slumped further into my seat, I refreshed my apps for the fourth time in a row as if I was tracing the outline of my own enclosure. Being stalked for years had turned me into a nervous wreck, and I often felt as though I was in an abusive relationship with my own phone.

Then an email came through. I felt my breathing pause as I waited for it to download fully. Every notification, on every app, at every time of the day filled me with dread.

My eyes filled up with tears.

"What's the matter? What's going on?" Jay questioned.

I snapped back, trying to read through blurry eyes. "Can you just give me a minute?"

Dear Dr Taylor

My name's Joanna Londis, I'm the senior lead practitioner at Women's Advocacy Trust. We've had some concerns raised about your involvement in our annual conference, and I'd appreciate the opportunity to speak with you about them and gain some clarity.

My apologies for this being our introduction, but if you could just give me a quick call as soon as you can, we'd really appreciate it. You can find my contact details on the signature of this email.

Best,

Joanna

I sighed. Totally defeated.

"I've had another one," I said to Jay, completely unable to hide the shame and exhaustion.

"What?! I don't understand how this keeps happening. How are they even finding out so many of our partners and commissioners? All this information is private! Who's even contacting them?" Jay questioned, with the same familiar panic and bewilderment that seemed to dominate our lives.

I didn't have the answers for her. I never did.

"Look, I'm going to have to just give her a call." I pressed the number at the bottom of the email and put my phone to my ear. As I listened to it ring a few times, I couldn't help but hope she wouldn't pick up.

Just at that moment, of course, she did.

"Hello, Joanna Londis speaking," the friendly voice sang.

I tried to match her energy, but I just couldn't. The best I could do was not cry.

"Hi there, it's Dr Taylor. You left your number and asked that I give you a call?"

I heard the woman hesitate for a second.

"Ah yes, thanks, Dr Taylor. What it is, you see . . . is that the organisation has come under some . . . uh . . . scrutiny for platforming you at our conference, and it's putting us in a rather difficult position, as I am sure you can understand . . ."

I wiped my eyes. I wasn't sure how much more of this I could take. I steadied my voice, and Jay stroked my hand.

"Right, okay. Would you be able to tell me some more about what the, uh, scrutiny is, and where it's coming from?"

She hesitated again, becoming slightly defensive.

"I'm sure you can appreciate, Dr Taylor, that I cannot give any details of the individuals raising these concerns."

"Individuals?" I questioned. "So it's more than one person then?" I knew I shouldn't be pressing, and I knew she wouldn't answer me, but this was like fighting a battle with an invisible enemy. Or *enemies*, rather.

"Dr Taylor, I really can't comment, however I must ask for your side regarding the concerns raised if there's potential of you speaking at our event."

I froze.

"Potential? Sorry, am I no longer confirmed to speak?"

The woman side-stepped my direct question.

"At this stage, I'm just looking to get your side."

I knew what that meant.

"Oh. I understand, it's just that, well, whoever this group of people are, they're absolutely set on destroying me."

I tried to control the speed of my words as I continued "They're . . . they're . . ." I stumbled over my words as I tried to get them out as quickly as possible.

"They're managing to find everyone I work with and posting all over the internet these horrific made-up allegations. I don't even know where to begin. They've said I'm trafficking people, that my PhD isn't real, that my company is a money laundering scheme, that my wife is . . . is . . .' I tried to continue but the woman stopped me.

She sounded annoyed, as if I was telling her some Jackanory story and wasting her time.

"Dr Taylor, I can assure you that they are not the allegations we've had, or what we're looking into." She paused, and then lowered her tone. "The concerns we've had raised pertain to your work, and that it led to a suicide."

I was horrified. My heart pounded in my chest. The thought, even the slightest chance, that my work had caused someone to kill themselves burned through me. And then, as if I had suddenly come to my senses, I forced myself to remember that none of this was actually true. Jay had told me that those were the next sets of rumours and lies being spread across the internet about me, so I suppose I should have known this was coming at some point.

"A suicide? That is not true at all. It's all part of a huge game for these people. Just the other day I had another organisation on the phone telling me they'd received emails from almost a dozen people, one of them even claimed he was a police officer. I've tried to get them to report to the police because clearly that's a crime in itself . . ."

I could feel myself overexplaining again, but I couldn't help it. In fact, the more I noticed I was doing it, the further I went. On and on, almost pleading for them to be the first person to validate me. It didn't matter who that person was, and I didn't seem to learn anything from the last time, or the time before that, but the desperation was pouring out. I had so much to lose. So did Jay. So did the team.

I was desperate for just one person to realise what was happening to me. I was being stalked, and no one seemed to believe me.

"We're going to have to take the allegations seriously due to the nature of them, Dr Taylor."

Maybe she heard me sniffle. Maybe she could tell I was crying in silence at the other end of the phone. Her tone softened again.

"Have you thought about getting any help whilst you're dealing with this?"

I sighed. I knew what was happening. My own commissioner was slipping into seeing me as a client or a victim. She wasn't communicating with me on the same level anymore and her 'duty of care' had kicked into action.

She continued, "I hope I can put your mind at ease for a while and let you know that this isn't some huge conspiracy against you. We have been assured that the complaints are legitimate and the concerns have been raised internally for investigation."

I kept my nerve and kept my voice as steady as I could to finish the phone call, but inside I was breaking. There were no legitimate complaints, there never was. Every one of these investigations had finished the same way – months of being treated like I was a danger to society – only to receive a quiet email explaining that the complaints were baseless and they were sorry for what had happened to me, but that they couldn't continue working with me as they were being bombarded with threats and abuse.

By this point, I didn't know which of our partners had been contacted, who had seen what, and who had been made aware of everything going on. It was impossible to pre-empt and whenever I tried to, I just sounded, well, like a conspiracy theorist, just as Joanna, and several others had implied.

Jay was sat next to me, furiously opening up the forums to look for evidence of what was happening to us. And boy, did she find it.

Candles64: *I heard she's losing all her work, and the company is on the brink of collapse >.<*

Traveltime89: *Yep, heard through the grapevine she's going to make redundancies. All she ever does is prove us right. Claims to be a wonderful person to work for. 6-bedroom house with a swimming-pool but is making these poor women redundant and forcing them to rely on foodbanks? Disgusting, selfish bitch.*

AlabamaMama: *And of course it's all our fault! Ummm NOPE. Everyone is just learning the truth about you, 'Dr' Taylor, and they're all sick of your shit!*

OrangeDoor67: *At this point, her refusal to take accountability is just delusional – she's seriously sick in the head. It's always someone else, isn't it, Jess?*

Candles64: *I think we have a duty to ensure these organisations are doing due diligence!! She's a dangerous fraud! I've put another 4 complaints in about her this week . . . and it's only Tuesday! I still have an entire list of organisations to work through yet.*

Handbasket32: *I think we should all be doing this! I know I am! She's working in Australia in the Autumn, so I am just digging to find out where she will be and who is funding it, so we can target them next.*

AlabamaMama: *I've done a couple anonymously, including some organisations in New Zealand she is working for, but they don't seem to go anywhere . . . shock horror! They say I have to leave a name and details if I want them to follow up which I'm just not comfortable with. If she found out, she's the type to come after my livelihood . . . some feminist she is. The way she treats women is evil.*

Handbasket32: *She'd probably claim you're obsessed with her or say you're stalking her. It's absolutely fucking delusional she thinks anyone even cares about her enough to stalk her. Pathetic. She needs ending.*

* * *

So many times when I was being stalked, I questioned myself. And I wasn't the only one – because many people were questioning me, too.

Are you sure this is really happening? Are you sure you're not overreacting?

Have you considered that this might be anxiety? Doesn't this all sound a bit . . . tinhat to you?

Why would anyone do this to you? Maybe you are reading too much into it?

Did you really do the things they are saying? Did you do something to deserve this?

The shift is subtle but devastating. The focus moves from their behaviour to victim perception. From evidence to observer interpretation. From the perpetrator's conduct to the victim's mental state. Always.

This is something I see and have written about for years. It happens in domestic abuse and coercive control. It happens in sexual violence. It happens in child abuse and neglect. It is no wonder that this same framing of victims as paranoid extends to stalking, but in some ways, it is even more profound (and effective) in this online context.

Are you really being stalked, or are you just paranoid? Maybe you should get some help?

This has to be one of the most effective tools in a stalker's arsenal and one of the most damaging failures of our systems. And yet, within the academic literature, it is abundantly clear that stalking is common and that online stalking is increasing. Whilst there are many stereotypes of stalking victims, I have collated some of the prevalence statistics which demonstrate just how common stalking is and how diverse the victims really are.

Prevalence of stalking victims

Victim	Prevalence	Notes of interest
Women (general sample)	20%	43% were stalked by ex-partners, 57% were stalked by acquaintances, strangers, and colleagues
Men (general sample)	6%	28% were stalked by ex-partners, 72% were stalked by acquaintances, strangers, and colleagues
Doctors	15%	Stalked by their patients
NHS staff	25%	Stalked by their patients
Psychologists	20%	Stalked by their clients
UK Members of Parliament	81%	Stalked by members of the public
NHS mental health nurses	50%	Of these, 31% were stalked by their patients, 27% were stalked by their NHS colleagues, and 20% were stalked by their ex-partners
NZ Members of Parliament	87%	Stalked by members of the public
Psychiatrists	21%	Of these, 60% were stalked by their patients, 40% were stalked by colleagues and others
Lawyers	37%	Of these 95% were stalked by colleagues, other lawyers, and those they worked with
Health care professionals	14%	Of these, 14% were stalked by colleagues, and 33% were stalked by ex-partners
US counsellors	6%	Stalked by their clients
Instagram influencers	63%	Stalked by members of the public, with an average of 3 stalkers each

Sheridan et al. (2019); ONS (2016); Harris et al. (2023); Fox et al. (2024)

In 2025, I met with several mental health professionals, including some therapists and psychologists, who were all noticing the same thing. Increasing numbers of women who were being referred to them as delusional, psychotic, or as having personality disorders were in fact being stalked. In some cases, the mental health professional was then having to argue with the referrer, usually a doctor or even the police, who were convinced that she was imagining or lying about being stalked.

In most cases, the women being referred were described as paranoid.

When a person reports stalking, especially digital stalking, they are often reporting patterns: repeated monitoring, coordinated posts, false allegations, escalating intrusion. Patterns require interpretation. They require connecting dots across time. And in connecting those dots, victims frequently display behaviours that psychiatry might label as hypervigilance or suspiciousness. This presents a big problem.

When people are connecting dots like this, and able to see patterns in incidents, some medical model practitioners are going to perceive them as delusional. It is likely that they will ignore the substance or evidence of the patterns the person is talking about and instead begin to reframe their fears as persecutory delusions and psychosis.

What makes this even more dangerous is that stalking and harassment is defined as a course of conduct, meaning that when victims are trying to seek help, or get justice, they will be required to demonstrate evidence which aligns with that legal definition. In many cases of stalking, the course of conduct is complex. It could be that the stalker has tried to hack their emails several times, then added them on fake accounts on Facebook, then sent threatening messages using an anonymous account, so that the victim cannot prove their identity. Then a website about the victim is set up, leading to mass abuse and complaints to their employer. And the victim is left to piece it all together, like an amateur detective, whilst professionals roll their eyes and tell them that they are suffering from paranoia and that they are seeing connections and patterns where there are none.

Common stalking behaviours

Stalking behaviours	Workplace stalking	Ex-partner stalking
Watching, spying or following you	67%	74%
Harassment and stalking via social media	49%	49%
Using other people to get to you	47%	58%
Contacting your workplace or colleagues	47%	29%
Turning up at your home or workplace	45%	71%
Monitoring on the internet	41%	36%
Phone calls	39%	76%
Threats to hurt or kill	37%	42%
Contacting people close to you	37%	55%
Emails	33%	38%
Text messages	31%	75%
Damage to property	31%	28%
Stealing personal property	31%	23%
Posting of information on the internet	29%	24%
Letters or gifts	29%	36%
Threatening to hurt adults close to you	14%	17%
Threatening to sexually assault you	12%	12%
Ordering or cancelling goods	10%	6.5%
Physically hurting you	10%	30%
Threatening to hurt your children	8%	17%
Physically hurting people close to you	8%	9%
Sexually assaulting you	8%	15%
Threatening suicide or self-harm	8%	43.5%

N = 191 Sheridan et al. (2019)

As the table above clearly shows, it is likely that victims will be subjected to a range of overlapping and overwhelming stalking tactics, regardless of who they are being stalked by. Trying to explain this to professionals who do not understand the depth and breadth of stalking can easily result in those professionals disbelieving the victim or framing them as delusional.

Stalking, therefore, is a serious danger zone for pathologisation and framing the victim as paranoid. Completely natural and rational responses to the trauma of being stalked can easily be categorised as symptoms of mental disorder.

Let's take hypervigilance as a common example.

Hypervigilance is a trauma response. It is a state of heightened alertness to an actual or potential threat. In stalking, hypervigilance is adaptive and required. If someone has demonstrated a pattern of intrusion and intimidation, it makes sense to scan for recurrence and risk. It makes sense to document (especially as the police ask victims to do this), and of course, because stalking and harassment is repetitive, it then makes sense for the victim to anticipate that something is coming next.

But within mental health systems, hypervigilance can be reframed as paranoia. Many women I mentor who have been stalked will describe themselves as 'para' (short for paranoid). Some of them even tell me that they feel like they 'went crazy'. They will say things like, "I ended up so paranoid, I was always checking the doors and windows, I was always worried what would happen to me next. I was always on high alert . . ."

But I always say the same thing to them: "That isn't paranoia. That is fear. Valid fear."

Paranoia, in psychiatric terms, refers to persistent, unfounded beliefs that others intend to harm you. The key word there is 'unfounded'. But in practice, the distinction between founded and unfounded is not always treated with rigour. Particularly when the alleged harm is digital, distributed or reputational rather than physical. Professionals simply decide that what the victim is saying is unfounded, despite having no evidence of this.

When I wrote *Sexy But Psycho* back in 2022, I included the story of a woman who had been labelled as paranoid and delusional because she kept reporting that someone had put a hidden camera in her hostel room. Everyone had treated her as if she was beyond help and completely delusional. Until one day, she set up a trap and caught one of the hostel staff coming into her room whilst she was out and moving her belongings into different places, in order to toy with her and make her feel like she was losing her mind.

Up to that point, this woman had been diagnosed, labelled and medicated for a so-called delusional disorder that she didn't have. A psychiatrist somewhere had listened to her concerns that people were coming into her room, moving her things and secretly recording her, and decided that her fears were unfounded. There is rarely any investigation of the fears. The diagnosis, in the absence of any scientific tests, is the opinion of the doctor.

And I have seen this reframing repeatedly.

A woman reports that an ex-partner is monitoring her online activity and contacting her employer. She is told that she is catastrophising. A professional documents hundreds of coordinated posts targeting her work. She is asked whether she might be misinterpreting online criticism. A mother reports that anonymous complaints to social care have triggered repeated investigations into her and her children. She is advised to consider therapy for anxiety and paranoia.

This is actually more common than people realise, and it often leaves me wondering how many victims of stalking are currently in mental health systems, being convinced that they are mentally ill.

The behaviour of the perpetrator fades into the background. The mental state of the victim moves centre stage.

In my own experience, there were moments when the insinuation was explicit. Was I reading too much into it? Was I amplifying it? Was I sure the coordination was real? Even when there were screenshots, timelines, and hundreds of documented complaints via email, the tone always implied exaggeration.

There is nothing coincidental or benign about this. There are structural reasons why stalking victims are pathologised.

First, psychiatric frameworks have long been more comfortable diagnosing individuals than interrogating systems that fail on such a grand scale. It is simpler to assign a label to a victim than to unravel a network of coordinated harassment. The medical model prioritises internal states over external contexts. It always has, and that is arguably its biggest weakness. Distress is often located within the person rather than in the environment, so no one needs to look at the distressing, traumatic or oppressive situation that someone is living in. Victims of abuse and stalking are often framed as mentally ill or delusional, whilst the person abusing and stalking seem to get off scot free.

Second, women in particular are historically over-pathologised (Taylor, 2022). From hysteria to borderline personality disorder, the cultural script of the unstable woman runs deep. Women expressing fear, anger or distress are more likely to be labelled dramatic or emotionally dysregulated. Interestingly, this was the entire thesis of my 2022 book, *Sexy But Psycho*, which escalated the stalking and harassment against me on the day it was announced a *Sunday Times* bestseller.

When a woman says to her doctor or to a police officer, "I am being watched, discussed and targeted by multiple people," the response is not evidence-based or scientific. It is filtered through centuries of suspicion, misogyny and bias.

Third, stalking disrupts the neat boundary between rational fear and 'psychiatric' symptoms. Trauma responses are interpreted by doctors through a medical lens and then seen as symptoms of an illness or mental disorder. Sleep disturbance, scanning behaviour, intrusive thoughts, emotional reactivity and suicidal thoughts are all common trauma responses. In the medical model of mental health, these might appear clinical and in requirement of 'treatment'. But in the context of stalking, they are proportionate and appropriate responses to risk and harm (Taylor and Shrive, 2023).

The problem arises when context is ignored.

Forensic research has shown that stalking victims frequently exhibit many trauma responses and coping mechanisms (Taylor and Shrive, 2023). They may avoid places, monitor surroundings, document incidents for months or years. These behaviours are not evidence of delusion, rather they are evidence of sustained threat. Yet research, case studies, and current clinical practice reveal repeated instances where victims have been misdiagnosed with mental disorders and personality disorders for merely reporting that they were struggling with being stalked.

There are documented cases in which women reporting harassment by ex-partners were diagnosed with delusional disorders, only for subsequent evidence to confirm the stalking. In some instances, protective orders were delayed or denied because the victim's credibility was undermined by psychiatric labels, something that is frighteningly common in family court.

Within NHS contexts, I have encountered examples of women presenting with 'anxiety' linked to ongoing stalking, only to receive diagnoses of generalised anxiety disorder or personality disorder without thorough exploration of environmental threat. Their fears were ignored and cast aside in favour of a medical label. The label then becomes part of their record, and it can then be used by police, in criminal and family court, employment disputes, or in further complaints to discredit them.

I have seen far too many cases where women who were being abused and stalked were told to go to their doctor, only to then have their medical records and mental health used against them to claim that they are not credible witnesses.

It is a very common cycle, as I demonstrate below. Many thousands of women have experienced this, meaning that their own help-seeking led to them being framed as paranoid or mentally ill, when in fact they were being stalked, threatened and abused.

Cycle of pathologisation of stalking victims

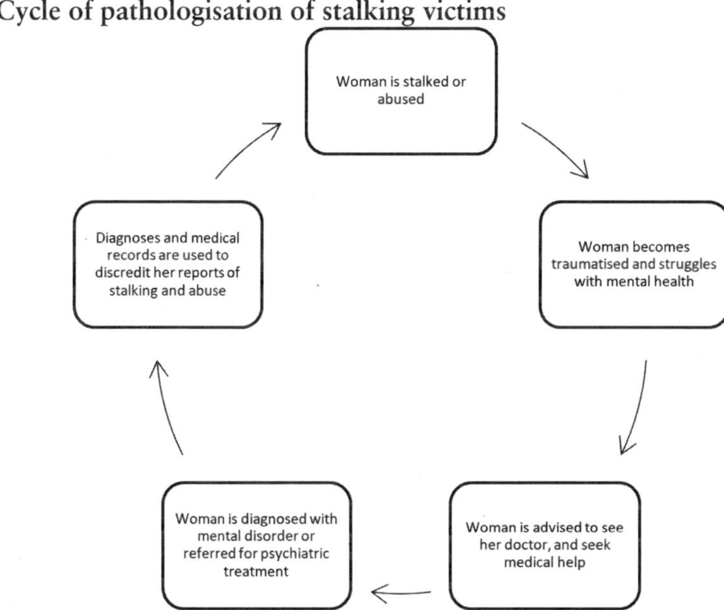

Taylor (2026)

This happens because diagnosis is not neutral. It never was and never will be. It carries immense social power. It shapes our credibility. It influences how police, courts, social care, and employers interpret behaviour – it even changes the way our family and friends treat us.

When a stalking victim is labelled as paranoid, every future report is filtered through that lens. Documentation becomes their 'obsession'. Fear becomes 'instability'. Anger becomes pathology. If they make complaints that they are not being listened to, these become framed as 'vexatious'. If they continue to report the stalking and harassment to the police, they can be labelled on police systems as 'repeat callers' or 'nuisance callers'. Even family courts can frame them as 'vexatious litigants', and I have met several women in the US and Canada who have had this levelled against them when they presented evidence to family court judges that they were being stalked.

In police systems, they have codes that the call handler can add if they 'suspect mental health issues' whilst on the call to the victim, meaning it can be added to a report purely on the opinion of the unqualified call handler. When and if (let's be real here) the case is then passed to a police officer, they receive the case file with the code that the call handler suspected mental health issues during the report. And from thereon, the pathologisation begins.

The scrutiny and framing of the victim is profound, meanwhile, the perpetrator remains unchallenged. Truth be told, they fade into the background as if they don't even exist.

The anti-pathology lens I have developed over years of work is crucial here. We must recognise rational responses to harm. We must validate trauma responses and coping mechanisms (Taylor and Shrive, 2023). Intense emotional response is not evidence of mental disorder. When people are being stalked, vital pattern recognition is not a paranoid delusion.

Victims often begin to doubt their own reality precisely because of this pathologisation. Gaslighting, whether intentional or systemic, destabilises perception and places victims at further risk. When professionals suggest overreaction, victims question their interpretation, begin to minimise incidents, stop documenting, stop reporting, give up hope of any justice, and they may even withdraw complaints.

This self-doubt is dangerous because it gives stalkers more room, and more time, to escalate. In some cases, stalkers actively weaponise psychiatric language. Online, they pre-emptively describe the victim as unstable in complaints and public posts. They may suggest that she is paranoid or obsessive. They may frame her documentation as evidence of mental illness, or even as evidence that she is stalking them. In online forums, this narrative can spread rapidly.

She's unhinged. She's spiralling. She's imagining enemies. She's delusional. She believes she is being stalked. She's psycho. Insane. Lunatic. Mental.

Psychiatric terms are used as slurs because they work. Again, this is something I teach and write about in my day job. We are encouraged to 'end mental health stigma', and yet everyone seems to know the exact terms and words to use to frame someone as mentally ill. They know, professionals know, perpetrators know, institutions know, employers know, ex-partners know. Stalkers know this. Psychiatry is no friend to victims of abuse and trauma, it is only ever used against them (Taylor, 2022).

It's a troubling conundrum. The more the person tries to convince people that they are not 'mad', the 'madder' they look. Their defence is used against them to frame them as mentally ill. This is identical in stalking. The more the victim defends or explains herself, the more the label is reinforced. The more she tries to show evidence that she is being stalked, the more she looks like she is the obsessed one. I have even come across solicitors who have had to advise their clients (victims of stalking) not to produce huge files of evidence of stalking in case she was reframed as the stalker. Wild.

This dynamic is particularly potent in digital contexts where tone is easily misinterpreted and context stripped. If she tries to rebut the allegations, she is aggressive. She is a pathological liar. If she tries to explain to everyone what is happening, she is 'rambling' and 'spiralling'. If she presents documents, evidence, and timelines of her being stalked, she can easily be framed as delusional and fixated.

Police tell victims to document and report stalking.

A woman then documents hundreds of instances of harassment. She tracks timelines. She preserves screenshots. She compiles evidence. She creates files of emails. She chases police for updates. She tries to engage with lawyers and stalking advocates. These behaviours, which in any other investigative context would be praised as meticulous, methodical, and rational, are reinterpreted as obsessive. Her diligence becomes pathology, and then she is back to being framed as paranoid and delusional. This is a lose-lose situation for women.

Research consistently shows that women's reports of interpersonal harm are taken less seriously than men's (Taylor, 2022). Cultural stereotypes cast women as overly emotional. In stalking cases, this translates into suspicion of exaggeration.

Of course, the broader cultural discomfort with acknowledging coordinated harassment and stalking also plays a role. It is much easier to believe that one individual is simply misperceiving unrelated or exaggerated events than to accept that an individual or a group can mobilise stalking and abuse at scale. The psychiatric explanation is psychologically comforting to observers, which is something we see in all forms of violence and abuse against women and girls (Taylor, 2022).

If she is telling the truth, then digital culture is more dangerous than we would like to admit. If she is paranoid, then the world remains orderly and justified, and she is just another mental woman. *She's probably lying anyway, right?*

I have spoken to women who were admitted to psychiatric units whilst they were being actively stalked. Their reports were reframed as delusion. Only later, when independent evidence surfaced, was the stalking acknowledged. The trauma of not being believed compounded the original harm.

In a recent study of 105 women who were stalked, 95% were diagnosed with a mental disorder during or after being stalked (Short et al., 2023). Further to this, 46% of stalking victims were prescribed psychiatric medication, despite the fact that they were not mentally ill, but rather experiencing trauma as a direct result of being stalked. Of those prescribed medication, only 33% reported that it helped with their 'symptoms of mental illness', while 6% refused or did not take the prescribed medication.

The most commonly prescribed medications to victims of stalking were:
- Sertraline (11%)
- Citalopram (8%)
- Diazepam (5%)
- 10% were prescribed multiple medications for mental health symptoms

This raises serious concerns about the medicalisation of stalking victims and the potential for misdiagnosis. Many stalking victims will exhibit symptoms entirely consistent with trauma, including hypervigilance, anxiety, difficulty sleeping, catastrophic thinking, isolation, withdrawal, and panic episodes (Taylor and Shrive, 2023). However, rather than recognising these as expected responses to an ongoing threat, professionals may mistakenly interpret them as indicators of a primary mental illness. This is leading to inappropriate prescribing of psychiatric medication, rather than addressing the stalking. And this can have multiple negative implications for a victim, especially in legal contexts.

When Harris et al. (Spitzberg and Cupach, 2014) explored the way victims coped with being stalked, they found five common coping mechanisms:

1. Moving toward/with: any efforts to engage with the stalker to get them to stop, including reasoning, arguing, or yelling
2. Moving against: any intentional act to cause harm or damage to the stalker, including physically attacking, reporting to police, or attempting to damage their reputation or career to get them to stop
3. Moving away: any act of effort to avoid contact with the stalker including changing phone numbers, moving house, changing routines and email addresses, avoiding places or resigning from a job
4. Moving inward: any effort to repair the self, empowerment, or focus on the self to cope with being stalked, including therapy and meditation, but also including drugs, drinking, and even buying a weapon to protect themselves
5. Moving outward: any effort to seek assistance or guidance, or speak to friends or family about what was happening to them

Where studies have been conducted to explore which coping mechanisms are most common, it was found that victims would use multiple, usually because the stalking continued for extended periods of time which traumatised them further. 100% of stalking victims used 'moving away' coping mechanisms, 78% used 'moving inward' coping mechanisms, and 55% used 'moving against' coping mechanisms. Importantly, the latter usually involved reporting the stalker or trying to get protective orders against them, rather than physically attacking their stalker (Harris et al., 2023).

The central question should not be "What is wrong with you?" but "What is happening to you?"

When systems default to diagnosis of the victim, they are colluding with perpetrators. The phrase 'Stalked, or just paranoid?' encapsulates a false dichotomy. A person can be stalked and traumatised. They can be distressed because of real and documented harm. They can be vigilant because vigilance is required.

Pathologising victims of trauma is always harmful. And in the context of stalking, it may be one of the most powerful tools perpetrators have. Because once a woman is framed as paranoid, she is not only fighting a stalker. She is fighting a diagnosis and an entire system.

CHAPTER 9

There's nothing we can do

My wife burst into the kitchen, red in the face, tears in her eyes. She could barely get her words out as she charged towards me, phone in hand, shaking it in shock. It had been over a year of being stalked, harassed and abused online – day and night.

"I know who it is!"

Time slowed. My body froze. The air between us thickened with the dread we had carried for months. For a second, I thought I had dreamt it. I had indeed dreamt this exact moment countless times before.

"Lorraine," she gasped, almost choking on the name.

And with that, the ground shifted beneath us.

It took me hours, days even, to fully comprehend what she was saying: a woman in her sixties, a married nurse with adult children from Lincoln, whom I had briefly met twelve years earlier, was one of the people behind the anonymous accounts that had stalked, harassed and terrorised us for more than a year.

"Lorraine?" I whispered in complete shock. She was so unassuming. And . . . so nice to both of us.

She had sent us flowers. She had even offered us her home for safety during the peak of the stalking and when our home address and photographs of our house had been shared on Tattle Life and across the internet. She had played the role of a friend. All while orchestrating and escalating an online campaign to destroy our lives.

"I know! I can't fucking believe it!" Jay raged, pacing in front of me.

"Why would she do this?" My mind raced with questions and confusion until I suddenly stopped. "Hang on babe . . . how do you know this? Are you sure it's her?"

She stared at me, tears filling her eyes. "I'm one hundred per cent sure. Look at this!"

She showed me a file she had been making on her phone. Whilst I had been crumbling, she had been investigating. Screenshots of an anonymous account pretending to have studied her PhD with me, writing hundreds of posts and comments, spreading lies and rumours about us, our house, where we live, our dogs, our kids, our parents, our jobs, our education, our childhoods . . . It was terrifying. There were even disturbing comments about our sex life and our bodies.

"But . . . I haven't seen Lorraine in . . ." I tried to count in my head. "Twelve fucking years . . ."

Jay pointed to a photo of me that she had uploaded just a few hours ago.

"She didn't crop her own profile picture out of the screenshot. Look! That's her Facebook profile picture, isn't it?"

I looked closely, zooming in on the image. It was her, alright. I scanned her posts. Multiple per day. Claiming to be my best friend. Claiming to speak to me every day. Claiming I was mentally ill and that I deserved everything that was coming to me.

I paused.

"But . . . she knew we were being stalked. She messaged you . . . she wanted our address to . . ."

"Send us flowers? Oh, I know! It all clicked when I found it. Her trying to add me on Messenger . . . remember? Asking for our address. Telling us that we could go and stay with her when we got scared of the 'stalkers' . . . The fucking stalker is her!"

As I listened to Jay, every single betrayal sank into my body like stones sinking in a cold lake.

"Oh my god. And she was going to have us in her house . . ."

"And the kids!"

I shivered. She did invite us, and our kids, to stay in her house. She had messaged us when she 'saw' the harassment and stalking online. She had even told us that our address and our house had been posted online. She had messaged Jay to tell her that she was worried for our safety, and that we should come to stay with her.

And the entire fucking time, it was her.

I couldn't help myself. Rage coursed through me. I found her Facebook profile and messaged her the screenshot of her anonymous account. Within seconds, she had seen my message. She typed back, panicking, begging for forgiveness, promising to delete every post she ever made about us and the kids.

I scrolled back through unopened messages to me, and what I found was disturbing.

Your address is being shared online. I really hope you don't think it is me doing all this to you though! I wanted your address to send flowers to, that was all. I messaged Jay and she said you don't really like flowers. But I mean it, it wasn't me.

I am so worried about you. You don't deserve any of this! Are you safe? I am so sorry someone is doing this to you!

Do you have anywhere safe to stay for a while? How are you coping?

Every message, dripping with care and concern, whilst she was posting online multiple times a day saying that I was an evil, narcissistic, dangerous, and abusive piece of shit. That she hated me. That she wanted to see me fail. Watching my social media. Posting our address. Information about our kids. A photo of Jay's new car with the registration plate. Attending my . . .

I stopped. I suddenly remembered that she had attended my book launch.

The one where I had to hire security. My whole body tensed.

I scrolled back, certain I had seen something about the event. And there it was.

Hey Jess. Me and a few others are coming to your book launch next week but we have lost the address of the venue! Could you send it over please?

I froze. Surely . . . she was not involved in the boycotting of my event, the threats to the venue, the reason I had to get security . . . the posts online planning to attend to heckle and scare me . . .

I looked up from my phone.

"Jay . . . uhhh . . . Lorraine was at my book launch last year, right? But . . . did you see her with anyone?"

"No, she definitely came alone. I had the guest list . . . she only bought one ticket."

"Not according to this." I showed the message to Jay where Lorraine was talking of 'a few others' coming with her. I watched the realisation sink in for Jay, too.

We'd been played. We'd been stalked. We'd been toyed with.

It is incredibly hard to describe the cognitive dissonance of realising that someone who smiled to your face and sent gestures of support was also the person keeping you awake at night, sabotaging your career, and driving you to the edge of suicide. When I tried to explain this to the police later that day, they were less than helpful.

"So, let me get this straight. Sorry to go over it again . . ."

I groaned quietly, sick of going around in circles with a police officer that was either being deliberately obstructive or struggling to grasp the basics of stalking.

"So, a woman has posted some stuff about you online, but at the same time, she was messaging you being nice to you? And you think that's stalking, do you?"

My head pounded with what must have been my tenth headache that week. I reached for the paracetamol. I didn't have any energy left to correct the minimisation, and so the officer took the opportunity to continue.

"I don't know what you think we can do about that, but it isn't stalking. There is nothing we can do. If she turns up at your door, call 999, but otherwise, that's it. It's not a crime for her to write things about you on the internet and it's not a crime for her to be messaging you, offering you flowers and gifts. I know you think that is stalking, but it isn't. Okay?"

* * *

There are three sentences that stalking victims hear so often, they can lip sync them as the professional says it.

There's nothing we can do. It's not a crime. You need to get a solicitor.

They are delivered with a sympathetic shrug. Sometimes with genuine regret. Sometimes with impatience. Occasionally with irritation, as though the victim has misunderstood the limits of the law. But the effect is the same. The harm continues. The system retreats. The perpetrator carries on, unabated.

When the stalking is digital, this sentence is almost predictable. Indeed, in over half of the stalking cases reported to police from my Tattle Life research, the victim was told that no crime had occurred, and a third were told there was nothing they could do about it anyway.

Most victims of online stalking do not report it to the police because they do not think it will be taken seriously, or they do not understand that what they are being subjected to is a crime (Taylor, 2025). In Sheridan et al. (2019), researchers examined the 'tipping points' for victims; the moment they realised they were being stalked and needed to seek help.

Overall, they found that the most common tipping points for victims being stalked by their ex-partners and by work colleagues were when they became frightened for their physical safety, when they realised it was never going to stop and when they realised that the stalking was escalating. What was interesting was that people being stalked by their ex-partner were half as likely to experience direct threats of violence as their 'tipping point', whereas this was a common tipping point for people being stalked by their work colleagues (Sheridan et al., 2019). Uniquely, and understandably, victims being stalked by their ex-partner were twice as likely to experience fear for their children's safety as their 'tipping point' compared to people being stalked by work colleagues.

As we have discussed, when these crimes are reported, many officials will imply that the digital world is not quite real. No matter what is being done to you online, it does not carry the same weight as physical presence, smashed windows or men standing outside of houses. The online world is treated as virtual commentary, not crime at all.

This conceptual gap is one of the most significant failures in the modern response to stalking and online stalking. Stalking legislation in many jurisdictions around the world was drafted with physical behaviours in mind, and even then, it took decades to be defined at all: following, loitering, sending letters, turning up at workplaces. Even when laws have been updated to include digital communication, the investigative mindset often remains anchored in that older imagery.

From my experience of training police forces, many officers and call handlers switch off the moment that the victim mentions the online space. "They threatened me on Facebook" or "They are watching all my social media on anonymous accounts", and the officer has zoned out of the conversation.

When I have personally challenged this response, officers often tell me that it is related to their own burnout and exposure to such serious crime. Rightly or wrongly, when a police officer must move from job to job every day for years, whether that be a burglary, an assault, a suicide, a fight in a bar, domestic violence, a drug overdose, a fatal car accident, child abuse, they do become rather jaded. They are used to dealing with traumatic events and often their only coping mechanism is desensitisation and minimisation. They start to rank crimes in their mind, and quite simply, most of them don't see the online world as 'real' in comparison to crime happening on our streets.

I've had police call handlers tell me that they hate taking calls from people being stalked or threatened online, because they don't think the police should have to deal with them at all. Even when the stalking online is profound and extremely abusive, with specific threats to the victim, police forces lack the digital tools, skills, knowledge or capabilities to investigate the users properly.

As an example, whilst I was being stalked, an anonymous account popped up overnight and began offering my home address to anyone who wanted it on Twitter. They had no name, no profile picture, and no identifying details. Police told me that there was nothing they could do, as they would have to subpoena Twitter to hand over the account details, which they didn't know how to do.

Similarly, when I opened my phone at the dinner table one night and found messages and comments from an anonymous account, describing how they wanted to "rape you with a metal bar until you die" and "slice your clit off", I was told that nothing could be done to protect me or find the perpetrator.

I was left to deal with threats and abuse like this for years, with no intervention, no protection and no support.

And I am not the only one to find this. Ivask (2025) titled their paper "It is easier to leave a death threat on social media than to get it removed!" for a reason. They explored stalking, threats and abuse online, and frankly, their findings are right. I have never had a positive outcome from any of the reports of death or rape threats I have ever reported, whether that was a report to police or to the social media platform itself.

Having trained police for over a decade, it is evident to me that general police training has not kept pace with technological evolution. Many frontline officers receive minimal training in stalking. Digital literacy varies widely between officers and forces. Understanding of online platforms, forum culture, distributed networks, and algorithmic amplification is inconsistent, or non-existent. What a victim reports as coordinated stalking or harassment may be interpreted by an officer as mere online disagreement.

In my own case, I had to provide over one thousand pages of evidence to demonstrate that I was being stalked by a group. For the first few meetings, I am absolutely certain that I was perceived as having gone totally crazy. When I handed over the huge stacks of paperwork, the officer looked at me like she was going to bang her head on a wall. Thousands of posts. Hundreds of emails to my colleagues, friends, commissioners, partners, publishers, agents and producers.

Having asked me to collate evidence and present timelines, I don't know if she knew whether to laugh or cry when I actually did it. Well, I say me, Jay did it. I was too traumatised to even look at it. As I write this in 2026, Jay still doesn't let me look at it.

The policing imagination still tends to require dramatic scenes in order to get their attention. It often feels as though they want to wait until the stalker has tried to burn your house down or stab you to death on your driveway for them to take action. The justice system struggles to validate and conceptualise harm that is cumulative rather than explosive – which is why we have such low rates of convictions in crimes such as domestic abuse, sexual abuse, child abuse and coercive control.

CPS thresholds often require evidence of a course of conduct causing fear or distress. But when each individual act appears lawful – a post, an email or a complaint – the cumulative pattern can be overlooked by inexperienced or uninterested officers. The burden falls on the victim to document extensively, demonstrate impact, and to prove intent. And proving intent in digital stalking is subtle.

There may be no explicit statement of threat. In many cases that I analysed, there was a distinct lack of direct death or harm threats. Instead, there was persistent insinuation. Talks of the victim dying or hoping that the victim would die soon. Wishing that something terrible would happen to them. Joking about killing them. Telling them to kill themselves. Sometimes it is even more subtle than that. Incessant monitoring, reporting, archiving, or carefully suggesting that the victim is mentally ill. The language may be couched in responsibility, concern or accountability. The effect, however, is always domination.

Police responses frequently reflect outdated assumptions. This response reveals a belief that digital harm can just be switched off by the victim's behaviour. As though logging out erases what has been written, and as though logging out means that employers will not be contacted. As though children will not be discussed any longer if you just stop looking at it. As though false reports will not trigger real investigations, if you just ignore it all and pretend it is not happening.

The digital world is not a simulation. It is not separate from our lives.

Perhaps there was a point when it was separate, in the late 90s or early 00s, when the digital world was confined to the mind-blowing ability to send basic emails to each other, download illegal music, and maybe even read the news. Only 1% of households even had access to the internet back then (jumping to 15% by 2005) according to Our World in Data (2026), and so, whilst I am sure that people did use the earliest email clients to send malicious communications, there was nowhere near the technological possibilities of today.

There were no social media platforms to seek out victims, no algorithms pushing outrage and hatred, no mass surveillance, no camera phones, no influencers, no endless feeds, no platform-wide instances of harassment and abuse, no real-time stalking 24 hours a day.

Contrast that with the digital world of today, which intersects with (and is vital to) employment, parenting, finances, communication, family, health, education, news, media, politics, personal lives, dating, and even our reputation. Online allegations do trigger offline consequences. Emails sent to institutions can result in police arriving at your door within a few hours. Forum threads can influence professional standing. Anonymous complaints organised online can lead to your children being removed. The boundary between digital and physical has collapsed.

Yet many systems still operate as though it exists.

National reports have repeatedly highlighted gaps in stalking responses (Suzy Lamplugh, 2022). In 2022, the Suzy Lamplugh Trust submitted a formal super-complaint to the police watchdogs (HMICFRS, the IOPC and the College of Policing), arguing that policing responses to stalking across England and Wales were fundamentally failing victims. The super-complaint mechanism allows designated bodies to raise systemic concerns about policing. The resulting joint investigation, published in 2022, found widespread under-recording and misidentification of stalking, frequent down-grading of cases to harassment, poor risk assessment, inconsistent safeguarding and a failure to recognise patterns of fixation and esca-lation. It concluded that victims were often left unprotected, that officers lacked specialist training, and that stalking was not being treated with the seriousness required despite its well-established links to serious violence and homicide.

Survivors often describe being passed between departments and being told that incidents are isolated, being advised to collect more evidence before action can be taken. By the time a case is recognised as serious, escalation has often already occurred. Academic research on policing responses to stalking consistently identifies themes of minimisation and disbelief. Officers may lack confidence in identifying patterns. They may conflate harassment with interpersonal conflict. They may prioritise cases involving explicit threats over those involving sustained intrusion (Martellozzo et al., 2022; Suzy Lamplugh Trust, 2022).

Digital cases are particularly vulnerable to dismissal. Part of the diffi-culty lies in scale. When hundreds of individuals are involved, identify-ing a single suspect feels impossible to the police officer who can only just manage the caseload they have. The distributed nature of online harassment does not fit neatly into traditional investigative models.

Who is the offender? The original poster? The commenter? The anon-ymous reporter? What if there are hundreds of potential offenders? Is there one central person to pursue? How is the victim collating all this evidence? Couldn't the victim just stop looking at it? How do we get the data from the social media platforms who are not even based in this jurisdiction? Who do we contact for evidence?

The complexity becomes a deterrent and officers with thirty cases to investigate have no incentive to go off on a wild goose chase, trying to track down anonymous accounts all over the world.

Systemic misogyny also plays a role. Women reporting stalking, especially when the stalking is reputational or relational rather than physically violent, are often perceived as dramatic, exaggerating, or overly sensitive. The stereotype of women as conflict-driven or attention-seeking influences perception. When the victim is a woman with a public platform, the minimisation intensifies ever further.

She has thousands of followers. She's used to attention. She can handle it. She chooses to expose herself. She wants it. She makes money from it. She likes the drama.

These assumptions obscure or completely erase vulnerability and victimhood. The experience of being a victim of crime disappears behind these kinds of phrases.

In my own experiences with police, there were moments of clarity and moments of profound disconnect. Officers acknowledged breaches of court orders and breaches of the law yet struggled to translate digital monitoring into any actionable concern. Apologies were offered privately, they sympathised and shook their head at how bad the stalking was, but nothing was done. Safeguarding was inconsistent at best.

This inconsistency reflects a system grappling with a phenomenon it has not fully understood. Outdated legislation compounds the problem. While many jurisdictions have updated stalking laws to include electronic communication, which is vital, the evidential thresholds remain very high. The specific requirement to prove fear or serious alarm can be interpreted very narrowly, leading the officer to question whether there is adequate evidence to suggest that hundreds of stalkers 'intended' to cause distress to the victim. And if the victim is articulate, professional, or outwardly composed, her distress is often underestimated.

Increasingly, perpetrators operate in the grey areas between legality and illegality. They exploit procedural rights. They file concerns and complaints. They submit data access and information requests. They coordinate posts that stop just short of explicit threat. Each act may be defensible in isolation.

Police then investigate incidents rather than patterns, despite the pattern being central to the definition of the offence. When a victim presents with dozens or hundreds of incidents, the administrative burden is immense. Officers may triage based on immediacy of physical risk. Digital harm becomes secondary unless accompanied by explicit threats of violence, and even then, the reaction is slow or absent.

In one study, when presented with short stalking vignettes in which the prior relationship between victim and stalker is manipulated, all respondents, whether male or female, general community or police officers, are more likely to identify unwanted intrusions by strangers as stalking. Strangers are also judged to present a greater threat and require more police response than ex-partners or acquaintances. I find this particularly interesting, as this identification of threat is neutralised by the online element. People generally feel as though online stalking is not harmful to the victim, even though the stalker is often a stranger or anonymous.

Sheridan and Scott's (2010) findings suggest that people rely mostly on evidence of overt aggression when identifying stalking, to the exclusion of all other indicators. Their sample of British undergraduates judged persistent relationship pursuit lasting for 12 months to be stalking only when it then culminated in physical violence or a serious threat. The study found that other kinds of verbal abuse had no effect on judgements.

The reliance on overt aggression in perceptions of stalking is concerning because the majority of stalking victims (whether online or in person) are not subject to physical assaults. Only around 20% of stalking cases include physical attacks and violence (Mckeon et al., 2015). Threats, although very common, are not present in all cases (Dressing et al., 2020).

Moreover, persistent stalking is associated with harm to victims, regardless of whether the stalking involves overt aggression (Purcell et al., 2005). These findings suggest that the experiences of many victims go unrecognised or that they are dismissed or minimised by family, friends or police, blocking access to necessary support and protection.

Many assumptions and myths seem to affect the way systems respond, too. Technology affords greater accessibility to perpetrators who are unknown to the victim, but most officers have been trained to look for cases where the perpetrator is known to the victim. Based on very limited information, the online stalker is now able to contact nearly anyone from anywhere with little to no fear of being identified (Ahlgrim & Terrance, 2021). The internet has allowed for an almost endless supply of victims for online stalkers who can inflict harm from any distance. Victims of offline stalking are more likely to be stalked by ex-partners, whereas cyberstalking victims are at increased risk of being stalked by a stranger as well as by ex-partners (Lambert et al., 2013; Reyns et al., 2012; Ahlgrim & Terrance, 2021).

The relationship, or lack thereof, between stalker and victim may impact perceptions regarding the seriousness of the behaviour and whether it is seen as a crime or not (Ahlgrim & Terrance, 2021). Cyberstalking perpetrated by ex-partners may be taken more seriously due to misconceptions. Taken together, although cyberstalking behaviour may be engaged at relatively comparable rates by men and women, perceptions of the seriousness of the behaviour and the legitimacy of the police reports made by victims may be influenced by perpetrator and victim gender, regardless of evidence, and regardless of the motive.

Research on stalking has long shown that fixation and grievance can intensify over time (Weekes and Storey, 2025). The absence of early intervention may embolden perpetrators. When systems respond with "there's nothing we can do", the message received by the stalker is ultimately permission. No one is going to stop them.

This chapter builds towards an unavoidable conclusion: incremental reform is not enough.

Police training must urgently incorporate digital literacy at depth, not as an optional extra. Investigative frameworks relating to stalking must prioritise patterns over isolated acts. CPS thresholds must reflect cumulative harm. Safeguarding must recognise reputational and psychological risk as legitimate.

Above all, the justice system must abandon the idea that harm requires physical proximity and violence to be real.

"There's nothing we can do", is not fact, and it is not legally correct. It is a decision to conceptualise digital stalking as peripheral and then relegate it. It is a decision to ignore or minimise 'grey area' behaviours and a decision to leave victims navigating relentless stalking and abuse alone.

If we are serious about confronting modern stalking, that sentence cannot remain the default response.

CHAPTER 10

DARVO: how victims become perpetrators

My phone rang twice whilst I was driving home from the recording studio. The first time, I had glanced at the screen and saw the name but assumed it was a mistake. The second time it rang, I picked it up.

Leanne Davidson hadn't spoken to me for five years, not for any particular reason. We had worked on a project together and then lost touch after it ended. I didn't realise I still had her number, and I wouldn't have expected her to still have mine. I pulled over into a layby, intrigued.

"Hey Leanne, long time no speak!"

"Hey Jess, I know! Listen, I know this is out of the blue . . . I just need to talk to you about something . . ."

I knew that tone. The tone I heard time and time again. I steadied myself for the blow, glad I was in a layby.

"Sure, go on," I said breezily, not feeling at all breezy.

"So, I was at an event in London last night for psychologists. Lots of us were there. Your name came up, and I was talking about your books and your research, and this woman totally shut me down in front of everyone in the room . . ."

I could feel my adrenaline rising in my body.

"Well, umm. The woman was really rude, and said that no one was to support or share your work any longer, and you shouldn't be cited or referenced at all . . ."

"Oh right . . ." I mumbled, dreading what was coming next.

Leanne went quiet, hesitated and tripped over her words, and then started again.

"So . . . uhhh . . . then she said something really bad. And I wouldn't call you and tell you if . . . you know . . . I believed it. I just want you to know that I don't believe a word of it . . . but I do think you need to know what is being said in these spaces. Okay?"

I could feel my heart galloping already, and she hadn't even said the bad bit yet.

"Yeah, fine," I snapped at her, wanting it to come out of her mouth, to get it over with.

"Um. She said she had been sent an email with all these links to a website . . . saying that . . . ummm . . . you were sexually abusing your wife, and ummm, you had been grooming her as a child . . . to umm . . . become your wife when she was old enough . . . to umm . . . marry you. And she said that the email said that Jay was a victim of domestic abuse, and was trying to leave you . . . and that you were going to be investigated by the police . . ."

My head spun out. My body trembled. I felt freezing cold and boiling hot at the same time. I couldn't breathe. Every single possible trigger point had been hit at once. I instantly wished she had never told me.

How I wished I had never heard those sickening words.

I don't know if I was silent for a few seconds or a few minutes.

"Hello? Hello? Jess, are you still there?"

I tried to muster up some strength to speak, "Yeah, I'm ... here still."

"I am so sorry, Jess. I debated calling you at all, but ... everyone ... believed her. And then there was all this noise and chaos, and people saying you should be struck off ... and professors saying they would stop their students from reading your work. And it turned into carnage. I just ... I didn't know what to do. I tried to defend you and say that you are nothing like that, and you and Jay are obviously really happy together, but no one would listen to me ..."

I could still hear her, in some distant realm somewhere, but my mind had long disconnected and was imagining the moment I had to sit my beloved wife down, the woman I cherished and adored, and explain what was being done to me, and by extension, to her.

As a woman who had been sexually abused myself and as my wife had been a victim of abuse in her own childhood, for both of us to be framed like this – me as a perpetrator and her as a naïve victim – I don't think I had ever felt shame or humiliation like it.

I drove home, crying for over an hour. I kept imagining how to explain it to Jay. I kept playing the scene over in my head: how she would react, how she would burst into tears, how she would ask me what we should do. The way I would inevitably tell her that I didn't have any answers, and I didn't know how to make it stop. However, that imagined scene never came true, because instead as I walked through the door later that day, I found her sat at the kitchen island, crying.

I parked my own troubles for a moment and wrapped my arms around her. Between sobs, she explained what she had found whilst I was out and it was so much worse than I thought.

"This! Look at this shit! It's all over the fucking internet, babe! They are saying you're abusing me! The fucking bastards have even commented it all over my Instagram posts. Look! They've put under my holiday photos 'Give us a sign if you need help' and . . . this one . . . 'We will help you escape from Jess'. One woman has put a fucking post up on Twitter, saying that she will 'stand by Jay when she realises she is being abused'. And guess where it all originates from? Fucking Tattle. Again!"

My heart dropped. Of course it did.

The comments under her happy holiday pictures broke my heart. It felt like our relationship was being dismantled from the outside, framing our love for each other as something abusive, violent and deviant, purely to get at me.

"They don't fucking care about me! I am just collateral damage in their sick game to get at you! If they really thought I was a victim of abuse, they wouldn't be commenting it on my fucking Instagram pictures, would they?"

I was still unable to speak. The shame and horror were pulsing through my veins and I had nothing useful to say to her. She was right. She was being used as a pawn and it was getting extremely serious.

"There's another post here, calling you a paedophile, making out I was a child when we met! I can't cope with this, babe. I can't. I can't fucking stand this. When will it end? How the fuck are we supposed to survive this?"

I watched her closely. She had clearly been crying for some time. I couldn't stand to watch her break down like this, and she didn't even know about Leanne calling me yet.

Just as I was about to speak, she started again.

"Oh, and that's not all. Guess what else these fuckers have done today?" she raged, pacing up and down the kitchen tiles. I didn't want to guess. I stayed silent. It was rhetorical anyway.

"They've written to my fucking Professors, Jess. Ask me how they found them. Go on. Ask me. Because I have no fucking clue! I have kept that PhD private from the beginning because of the stalking. I have never posted about it. I have never even named my university. How can the police say that this isn't stalking? I've got to go in for a meeting about the emails next week!"

It's hard to describe how cumulative and crushing this conversation was.

I had only just got off the phone from Leanne and learned I was being publicly discussed at a professional networking evening as someone who abused my wife and supposedly groomed her for sex and marriage as a child, only to walk into my house to hear that my wife was being bombarded with messages and comments telling her that she was being abused and that anonymous accounts would help her to escape from me. This extra news, that the stalkers had found her university and written to her professors, felt even more devastating.

The guilt churned inside me. The only reason they were coming for our marriage, and for my wife specifically, was because it was a direct way to inflict further harm on me.

I realised much later that the escalation to these tactics was because I had not publicly cracked as a result of the previous tactics. Where once, the stalkers had focused on breaking down my career and my reputation, now we found posts online that had placed bets on how long we would last, when we would divorce, and how much they wanted to see our marriage fail. It is a testament to both of us that we are still together and still loving each other.

But Jay was right. No one cared about her and if those people really believed that she was a victim of any form of harm, posting it all over the internet for entertainment was a very strange way of safeguarding her. Jay and I knew that this was not genuine care. Of course, it was just another planned tactic to destroy my life, but this time through my beloved wife. And I must admit that around this time I asked her several times whether her life would genuinely be better, happier, and safer without me in it, however that circumstance occurred. There were several months where I wondered if my mere existence was affecting her life, and whether she would be better to find someone else who wouldn't be targeted in this way. It is hard to admit that there were times when I imagined that she could meet someone new, fall in love, live a happy and normal life with someone else, and it made me feel relieved for her. I didn't want her to suffer any longer and I knew that I had no control over the stalkers, or what they planned to do to me, or her, next.

We fell silent as I held her tightly. She sobbed into my chest and I kissed her forehead and stroked her hair, whilst all three dogs looked up at us, trying to decipher what the hell was going on.

* * *

By far, this was one of the worst things that was done to me, and to Jay, as part of the stalking. Not only had I been reframed as a villain that needed to be destroyed, but being accused of such serious, life-changing, disgusting crimes messed with me in a way I am still working through to this day.

There is a horribly disorientating moment when the ground flips on you. You report stalking. You document evidence. You ask for protection. And then suddenly, you are the suspect. You are being accused of things that never happened. You are being reported for crimes that never occurred. You pour energy into trying to wrap your head around being a victim of stalking, only to be redefined as a criminal, an abuser or a perpetrator. Sometimes it's rumours online, but sometimes it's real reports to police and authorities.

This is a recognised pattern that's common across many forms of abuse. Perpetrators often flip the script on their victim (Harsey and Freyd, 2022).

Psychologist Jennifer Freyd coined the term DARVO to describe a common response of perpetrators when confronted with wrongdoing: Deny, Attack and Reverse Victim and Offender. The sequence is deceptively simple. First, the behaviour is denied. Then the victim is attacked. Finally the roles are reversed so that the perpetrator presents as the 'true victim' and the victim as the 'aggressor'.

In digital stalking, DARVO is a central strategy. On Tattle, this is one of the most common elements to the threads. When stalkers are challenged, they rarely retreat quietly, no matter their typology. When they are exposed, it threatens their carefully curated identity. It disrupts the grievance narratives that they have created to frame themselves as the true victim. It risks consequences for them.

And so, they pivot. They deny that they are engaging in any form of abuse or stalking: "I haven't done anything wrong. I would never behave like that."

They attack: "She's unstable, obsessive, and dangerous. She is a pathological liar. She is mentally ill."

They reverse: "I'm being harassed. I'm being targeted by her. I am being attacked for no reason. I'm the victim here."

The speed of this reversal can be breathtaking and extremely disturbing. I have lived it.

In one of the cases of stalking I experienced, the stalker who was placed under court orders claimed that I was committing harassment by reporting the stalking to the police, and then claimed that they were the true victim. Those claims were spread online, despite the stalker being under a court order. The truth didn't matter to anyone. Only the narrative that kept the grievance alive mattered.

The hurtful realisation here was that no one wanted to see me as a victim of crime, or of stalking. Instead, they wanted me to be the perpetrator. They wanted me to the be the evil, dangerous, powerful, unstable person they had already cast me as in their minds.

As any victim of stalking will know, when there is any kind of police investigation or court order in place, the victims are gagged more than the perpetrator. I was under strict expectations not to talk about the police investigations, not to publicly name my stalkers, not to confirm that they were placed under court orders, and not to continue defending myself or posting about being stalked. This advice leaves victims in a vulnerable position to be reframed as a perpetrator, because no matter what their stalker or abuser says about them, the police expect them to remain silent.

Some of this is borne out of a belief that if victims of stalking or abuse confront, retaliate or expose their abusers then they are complicit or mutually abusive. This means that when a victim has been abused, assaulted, threatened, attacked or stalked for months or years, the simple act of speaking out or even indirectly mentioning what is happening to them is seen as equally weighted.

As you can imagine, I come across this contradiction a lot in my work with women and girls who have been abused. It is becoming increasingly common, for example, for women to be sued or taken to court for naming their abuser. Women are routinely grilled by lawyers in a courtroom or even interviewed by police in custody for making social media posts, writing blogs, writing memoirs or telling family and friends that they are being abused or stalked. And it is not restricted to specific, detailed posts either. In some cases, women are investigated or punished for sharing general memes, posts, and articles about abuse, DARVO, parental alienation, trauma and violence.

In one case I examined, a woman who had been abused by her ex-husband and then stalked for many years had over 1000 of her private social media posts submitted to the family court during proceedings. These were used against her in order to allege that she was the perpetrator, and that she was 'harassing' her violent and abusive ex-partner subliminally by sharing benign quotes, pictures, articles, and memes about everything from mental health to new year resolutions.

Ultimately, that was the crux of the Depp v Heard case, in which actor Johnny Depp sought to sue Amber Heard for writing an op-ed in which she wrote the words, "Two years ago, I became a public figure representing domestic abuse, and I felt the full force of our culture's wrath for women who speak out."

No names. No specifics. No dates. No details.

And yet, she ended up the respondent in the most high-profile televised lawsuit in the world in which she was publicly destroyed and humiliated for weeks, which was exactly what Depp had threatened her with.

The world watched whilst she was subjected to DARVO on a grand scale (Harsey and Freyd, 2022).

When I worked with Amber during her case, she was being framed as mentally ill and being deliberately diagnosed with histrionic personality disorder by Depp's commissioned psychologist. I think it is safe to say that Amber had never considered that such a vague nod to her previous experiences of abuse could cause her to be sued. Especially as, in 2020, the High Court of England and Wales had already found that *The Sun* newspaper had not committed libel by directly calling him a 'wife-beater' because 12 of the 14 allegations of abuse and domestic violence were found to be 'substantially true' when examined. The judge concluded that Johnny Depp had assaulted Amber Heard on multiple occasions and that the assaults had made her fear for her life at least three times.

Therefore, I am not sure anyone, including Amber, could have predicted that several years later she would be successfully sued for such a vague statement. In the second trial in the USA, she was found to have defamed Johnny Depp by calling herself a victim of domestic and sexual abuse in the *Washington Post* op-ed and Johnny Depp's former lawyer, Adam Waldman, was found to have defamed Amber

Heard by stating in the press that her allegations were 'fabricated', 'staged' and 'a hoax'.

And she isn't the only one this has happened to. One lawyer reported that in the past, only around 5% of her university campus sexual assault cases included a defamation lawsuit against the victim, but more recently that number had jumped to about 50% (Harsey and Freyd, 2022). Similarly, Equality Now, a women's rights organisation, reported seeing a worldwide increase in perpetrators filing defamation lawsuits against victims of gender-based violence (Dugan, 2022).

UN Special Rapporteur for Freedom of Opinion and Expression, Irene Khan, wrote that "women who publicly denounce alleged perpetrators of sexual violence online are increasingly subject to defamation suits or charged with criminal libel or the false reporting of crimes" (Harsey and Freyd, 2022). Indeed, this was the focus of the book *How Many More Women? The Silencing of Women by the Law and How to Stop It* by Jennifer Robinson and Keina Yoshida. The book drew on several high-profile US and UK defamation cases and non-disclosure agreements to show that these types of lawsuits are increasingly used against women who disclose abuse.

It's not just the growing number of cases that's concerning. The threat of such lawsuits against people reporting or disclosing abuse is also something that many victims fear or experience. A recent survey of over 100 women subjected to sexual violence who reported their assaults to their college campus found that 23% were threatened with a defamation lawsuit by either their perpetrator or their perpetrator's attorney (Nesbitt & Carson, 2021). According to this survey, nearly 20% of victims were also warned by their school that they may be at risk of being sued for defamation if they reported their perpetrator.

When I tried to speak publicly about what had happened to me, and despite having court orders and police investigations against multiple stalkers, I was laughed at, publicly mocked and accused of lying. The very act of self-defence became proof of my imagined guilt.

This is the genius of DARVO. It exploits systems that are primed to assess behaviour symmetrically. If both parties appear to be accusing each other, institutions and observers default to neutrality, or switch sides. Conflict is assumed, which minimises the stalking or abuse to 'drama' and the original harm is blurred or flipped over, so that the stalker or abuser becomes the 'real victim'.

False allegations made by the stalker are central to this manoeuvre. A stalker may accuse the victim of harassment for responding publicly or try to claim 'defamation' for being named. They may file complaints alleging bullying, misconduct, or safeguarding concerns. They may report to the police that they are being stalked themselves. I have found that the content of these allegations often mirrors the accusations originally made against them, something that Harsey and Freyd (2022) argue too.

With Tattle Life users in particular, when victims did find out who they were, or posted their real identities on their social media platforms, perpetrators were outraged, indignant and instantly converted to 'victim' status. They were being abused, they said. Targeted, they said. Stalked, even.

Some Tattle users even complained that their privacy was being breached and that they were being put at risk by their victims publishing their identities. The cognitive dissonance was something to behold, especially whilst other Tattle users rushed to the aid of the exposed stalker, commending them, supporting them, and telling them to go immediately to the police.

These perpetrators, despite having had so much power over their victim for so long, suddenly realise that their power has been erased, and the playing field has been levelled, when they are exposed as a completely average, normal person with kids and a job. It is at this point, with the absence of power and anonymity, that they must reframe their victim as a powerful perpetrator who is out to get them. This is particularly true when their victim has a large platform, like a celebrity or influencer.

When this is the case, the stalker has wielded life-changing power over their victim as an unknown threat, but once unmasked, they suddenly reposition themselves as a victim of a powerful public figure who can ruin their life in one Instagram story.

It is psychological projection, sure, but it is enacted through bureaucracy and complaints systems are particularly vulnerable to this.

Regulators, professional bodies, employers, commissioners, and publishers are structured to respond to concerns raised about individuals. When a complaint arrives, it must be processed. Even if it is baseless, even if it is from a dodgy email address. The administrative mechanism is still triggered. Emails are sent to the victim. Statements, explanations and evidence is requested. Investigations are initiated and these sometimes take months, or even years.

Sometimes the investigating organisation is going through the motions and doing this purely to cover their own back. They don't believe any of it to be true, but sometimes the organisation becomes more concerned with their own reputation and processes than the safety and wellbeing of the victim being targeted. In many of the Tattle cases that I explored, the victim was dragged through investigations in which their wellbeing, privacy and safety was compromised throughout, but because they were being framed as the wrongdoer, no one really cared about the impact on them. They had to comply with all requests, meetings, hearings, interviews and processes – no matter how much they harmed them as the victim of stalking.

When DARVO is used, the victim is subjected to scrutiny, interrogation, challenge and intrusion. Any potential for protection disappears, people stop believing them, and instead, they are required to defend themselves fiercely. In this way, they take up two positions at once. They are simultaneously being victimised, abused, stalked, and harassed whilst also having to prepare defence statements, evidence files, legal documents, timelines, and interviews. The result is usually collapse from exhaustion, but also significant psychological trauma from the experience of being gaslit to such an extent.

In my own experience, DARVO was used to great effect. The whole time I was being stalked and being supported by police as a victim in a large police investigation, I was being constructed online by stalkers and unwitting bystanders as a serial criminal. I wasn't able to speak out or correct anyone, because police were asking me not to post about or discuss the investigation publicly.

The tough reality, for me, was this: no one believed I was being stalked. Many people still do not believe that I was stalked. Instead, they were sucked into the narratives of a small group of people and I had to weather a storm that lasted years of my life. I was recast as a bully when I did try to shut down lies and rumours, and when I became more withdrawn, I created boundaries which were then recast as guilt, hostility, and a general sense that I believed I was better than everyone else.

At conferences, I became so frightened about how I was being perceived that I would turn up, hide in the green room, give my speech, retire back to the private room and then get in my car and leave. It created a powerful rumour that I thought I was some sort of A-list celebrity when in reality I was having panic attacks and trying not to throw up.

I am sure by this point that some people will be asking why on earth I didn't just retire, step away or stop appearing in public. I thought about it daily and that was what I wanted to do. In fact, much further than that, there was a point in the stalking where I longed for annihilation; something that would mean I could disappear, or quite frankly, stop existing. I was desperate to escape, emigrate, delete all of my social media accounts, delete my websites, and simply melt into anonymity.

But I couldn't. I had people who relied on me, financially and emotionally. I had responsibilities. I had deadlines. I had obligations. I knew that if I took a normal 9–5 somewhere, the stalkers would bombard that new employer until I was sacked. I knew that if I deleted my social media accounts, they might temporarily feel they had 'won', but would then escalate and find another way to harass and stalk me. I felt that I had to stay strong for my wife and my children. My wife needed someone to support her too and my children needed a safe, stable role model. I was completely trapped.

In the famous words of Alanis Morissette, I came to realise that "the only way out is through". And if that meant that I was publicly trashed and recast as a dangerous, abusive, egotistical bitch for years, then that was my path. I knew I was no match for a group of fixated stalkers. I couldn't possibly dream up the things they were doing to me and I couldn't retaliate or do the same things back to them because then, of course, I would confirm their DARVO.

In the online stalking world, DARVO thrives because access to the victim and 'evidence' is abundant, but interpretation is entirely malleable.

Did she post that on purpose? What does that Instagram quote really mean? Why has she cropped that photo? Why isn't she defending herself if none of this is true? Why does she keep claiming she is being stalked? Why is she pretending that nothing is happening to her?

She's so fake. She's a liar. She's delusional. She's abusive. She's a fraud. She's deliberately withholding information so she can pretend that her life is carrying on as usual. She is trying to make out that she is happy and healthy, when in fact, we all know what is happening behind the scenes.

Why won't she just fucking break, dammitt?

DARVO is probably one of the most powerful tools of the online stalker. After all, it's not stalking if you are 'exposing a fraud' or 'calling out an abuser' or 'raising concerns'.

And because of this inversion, victims begin to weigh the risk of reporting. Will this result in more complaints against me? Will I be investigated? Will my record be stained? The protective act becomes perilous. Victims begin to realise that they look unstable themselves because they have called the police ten, twenty, fifty times. Their tone is changing when they pick up the phone. The calls are dealt with as if the victim is a complete waste of their time.

In cases involving children, perpetrators often report the victim to social care under the guise of concern. The mother who reports stalking may well find herself investigated for instability, or mental illness, or even for being a risk to her own children. The act of seeking help is reframed as evidence of distress severe enough to question parenting.

When I analysed cases of stalking for a UK police force back in 2024, I learned that this was fairly common where the stalkers were ex-partners or ex-partner's family members. Endless complaints to social care that the woman is abusing her children, that she is mentally ill, paranoid and delusional are 'confirmed' when social workers then turn up, and the woman becomes defensive and distressed whilst trying to explain that she is being hounded by anonymous accounts and years of malicious reports about her.

Why do so many stalkers seek to position their victims as offenders like this?

Because they understand that credibility is power. Not in some intellectual criminal mastermind way. But in a deep-seated common-sense way. The social understanding that if you can affect the credibility and character of the person, no one will believe them. This is a tactic we see across all forms of abuse, from sexually abusing children through to systemic abuse in institutions such as the church or care homes. People know that reframing their victim as the aggressor, or as unstable and unpredictable will cause institutions to hesitate, observers to stall, and supporters to withdraw.

Traumatised victims of stalking and abuse very often do lash out, become very distressed, get defensive, become argumentative with professionals, or sound as if they are exaggerating or losing control, whilst the perpetrator remains cool, calm, collected and unflappable. And because we pathologise and scrutinise victims so much, we still then see the trauma as evidence of aggression and deviance but see the perpetrator as the stable one.

Simply put, DARVO wins.

It punishes the victim for speaking and ensures that the perpetrator is recast as an innocent party, bewildered by the outrageous 'false accusations' of stalking and abuse. Crucially, though, they are always the calmer party. Always the one with the strategy. Always the one with the plan.

Research on DARVO suggests it is very effective. An experiment testing the effect of DARVO on third-party observers found that among those who were exposed to a perpetrator's use of DARVO, individuals perceived the perpetrator as less abusive and less responsible for their harmful behaviour compared to those who were not exposed to perpetrator DARVO (Harsey & Freyd, 2020). DARVO-exposed participants in this study also rated the victim as less believable, more abusive, and more responsible for the harm they experienced.

For those who have committed abusive acts, the ability to influence how others perceive them and their victims is indispensable. Convincing bystanders that no abusive behaviour took place (or that if something did occur it was not harmful) and that the victim is untrustworthy gives the perpetrator a clear advantage in both social networks and the legal system. Further still, convincing everyone that the victim is the real perpetrator, and that they are lying and attacking the perpetrator by claiming they have been abused or stalked is extremely common. If successful, the perpetrator can avoid blame, accountability, and exposure and thereby avoid any negative outcomes. In lots of cases, the victim's account is doubted and ultimately disregarded in favour of the perpetrator's narrative (Harsey and Freyd, 2020).

Systemic failure to recognise DARVO compounds the harm. Many professionals and institutions are not trained to identify reversal patterns. They treat each complaint in isolation. They may not connect the fact that the complainant is the subject of a stalking report. They may not analyse timing. They may not consider motive. They speak of cases as though they are 'mutual conflict' or 'six of one and half a dozen of the other'.

Without a DARVO lens, systems inadvertently assist perpetrators. That language of neutrality can mask injustice and move towards responses like, "we must hear both sides of the story", "it seems like an ongoing dispute", or "there are allegations on both sides".

But, by definition, stalking is never a mutual dispute.

When a victim is forced into defensive posture repeatedly, her energy shifts from protection to survival. The original harm fades into background noise while the new crisis, defending against false allegations, consumes her.

CHAPTER 11

Stalking as entertainment

Jennifer could hardly wait to open the app. The TV was paused on that woman's face, sat there in her blazer in some posh library, talking to the camera. Thinking she was all that.

OrangeDoor67: *Is anyone online? I just nearly threw up in my fucking mouth. I just saw her advertising a new TV show – who the fuck has let this idiotic bitch have a TV show? Also, she has put SO much weight on, I thought it was a documentary on whaling for a minute.*

CatsAndDogs78: *What! You're joking. Where have you seen that? How does she keep doing this? She's such a fucking manipulator. How do we get this TV show axed? Who else is in?*

Handbasket32: *Oh, I'm game! Whale reference killed me btw. She can't hide behind filters on the TV, can she? Benny the Baluga.*

AlabamaMama: *Why won't she just fucking disappear yet? I'm in. What's the plan?*

Traveltime89: *Me too. We need to coordinate.*

Candles64: *Just seen this! What the hell? That bitch is like hydra. Cut one head off her and two grow back in its place. Jesus Christ. Why won't she just fuck off?*

"What are you doing?" Neville asked from behind her, watching his wife giggle into her phone for the millionth time.

Jennifer snapped upright, realising she hadn't been aware of his presence.

"Uhh, nothing! Just texting . . ." She tried to brush it off, closing down the app for a moment.

She slid her phone into her jeans pocket and tried to walk away, but Neville stepped into her path.

"Who? You're constantly on your phone these days. Always saying you're texting someone . . ."

"My friend from work! Why are you being so fucking weird and jealous . . . God!"

Neville searched her face, unconvinced. Twenty-six years of marriage meant he knew precisely when she was hiding something.

"I am not jealous, but when your wife becomes literally obsessed with her phone, never discusses any of these riveting conversations, and I have never met these friends she talks to 24 hours a day . . . when she is always sneaking around and having these so-called work meetings . . . always laughing at her phone in the middle of the fucking night . . . something isn't right Jen, you've changed . . ."

Jennifer didn't have time for this, she needed to get back to the thread. Neville could have his tantrum later, but she needed to make sure she didn't miss any of the plans to take down the TV show.

She couldn't think of anything convincing to say.

"Oh, grow up, Neville. I'm so sick of you being paranoid and jealous just because you have no friends!" Jennifer deliberately lied, storming out of the room and into her study, slamming the door behind her.

As soon as the door was shut and she was sure Neville wasn't going to follow her in, she opened the app and carried on where she left off.

OrangeDoor67: *I did some digging earlier and surprise, surprise, she hasn't posted about this TV show at all. Trying to hide it from us, I think!*

Traveltime89: *Oh Jess, we know you read here – we are coming for you! You thought you could do this behind our backs . . . very silly. And now everyone is going to know what you are!*

AlabamaMama: *Hahaha hi Jess! Hope you enjoy what's coming next from your 'stalkers' hahaha*

Handbasket32: *She is defo one of those people who would want to be stalked though – she's desperate to present herself as a victim*

Candles64: *Oh, I know. All perpetrators do. She's evil. Have you seen all the info flying around about her abusing her wife? I mean, how didn't that destroy her? This TV channel must know nothing about her.*

OrangeDoor67: *Ok, well, we can solve that. I found the production company she's made the TV series with. I reckon we write to them all together, as many of us as possible – we can all send the same email template – and then we can all add what we want to it.*

CatsAndDogs78: *I met her wife once you know. Seemed nice enough but totally obsessed with that woman. Obvious that she was* *brainwashed and groomed, I mean, who could fucking love her unless groomed to? She's utterly despicable.*

AlabamaMama: *Ahhh yes! Send us all the template and we can do it today. The TV show starts airing on Friday, so we only have five days to get it down.*

BerryGirl: *Hey everyone. So happy to have found this site! I'm new here, but I'm in. I saw those adverts today, and I am livid. Who the fuck does she think she is? Send me whatever you need, I have contacts in the industry who will get that show taken down.*

Candles64: *Oh fabulous! The more the merrier!*

Jennifer quickly typed out a list of things to include in the complaint letters to send to the TV channel, putting as much in there as possible.

OrangeDoor67: *Okay, so here is the list to include – she's a fraud, abuser, exploits and traffics women, lost custody of her kids, pretends to be a lesbian to sell books, she steals data, she abuses her wife, she commits tax fraud, she is running an illegal pyramid scheme, she is currently under investigation by police and by many organisations, she committed embezzlement, falsely claims to have been abused and raped, supported Amber Heard, supports women committing suicide, is a pathological liar, her family abandoned her, she is clearly mentally ill, and she writes absolutely bullshit books and articles to make millions of pounds out of vulnerable people. Get as many of these into the email as possible – and let's get them all out today. Okay?*

Jennifer could have gone on and on but hit send as quickly as she could and then gave everyone the email addresses of the production company and the TV channel.

Handbasket32: *Oh my god, I cannot wait to see the shit she causes over this! There is no way they will work with her if we send enough emails. I've got five email accounts I can send this from.*

BerryGirl: *Done. Thank you so much everyone. I have just sent this to all of my industry contacts.*

Candles64: *She is going to haaaaaate us for this one! Hahahahaha!*

Traveltime89: *Are we using fake names, ladies?*

AlabamaMama: *We can do, but I don't think the production companies can show her the emails we send anyway because of GDPR. So, do what you like!*

CatsAndDogs78: *This is fucking brilliant! Who wants to take bets on how long it takes to get this show down?*

Candles64: *I give it a week. They cannot ignore this amount of pressure.*

BerryGirl: *Oh, it will be down before that, I will make it my personal mission for you girls! I am literally just on the phone now to one of her producers haha!*

OrangeDoor67: *No waaaay. Haha. I like you a lot. Good job! Hey Jess, you just didn't learn, did you? Fuck you and your fucking 'career'.*

* * *

If stalking is so harmful, so harmful in fact that people become frightened when they think they are being followed down a street by a stranger, so harmful that we make documentaries and films about terrifying stalking cases, why do so many people watch or laugh along as it happens in real time?

Not intervene. Not protect. Just watch.

Whether it is stalking in person or online, there is a strong tendency in all of us to simply do nothing. When victims are being stalked in person, being left gifts, sent letters, followed and obsessed over, people are quick to brush it off, make jokes about 'bunny boilers' and 'psychos' or suggest the victim is misreading signals in some way. And when victims are stalked and harassed online, observers either quietly watch, as if it is the storyline of a dramatic soap, or become involved in the stalking and harassment themselves.

Today, stalking can become spectacle. In a weird way, stalking, mobbing, harassment and online abuse has become content to be consumed, shared and dare I say . . . enjoyed.

To understand modern stalking, we must confront an uncomfortable truth: many people are not only indifferent to it, they are also entertained by it. The public consumption of stalking-like content is driven by deep cultural appetites. And sites like Tattle Life demonstrate that the people most amused and entertained by days, months and years of hounding victims are women.

If we cast our minds back through history, humiliation has long been a form of entertainment: public punishments, torture in the town square, public trials, gossip, scandal sheets and tabloid exposés. But now, the court of public opinion is vast. The digital age has democratised this possibility. Anyone can participate. Anyone can comment. Anyone can add a detail, a joke, a lie, a threat. Behaviour can escalate and escalate. And no one even needs to know who they are.

In a way, it reminds me of the case of the Serbian artist Marina Abramović. In 1974, she famously performed *Rhythm 0*: a piece in which she placed 72 objects on a table (including a feather, scissors, pens, a knife, an axe and even a loaded gun) and then waited and passively allowed the audience to do whatever they wanted to her for six hours whilst she did not move or retaliate. ·

At first, no one did anything. The atmosphere was awkward and uncomfortable. Some people came forward and posed her body gently, held her hand, and some kissed her. But once the ice was broken, the boundaries were pushed. People cut her clothes off. Thorns were pressed into her skin. Someone wrote on her body to see what she would do.

Once the audience fully realised that they could do what they wanted, and that they were surrounded by people who were encouraging and accepting the behaviour, Marina was fully dehumanised, and the violence escalated. She was stripped naked. Her skin was cut with a scalpel. Someone sliced her neck and drank her blood. Men sexually assaulted her.

Finally, a man placed the loaded gun in Marina's hand, put her finger on the trigger and aimed the gun at her neck. Another member of the audience then jumped forward and removed the gun, with a large fight breaking out amongst the audience. Some people defended his right to do what he did, and others felt that he had gone too far.

The purpose of the piece by Marina was to examine how quickly social norms and restraints will collapse if you give a group of people the opportunity to act, to encourage each other, but also to diffuse responsibility. Marina is quoted as saying that her piece taught her that if you leave it up to your audience, they can and will kill you. For entertainment. For thrill.

It remains one of the starkest examples of real-world group psychology, power, and violence. Ordinary people who went to an art exhibition one day swiftly and easily behaved in ways that mutilated, assaulted, abused, humiliated, and almost murdered an artist in less than six hours.

And that behaviour was in person, with witnesses. No masks. No anonymous usernames. No screens or digital barriers to hide behind. I cannot help but wonder then how groups of people escalate, encourage, observe and enjoy violence and abuse when perpetrated online.

For a lot of people in the online space, the spectacle of downfall is particularly intoxicating.

When a victim is singled out online – an influencer, an activist, a professional, even an A-list celebrity – the narrative quickly shifts from curiosity to dismantling. Everything they have ever done, said or supported can be used against them to create a new storyline. People quietly consume the content, fascinated and titillated, or they jump in too. This was something Suler (2004) theorised back before social media and huge forums even existed.

Research shows that this behaviour has links to sadism. Kircaburun et al. (2018) found that sadists were likely to engage in online stalking and trolling simply because they enjoy seeing their victims suffer. For some stalkers, if they cannot fulfil their need for cruelty and harm elsewhere, they will become increasingly obsessed with victims they stalk online, fantasising and planning how to make them suffer more and more (Kircaburun et al., 2018; van Geel et al., 2017). I discussed this with my wife whilst I was writing this book, and we talked about the way we struggled to know what to do about the sadism element.

Everyone gave us the same advice: "Do not let the stalkers see the damage they are doing to you – otherwise, they will enjoy it, and your responses will fuel them." Sounds a little bit like victim blaming, but honestly, at that point in the stalking, I would have cut my own arm off if it meant stopping the torture.

We came to the conclusion that several of our stalkers were sadistic and were certainly enjoying the harm they were causing to us. They were laughing about it online, posting about me suffering and struggling, and were generally treating the stalking of us both as if they were part of a soap storyline. When we showed any form of distress, they loved it. So, we took the advice from everyone – lawyers, agents, publishers, friends, colleagues – and we decided to stop acknowledging the stalking completely. We figured that if sadistic stalkers were enjoying our pain, we could just stop showing them any signs of impact.

However, this seemed to enrage and fuel them further, especially on forums like Tattle Life. When I simply stopped talking about it, stopped acknowledging it and just got on with my life, the women stalking me were outraged. They escalated considerably, upped the ante, submitted more and more complaints, did more and more damage, as if they were desperate for me to crack. They seemed intent on increasing the harm, especially if I was doing well, moving on, ignoring them, or having a nice time somewhere. If I was off doing great things, like TV interviews, filming a new TV series or writing a new book, they were relentless. But similarly, if I was visibly struggling and talking about being stalked and abused online, they were loving it.

From this reflection, Jay and I concluded that there were certainly some online stalkers who would get bored or stop if they were not getting the reaction they wanted, but there were others who would escalate if they were not getting the reaction they wanted. And so, as a victim, you find yourself trapped again in a game that is for the pleasure and entertainment of others. And if you are unlucky enough to be a victim of multiple stalkers, or group stalking, the likelihood is that where one drops off, another will fill their place.

The entertainment and pleasure they derive lies in exposure. Exposure promises revelation. It suggests hidden truths coming to light. But often what is exposed is not misconduct, but vulnerability. These cases of virtual public floggings often do not dig up actual wrongdoing, crimes or justifications for abuse and stalking. Instead, they become hyperfixated on the victim's mental health, their relationship struggles, their parenting decisions, their appearance, their body shape, their childhoods.

The audience gathers. The mobbing intensifies. People send the links to each other, utterly captivated whilst watching someone get taken apart, piece by piece. The victim is being destroyed in real time and observers cannot help but stare. Thousands of views and comments are racked up, everyone weighs in with their own opinions, stories, jokes, accusations and beliefs.

Online, everyone becomes a detective. Just like on Tattle Life, users of TikTok, Instagram, Facebook, Reddit and X become enthralled. They go and find their personal social media accounts, dig up their old photos, find out what school their kids go to, find their families on Facebook, figure out who their last employer was, use Google Street View to look at their house . . . and before we know it, stalking someone and causing them devastating trauma is something you do for fun.

But why do thousands of people join in like this?

Online disinhibition theory, first articulated by Suler (2004), provides a foundational framework for understanding the dynamics of digital environments. Suler identifies several critical components: anonymity, invisibility, asynchronicity, solipsistic introjection, dissociative imagination, and minimisation of authority, which together reduce self-monitoring and weaken normative pressure.

Suler's six components of the digital environment (2004)

Component	Explanation
Anonymity	People feel less accountable when their real identity is hidden or unclear. If others do not know who they are, they feel safer saying or doing things they would not say face-to-face. **Example:** Someone creates a username like TruthWarrior99 and posts abusive comments about a woman online. Because their real name and workplace are not attached, they feel protected from consequences.
Invisibility	Online, we cannot see each other's facial expressions, body language, or immediate emotional reactions. Without seeing someone's hurt, fear, or anger, empathy is reduced. **Example:** A person sends repeated threatening messages via direct message. They do not see the recipient crying or becoming distressed, so the impact feels less 'real' to them.
Asynchronicity	Online communication does not always happen in real time. People can send messages without having to deal with an immediate response. There is no instant social correction. In face-to-face interaction, someone might say 'That's not okay'. Online, the delay creates emotional distance. **Example:** A user posts a long, aggressive rant at 2am and logs off. They do not have to witness the response, confrontation, or consequences until later, if at all.
Solipsistic introjection	When interacting online, people may imagine the other person's voice and personality inside their own mind. The interaction becomes partly a conversation with themselves. The other person becomes less real and more like a character created in the offender's imagination. **Example:** A stalker reads a woman's social media posts and constructs a fantasy version of her in their head. They believe they 'know' her, despite never having met her, and begin responding to her as if she exists primarily in their internal narrative.

Dissociative imagination	People can experience the online world as separate from 'real life'. They may treat online behaviour as if it does not carry real-world consequences. Harmful behaviour feels like part of a game or fantasy, rather than actual abuse **Example:** Someone participates in coordinated harassment on a forum and later says, 'It's just the internet, it's not real.' They psychologically separate their online cruelty from their offline identity.
Minimisation of authority	Online spaces often lack visible authority figures. Without physical cues of power (uniforms, titles, professional roles), people feel less constrained by rules. The perceived absence of enforcement increases risk-taking and rule breaking. **Example:** In a loosely moderated discussion forum, users escalate from gossip to threats because there is no immediate moderator intervention and no visible consequences.

Part of the answer lies in social bonding (Mardon et al., 2022; Tajfel & Turner, 1979). Shared hostility creates cohesion. When people gather around a target, they form in-groups and out-groups. In-group and out-group theory, originating in social identity research (Tajfel & Turner, 1979), explains how people derive identity and self-esteem from belonging to a group ('us') while defining others as outsiders ('them'). In online stalking groups, members bond through shared hostility towards a target, constructing the victim as the out-group. This reduces empathy, normalises cruelty, and creates social rewards for escalating behaviour. Harassment becomes entertainment because group approval, status, and belonging are reinforced each time someone contributes to monitoring, mocking, or attacking the designated outsider. Agreement signals belonging. Mockery signals loyalty. The more cutting the comment, the more validation it may receive from the in-group.

This is collective cruelty disguised as community – thousands of strangers feeling as though they have 'found their people', whilst using immense digital power to destroy someone in a matter of hours. I cannot ignore the blatant issue here either: that misogyny is the unspoken engine of much of this entertainment. I have never seen mobbing, stalking or abuse of a man in the way I have seen it of a woman.

Women's behaviour has always been policed publicly, so maybe that's why it feels so natural and expected in the online world. The online world is only really a replication, or amplification, of the real world in that sense. The difference is scale. The digital world is multi-faceted, vast, abusive and built now with algorithms to push us into these behaviours and reward us when we engage. Women are the majority victims of stalking and abuse, and so it follows that we would be the same target group online, especially where people who would not normally commit stalking and abuse crimes in person can act out their behaviours in the comfort of their own home, behind a fake username.

The Tattle Life scandal illustrates this dynamic starkly. Threads about women stretch into hundreds of pages over many years. Users log in daily not because they have been harmed personally, but because the unfolding drama provides stimulation. The target's life becomes episodic content, it gets updated every day. Comments and replies are awaited. New developments dissected. As long as she breathes, there is new 'content' to find, collate, and use against her.

Even in death, the stalking and abuse continues. In at least four cases I know of, where the victim of online stalking has died, the momentum never slowed. In fact, in at least one case, the death led to the escalation of the stalking behaviours, with perpetrators sending letters and cards filled with abuse and mockery of the victim's death. Obsessive surveillance of the bereaved family. Speculation about the cause. Trying to locate which morgue the body was being transferred to. Seeking and paying for copies of the death certificate to upload online.

In two cases, both deaths of unconnected children, the news of each of them dying led to hundreds of accounts mocking, blaming, and abusing the bereaved family. It is no coincidence, either, that the main targets of the gleeful groups of stalkers were the mothers of the children, not the fathers.

Nothing stopped them, not even death. In fact, the deaths were one of the most exciting events they had responded to yet. It sent stalkers into a frenzy – digging up old posts, watching the social media of close friends and family, trying to find and share details of the funeral, screenshotting videos and pictures, laughing about posts and comments made by grieving commenters. Obsessive comments.

What if they are lying about the deaths? Probably making it up for attention. Does anyone know how they died yet? Does anyone know their friends or family? Anyone got them on Facebook? Where do they live? What hospital were they at? Which coroner would it be? Can we get access to the death certificates? Does anyone know people who work at the hospital? Why have they put a GoFundMe up? Who do they think they are? We should report them for fraud. They are disgusting . . .

I often wonder whether 'true crime culture' adds another layer.

For years now, true crime has been the money spinner inn books, in film, and in TV.

True crime has become one of the most consumed non-fiction genres across media, with 84% of the U.S. population reporting consumption of true crime content (including documentaries, podcasts, and shows) in 2024, and true crime often dominating documentary charts on major streaming platforms. For example, on Netflix in 2024 15 of the top 20 documentary titles were true crime by reach, up from six in 2020, showing significant commissioning and viewer engagement growth in the genre (Edison Research, 2024). Searches for 'true crime' exceed hundreds of thousands, and streaming services have repeatedly placed true crime documentaries and series among their most watched factual content (Vivint, 2024). Audiences worldwide continue to seek real-life crime narratives and are a core driver of the expanding documentary market, which itself was valued at over USD 5.3 billion in 2024 and continues to grow as platforms invest in original non-fiction content (C21Media, 2025).

Audiences are now accustomed to consuming stories of harm as narrative arcs. 'Real life stories' where there is a villain and a victim. Where there are twists. Suspense is manufactured by the producers and editors. New information comes to light. Everyone is shocked. Who is the real victim? Who is the real perpetrator?

Our TVs are full of this stuff. Victims are exposed as liars. Families hid their children for money. People faked their deaths for insurance payouts. Rapists were wrongly accused. Influencers faked their cancer diagnoses for clout. Men exploited women for their money. Stalker and serial killer, Ted Bundy is played by Hollywood heartthrob Zac Efron, for God's sake.

It feels as though we are being fed inverted storylines because if TV and film commissioned the most common cases, it would be millions of the same thing over and over again. Rapes are common. Domestic abuse is common. Cancer is common. Exploitation is common. Murder is common. Missing children are common. Victims of crime are common. Stalkers are common.

Would anyone really keep watching that kind of media, if it had no twists, shocks or mysteries to solve? Would people sit there for hours, thinking, 'Oh yeah. This will be like the other 14 episodes. Woman gets stalked. She reports to the police. No one does anything. Stalker carries on. Woman becomes traumatised. Still, no one does anything. I bloody love these shows. My favourite part is how repetitive and hopeless they all are.'

The answer is a resounding no.

But will people watch twisty, rare, uncommon, subversive storylines of vulnerable victims turning out to be manipulative liars? Will they watch documentaries about influencers pretending to have cancer for likes and shares? Will they sit still for hours, trying to figure out whether that nurse really killed all those babies? Will they follow, step-by-step, trying to solve the crime alongside the narrator as if the entire documentary is an interactive murder investigation?

Absolutely.

It interests me how this manifests online, when a real victim is being stalked, abused and mobbed. Do people really want to follow along whilst they watch a confused woman struggle to cope with being stalked, or do they want a thrilling story where someone digs up some evidence that the woman is actually a nasty, evil, dangerous fraud, who deserves to be exposed and destroyed?

You know the answer to that.

When digital communities frame a woman as dangerous or fraudulent, the storyline becomes addictive. Each new post feels like a clue. The voyeuristic thrill of destruction is powerful. Voyeurism, psychologically, involves deriving pleasure from observing others without their consent or knowledge. In digital stalking-as-entertainment, the observation is not only passive. It is participatory. The audience contributes to the storyline. They speculate, predict, diagnose, lie, and add details and accusations.

Watching a woman's life unravel offers a rush. Why?

Because it gives the observers power to watch someone else be destroyed in public. They feel safe, watching on. It isn't about them. Their life is not up for examination. It then reinforces or creates a social hierarchy, where the observer is above the victim.

If she falls, I am safe. If she is exposed, I am righteous. If she is mocked, I am superior.

Downfall is culturally satisfying. We are primed to enjoy narratives of hubris punished. When a woman is perceived as confident, outspoken or successful, her perceived misstep becomes narrative gold. The more visible she was, the sweeter the collapse is for the rest of us.

And it normalises stalking and abusive behaviours. Entertainment culture blunts empathy.

The target becomes a character in a play, rather than a person. Her children become plot devices. Her distress becomes content. Tears and breakdowns are interpreted as performance. Anger as proof of guilt. The more she responds, the more entertaining it becomes. The more she says, the more there is to talk about. The more she hides and withdraws, the more there is to discover and dox.

This structural reality explains why sites like Tattle Life exist at all.

There is a big market for dissection and humiliation. A market for gossip elevated to obsessive investigation. A market for mockery framed as natural critique. A market for devastating downfall packaged as justice against someone who deserved it. As long as audiences are willing to watch, click, post, and share, the platforms will continue to host, and they will profit millions from that choice.

Make no mistake, if we are watching as someone is being dismantled and doxxed by online mobs, we are watching stalking. And if we are finding it entertaining, we are watching stalking for fun.

There is something profoundly unsettling about this realisation. Stalking online does not persist solely because of individual perpetrators, it persists because there is an audience. A performance. The victim's humiliation generates clicks and likes, and so the spectacle will continue. It gives it life.

The question then, is not only why do stalkers stalk? It's why do we all watch it like a soap opera?

CHAPTER 12

Changing the landscape: what must happen now

It was a warm September evening in 2025 as I looked across the large room in parliament. After years of relentless stalking, I could hardly believe we were there. It was quietly filling with people I didn't recognise, whilst a man checked people's invites over at the door. I sat at the head of a large horseshoe-shaped table that was fitted with microphones and name place cards. Despite working alongside government for many years, I had only ever seen rooms like this on TV. I had not known what to wear for such an event and had opted for a burgundy blazer and the smartest black trousers I could find.

It would have been an understatement to say that I was nervous.

To my left was Jay, discreetly holding my clammy hand under the table. To my right was Donna and Neil Sands, accompanied by their lawyer and their forensic investigator. None of us would be there if it wasn't for Donna and Neil, a married couple from Ireland who had fought in the High Court for years to unmask the owner and operator of the website Tattle Life.

In June 2025, when I saw the headlines naming Sebastian Bond as the man running the site, I had burst into tears. Jay had, too. The website had been used as the core hub for the group of stalkers who had destroyed my life, but I hadn't been able to take any action because the site was owned by an anonymous person who had hidden themselves from public life through layers of connected companies and fake names.

The site, with millions of views per month, was a safe haven for stalkers. Anyone could be submitted to the site to be victimised for months or years of their lives. It was, and still is, described as a 'gossip forum' which targets people who share their lives and monetise content online. The threads are thousands of comments long, targeting everyone from Meghan Markle and Britney Spears to unknown micro-business owners who had opened a little shop in Cheshire selling organic soap. The site users were mostly women, and the site victims were mostly women. Comments and posts range from inane chatter to disturbing deepfake porn made of their victims. From silly jokes to months of obsessed stalking and abuse of victims and their children. From conversations about someone launching a new cookbook to users sharing NHS medical records and death certificates of their victims on to the site. From discussions about fashion and TV shows being cancelled, through to organised groups of users working together to submit mass complaints to police, employers, DVLA, DWP, HMRC, local authorities, planning permission panels, and social care to cause the complete collapse of their victim's lives.

Donna Sands had found herself submitted to Tattle Life when she set up her small boutique fashion business. She reported that she had been harassed, abused, bullied, lied about, and harmed via the website for months. Like most victims of the site, the users had then targeted her partner. Together with her husband Neil, she had started legal action against the website for harassment and defamation, something that no one else had ever achieved before. Their case was pivotal and meant that the High Court ordered that Sebastian Bond could be named publicly, as the sole owner of the site, raking in massive annual profits from the stalking, harassment and abuse of thousands of victims on the site. The judge in the case had made comments that the site had been set up to deliberately inflict hurt and harm on others by allowing the mass anonymous destruction of their reputations and lives.

If it wasn't for their lawsuit and the naming of Sebastian Bond, I would never have seen the headlines, reached out to the Sands, and then put the call out for hundreds of victims of stalking to come forward to submit their case to my parliamentary report.

To the left of Jay was Member of Parliament, Apsana Begum, who had supported me to raise the issue of the website and sponsored the event. A victim of stalking and abuse herself, she was intent on helping us finally take action against our online stalkers.

Sat around the horseshoe were women of all ages and backgrounds and also a couple of men who had been stalked online. I had invited them personally, and whilst their names were on their place cards, I didn't know any of them, had never met them, and didn't recognise them. Some were business owners, some were influencers, some were models and musicians. Some were campaigners for cancer screenings, and some were just regular people who had worked in local government or small businesses, and had been submitted to the site to be obliterated. To the back of the room were representatives from the police, Ofcom, ICO, charities, and government departments.

It was such an eerie atmosphere. We were all perfect strangers, and yet, we were all connected in such a terrible way.

We were all there because we had been stalked online, targeted in the same way. Some of us by the same people, and all of us, on the same website. For most of us, this would be the first time we had ever spoken about our experiences formally. It felt solemn and I could sense the uncomfortable fear in the room.

As everyone settled, I started to speak.

I suppose I would have been nervous no matter what – it was my first time hosting a parliamentary session after all – but there was something incredibly unnerving about hosting a session on something that had almost ended my life. After my messages had been leaked all over the internet, I had never told anyone else about how suicidal I had become during the stalking. I had been so ashamed of how it had harmed me, that I had never felt safe enough to admit how close I came, not once, but twice. Even after the attempts, the feelings didn't go away for a long time. I was left with gnawing catastrophic thoughts that frequently begged me to slam my car into a tree or jump off somewhere high. I spent many nights driving hours in the dark, sinking into music that screamed about death like it was a comfort blanket. I imagined how calm and beautiful it must feel to never have to feel anything ever again. The void used to frighten me as a child but during the stalking, I longed for it like the warmth of an old friend. I couldn't believe how traumatised I was.

I never thought I would ever be able to speak or write about my own experience of being stalked, but to be surrounded by other victims just like me, filled me with emotions that threatened to strangle my voice at the exact moment I needed it. They looked just like me. Normal, average people we would walk past in the street.

Before we all attended, I had analysed over 150 cases of online stalking and produced a report for members of parliament, police, and regulators. I already knew how many people had also made attempts on their own lives, and I knew how many people had suffered in the same way I had.

No amount of public speaking experience or professional practice could prepare me for that session. I was told that I did well, even though my memory of the few hours we spent there are scant. Where I have them, they are filled with horror, tears, sadness, and rage.

It was my job to chair the event, which meant giving an opening speech and then introducing and thanking every speaker, and every victim who came to share their experiences of being stalked online. I told myself to stay calm, composed, and to lead with dignity. I needed to be the strength in the room, the person who was robust enough to chair and manage the speakers.

I cried throughout every testimony. I tried not to, of course, but the stories got progressively worse, and none of my usual techniques were working. Even as I kept my face as neutral as possible, tears poured from my eyes. Victims broke down in sobs as they recalled losing their employment, their houses, their friends and family, and then, trying to take their own lives. Every crack in their voice pierced through me as they spoke about being bombarded with threats, abuse, and ridicule for years.

My back and shoulders stayed straight, my body stayed upright, my face stayed professional – but my soul was being crushed into dust as I listened to one woman recount the way a group of strangers online had submitted hundreds of false complaints to social services, which resulted in her daughter being removed from her school one day and placed in care for six weeks, until the social workers realised that the 'concerns' were nothing more than an organised campaign of online stalking. My heart ached for that little girl and her mother, whose lives were irreversibly changed by the actions of anonymous stalkers who were never identified, let alone brought to justice. Having worked in child protection, and undertaken consultancy in children's care homes, I couldn't bear the thought of such a small child being ripped from her mother and placed in a home on baseless accusations, only to be returned with a mere apology, and a lifetime of trauma.

Another woman was there on behalf of her best friend, who was targeted nonstop until she died from cancer. She held back tears as she recalled the abuse, stalking and obsession of online stalkers – and the huge impact it had on her and her best friend. Tattle Life users have a curious and toxic obsession with those who document their cancer and palliative care journeys, and some readers of this book will be appalled to learn that the site has submitted several people dying of cancer to be targeted up until, and beyond, their last moments. The late Richard Davies, a man who shared his journey with cancer – whom some of you will know as his online moniker 'Bowel Bro' – was targeted, stalked and abused on the site throughout his illness, his final days, and even after he died. He was mocked and repeatedly accused of faking cancer to steal money. A close friend and cancer campaigner, Stacey Heale, wrote an article in 2025 discussing the abuse of people with cancer on the site, and revealed that Tattle users had called the hospice, pretended to be doctors and tried to find out if he was really there.

When he died in 2023, Tattle users called funeral homes, crematoriums and even the local council to buy death certificate copies. After he died, his wife, Lisa Davies, was sent anonymous handwritten cards and letters to her house that mocked his death or demanded that she provide proof of his body. Some of those 'sympathy' cards were shared online by Stacey Heale. One of them wrote (around the pre-printed text which read 'Thinking of you at this difficult time'): *'Howdy Bitch. Conning money out of vulnerable people. Karma is also a bitch!'*

Similarly, when the late Dame Deborah James, who was a journalist, campaigner and podcast host was diagnosed with bowel cancer at 35 years old, she was submitted to Tattle Life to be victimised, mocked and bullied to the day she died. One of the posters on her threads claimed to have worked in direct cancer research for 15 years, but still apparently found the motivation and time to hound her online.

After every speaker, I managed to compose myself enough to thank them for their contribution and invite the next victim of stalking to begin their testimony. Towards the end, after over 15 testimonies and what felt like a thousand tears, we opened the floor to comments and questions from anyone in the room, but most importantly, to the government, the regulators and the police who were present.

As people began to stand, speak and ask questions, the horror set in. No one had realised how bad online stalking had become. Even victims, who had been understandably absorbed in their own hellscape of stalking for years, were devastated to be surrounded by victims telling the same stories. Professionals in the room raised questions about the Online Safety Act, the role of the police, and the role of government departments. They asked how such blatant criminality could be ignored or minimised for so long, and why the online world seemed exempt from the law.

Neil Sands spoke to the room before we left and raised his concerns that it was only a matter of time until someone ended their life as a direct result of the site, and as a direct result of online stalking. His warning seeped into everyone in the room, many of us knowing how close we had come to that exact fate.

After the event, people hugged, supported each other, swapped details and thanked each other for being brave. For speaking so openly. For sharing their stories of being stalked. For talking frankly and honestly about the trauma. For honouring those who had died, victims of the site.

And as we made our way back to Euston Station to go home, I turned to Jay and sighed, "This is going to be a huge job, but we have to carry on. That site has to come down. Online stalking has to be taken seriously . . . I don't ever want to be in a room like that again."

* * *

Recognising that you are being stalked is just the first step. Documenting harm and naming patterns is necessary. Seeking help and protection is too. Of course, processing the trauma and finding a way to survive is also necessary. But none of these, on their own, alter systems.

None of those things will prevent other victims or stop the thousands of online stalkers who are running riot.

Cyberstalking legislation has largely been adopted from existing offline stalking laws, with only a few states and countries creating distinct and explicit cyberstalking legislation (Ahlgrim and Terrance, 2021). Legislation that has been adopted from offline stalking often fails to adequately address cyberstalking and technology use in victimisation.

Systemic intervention, accurate recognition and categorisation of online stalking and criminal justice reform is imperative if we are to address online stalking. However, I recognise that this is going to be one almighty fight.

If stalking has evolved into a distributed, networked, algorithmically amplified phenomenon, then the response must evolve beyond individual complaint and isolated prosecution. For me, the past few years has demonstrated the depth of institutional unpreparedness and the possibility of structural change when evidence, pressure and public scrutiny converge.

For too long, online stalking was treated as peripheral to 'real crime'. It was framed as the inevitable by-product of visibility, a regrettable but unavoidable consequence of participation in public life. Or it was framed as paranoid, delusional, mentally ill victims believing that they are being abused and stalked online by anyone from their ex to their boss. That narrative has begun to fracture, not because platforms voluntarily recalibrated their systems, and certainly not because they care about their ethical duties to their users, but because hundreds of victims refused to remain silent and because mounting evidence is becoming impossible to ignore.

The legal turning point in the United Kingdom was marked by the legal case, *Sands v Tattle*.

For the first time, the High Court was compelled to examine the infrastructure of a large anonymous gossip forum not merely as a host of opinion, but as an ecosystem capable of facilitating sustained harassment and reputational destruction. The case forced judicial consideration of anonymity, disclosure obligations, data protection, and the real-world impact of forum-based targeting and group stalking. It challenged the assumption that what occurs on a 'gossip site' is culturally trivial or legally neutral.

The significance of *Sands v Tattle* was not solely in the individual proceedings. The case signalled that courts are willing to interrogate platform architecture, not merely user behaviour. It demonstrated that anonymity does not extinguish accountability and that sustained digital targeting can cross many legal thresholds when properly evidenced.

Legal action alone, however, is likely to be insufficient without wider political engagement.

Over the past year, I have provided detailed reports to Members of Parliament outlining the structure and scale of online stalking networks, including specific case studies drawn from extensive analysis of Tattle threads and related digital ecosystems. Alongside my work, Neil and Donna Sands have been generating reports and evidence files in Ireland, and consistently meeting with Google, OfCom, ICO, and ISPs. These reports moved beyond anecdote. We are not a collective of people with sad stories. We are not moaning about silly gossip. The reports clearly document patterns: coordinated complaint campaigns, systematic archiving of personal data, doxxing, impersonation, abuse of regulatory processes, stalking, threats, abuse, harassment, defamation, DARVO, death wishes, and repeated targeting of children of all ages.

When the news broke that Tattle was owned by Sebastian Bond, Jay and I both cried. I am still not sure why that was. I suppose, part of it was that I realised that if a human being owns the site, someone who is based in the UK and has now been publicly identified, then there can be action taken against that person. Accountability is impossible when faced with an anonymous avatar, but the whole game changes the moment you can correctly identify the person who creates, and profits from the stalking.

Sebastian Bond had deliberately concealed his identity for years. He even posed as a woman, Helen McDougall. He allowed everyone to believe that the website which hosted thousands of women abusing, harassing, stalking, humiliating, doxxing, mocking, and bullying women was owned by some middle-aged woman somewhere.

But of course, of course, the owner is a man. Whilst women tear each other apart, and destroy each other's lives for entertainment, a man is sat raking in his profits from traffic and ads placed on his website.

Another part of it, I suppose, was that many victims had tried to take action against the site but police had told them that there was nothing they could do because the owner of the site could not be found. No one knew who 'Helen McDougall' was and there was even a rumour spread that the real owner of Tattle was a very famous female British TV presenter. I will not repeat her name here, as that rumour was evidently untrue, and come to think of it now, was probably shared for a specific reason.

Influencers, bloggers, business owners, authors, presenters, writers, musicians, and activists targeted on the website posted about Sebastian Bond being finally unmasked. I read their stories and posts, realising that there were thousands of victims out there in the world, who had been living in terror because of this site. I knew immediately that I must collate those cases and present them to police and government.

I put a call out on social media and was inundated with responses. I was hoping for 30-50 responses, but instead, I got hundreds. I quickly developed a framework and online form for victims to submit their case and report their abuse, which could categorise the type of stalking behaviours they were subjected to, the psychological, physical, financial and social impact on them, and their contact with police and authorities.

The data started to come through immediately, and it was terrifying. Whilst I have included some of it throughout this book, I include some key statistics from the report below.

> **Key findings from the Tattle Report (2025)**
> - 150 cases of victims stalked and targeted on Tattle Life were analysed
> - Over 80% of victims of the site were targeted for more than a year, with more than half experiencing abuse for 3–5 years or longer
> - The most common tactics include: sustained ridicule, doxxing of home addresses and personal data, public discussions and doxxing of victims' children, and malicious allegations such as child abuse, fraud, or faking serious illnesses
> - Victims of stalking on the site have been followed in person, detained by border control, forced to emigrate, and lost their employment and incomes
> - 89% of victims reported being extremely distressed or traumatised
> - 77% became socially withdrawn and isolated
> - 42% became suicidal due to being targeted on the site
> - 11% attempted suicide due to being targeted on the site
> - 96% of victims lost income, employment, contracts, and business opportunities. Some victims estimated losses of over £250,000, with 11% reporting business and employment losses of between £100k and £1m+ due to the site
> - In 79% of analysed cases, Tattle users targeted the partner of the victim and in 72% of cases, the users targeted the children of the victim
> - In 12% of cases, the victim had to move house
> - In 19% of cases, the victim was sacked or forced to resign due to being stalked and harassed on the site.

I reached out to MPs, and they suggested that we host an event where victims could speak about what had happened to them. The parliamentary roundtable was convened in September 2025 to hear directly from victims and professionals. Correspondence was exchanged with ministers responsible for the online safety Act framework. Letters were submitted raising concerns about regulatory blind spots, particularly the failure to conceptualise distributed harassment as stalking rather than mere 'user-generated content disputes'.

This engagement contributed to a shift in discourse. Digital stalking is increasingly recognised within the Online Safety conversation not simply as abuse, but as a structural harm requiring regulatory attention.

Simultaneously, work was undertaken with police leadership. Chief constables and national leads were provided with collated evidence demonstrating that digital elements now feature in the majority of stalking cases. This has begun to inform national discussions about training, data collection and the need for consistent identification of stalking patterns across forces.

Historically, stalking data has been fragmented. Digital harassment was often recorded under disparate categories: malicious communications, harassment, public order offences. This fragmentation obscured prevalence and hindered strategic response. The collation of cases at senior policing levels represents a necessary step towards acknowledging digital stalking as a distinct and systemic issue rather than a series of isolated incidents.

This is especially important given the findings of Martellozzo et al. (2022), who found that police officers widely varied in their confidence levels related to identifying and responding to online stalking. In their paper, they surveyed UK police forces about how they were responding to the rise in general and online stalking and found that 38% of officers said they were unconfident or extremely unconfident in dealing with online stalking, and 28% were unconfident or extremely unconfident in understanding the risks of online stalking. Just under 30% reported feeling unconfident or extremely unconfident in knowing when and how to use stalking orders and stalking specific interventions or protocols. 28% of officers also agreed or strongly agreed with the item, "I find it difficult to understand cyber-stalking behaviours".

One officer is quoted in the study as saying:

'The one that scares me the most is the stranger element. When, for example, the victim certainly hasn't got any genuine ideas who this person is contacting them, I think social media is to blame for quite a lot.'

Clearly then, some officers are worried about online stalking and also report their lack of confidence in dealing with it.

But what I also found interesting, as someone who regularly trains officers and detectives, and as someone who has had to report stalking, go through multiple investigations, and has had stalking orders and other protective court orders granted, was how confident the majority of the officers seemed to be on the other items. For example, Martellozzo et al. (2022) found that 96% of officers reported being extremely confident or confident in their understanding of the difference between the stalking and harassment categories, and yet, when I have been analysing real police data for UK forces, one of their biggest reported internal problems is that stalking is usually incorrectly crimed as other things on their systems, meaning stalking victims rarely get the right support, access to stalking orders, or justice. Similarly, 92% of officers reported that they felt extremely confident or confident that they knew the legislation relating to stalking and harassment, which does not align with what I am seeing in police forces all over the UK in my research, where most officers don't even know what a Stalking Protection Order is, how to apply for one, or what the criteria are for them.

Simply put, self-reported officer confidence is not the same as practice and this is something I work hard to test and evaluate when I am working with forces. Just because officers (and leadership) tell me that they are brilliant at something, doesn't mean they actually are.

Regulatory bodies have now also been drawn into this evolving landscape.

The Information Commissioner's Office (ICO) has been engaged regarding the weaponisation of data protection mechanisms. Subject Access Requests (SARs) and Freedom of Information (FOI) requests, designed to ensure transparency, have been used by some perpetrators as instruments of harassment. The distinction between legitimate data access and malicious burdening has required careful articulation. Engagement with the ICO has centred on the need for clearer guidance regarding vexatious or abusive use of data rights in stalking contexts.

Ofcom, tasked with implementing the Online Safety Act, occupies a pivotal role. Submissions have been made urging Ofcom to treat coordinated harassment and stalking networks as foreseeable platform risks. The regulatory focus must extend beyond extremist ideology and child sexual exploitation to include sustained, targeted campaigns against identifiable individuals. The design features of platforms (algorithmic amplification, frictionless account creation, opaque reporting systems) cannot remain outside scrutiny.

Media scrutiny has further altered the terrain. Newspapers have slowly started to report on the site, and online stalking in general. I appeared on *Good Morning Britain* to discuss the report with Jenna

McCusker, another Irish victim of stalkers on Tattle Life. Interestingly, when the ITV legal team sent a private description of me and my work to Sebastian Bond for his right to reply, he took a screenshot the email and immediately uploaded it to Tattle Life to encourage users to 'find out more information about me' – and ultimately harass me further.

He seems lovely, doesn't he?

In Summer 2026, a dedicated BBC documentary examining online stalking and harassment ecosystems on Tattle Life brought mainstream attention to behaviours that victims had long described but institutions had minimised. Public exposure can be frightening but has a regulatory function. It shifts perception from niche complaint to societal issue. It reduces the plausibility of dismissal.

I have filmed for many documentaries and TV shows over the years, and it is very much part of my job these days. I never get nervous and I love working with production teams. But when I was filming for the documentary, I was so nervous that I was shaking as I spoke to camera. It is one thing being a talking head on a documentary, where I am explaining psychology or research, but talking about my own personal trauma of being stalked and abused for years was genuinely terrifying.

Despite my reservations about speaking publicly and even writing this book in so much detail, I do think that we need to lead from the front and put our money where our mouth is. I cannot be a role model for women processing and validating their trauma from abuse and stalking, if I won't do it myself. And the BBC documentary (and hopefully, this book) is the beginning of a very important conversation about online stalking tactics and perpetrators.

The cumulative effect of legal action, parliamentary engagement, regulatory submissions and media investigation has been to destabilise the assumption that online stalking is culturally trivial.

Yet structural change requires more than reactive responses to individual cases. A comprehensive national strategy for online stalking is urgently required. This problem is not going away; if anything, it is growing every single day.

This strategy must operate across agencies and include:

- Explicit recognition within stalking legislation that cumulative digital conduct constitutes a course of behaviour capable of causing serious alarm and distress.
- Revised evidential guidance that enables prosecutors to assess distributed harassment networks rather than single perpetrators in isolation.
- Mandatory digital literacy training for frontline police officers, incorporating understanding of forum culture, coordinated pile-ons, DARVO dynamics, online stalking tactics, stalking by proxy, doxxing, and bureaucratic weaponisation.
- Integration of data-sharing mechanisms between police, CPS, and regulators to prevent perpetrators exploiting institutional silos.
- The introduction of a mandatory online stalking and harassment code of practice for all social media and forum platforms.

As simple as this sounds, all platforms must be subject to a stalking code of practice. Such a code should include clear obligations to identify sustained targeting of individuals, mechanisms for pattern detection across multiple accounts, transparent escalation pathways for victims and mandatory retention of relevant data to support criminal investigations. Platforms routinely refine algorithms for commercial optimisation; they must demonstrate equivalent commitment to harm mitigation.

Platforms should not be able to hide from the police, and police officers should not feel like they are begging for scraps from anonymous giants when they require evidence and IP addresses to investigate online stalking. The process between online platforms and police should be smooth, recognised and formalised, so that officers are able to request data from websites and social media platforms as a line of enquiry, and those platforms should have to respond and comply immediately.

If a police officer requires CCTV from a shop to investigate a theft, this is a relatively simple process. If a police officer requires address information from a housing association in order to arrest someone for whom they have a warrant, this is also relatively simple.

And, yet, when an officer requires the details, email address or IP address of someone who is stalking, abusing and harassing someone online, this simple request is treated as if they are asking someone to decode ancient hieroglyphics inside a hidden crypt somewhere in the middle of the desert.

It is too hard. It takes too long. No one knows the right people. No one knows how to get there. No one knows if it can be accessed. No one knows how to do it.

And yet, as I write that, I know that is not true. I know we have teams who can access that information extremely quickly. I know that if there is cause to, social media accounts can be accessed and investigated. IP addresses can be obtained and verified. The world is online and the right teams with the right technology can access everything from our NHS records to our Twitter accounts. And so, I often wonder if this is less about capability and more about capacity.

Police forces and CPS are not equipped for the modern world of stalking and digital crime. They can barely cope with the daily calls they receive about thefts, domestic violence, criminal damage, antisocial behaviour, and violent assaults. I think they might fully collapse if they attempted to respond to the crimes being committed online.

Having said this, it is not a good enough reason – and is not a good idea – to ignore online stalking, minimise it, dismiss it and hope it will go away. If anything, online stalking will increase and become the most common form of stalking as offenders realise that they can do incredible, life-changing damage to their victims without ever risking themselves.

Anonymity requires recalibration, not abolition. Anonymous speech protects dissent, which of course, is vital. I hold lots of views that others would consider to be dissent, including my views on anti-pathology psychology. I support our rights to hold those views without ending up in prison, injured, or dead. However, anonymity without traceability or consequences when people are committing crimes and abuses of each other enables impunity. Platforms and Internet Service Providers should be required to maintain verified identity records accessible through lawful process, ensuring that victims are not forced into prohibitively expensive civil litigation merely to identify perpetrators.

Algorithmic reform is equally urgent. Content repeatedly targeting a single individual should not be amplified simply because it generates engagement, traffic, or profit. Downranking sustained harassment is not a form of free speech censorship. Harassment and stalking pipelines must be recognised alongside radicalisation pipelines. Arguably, people are being radicalised and emboldened, and they are becoming prolific online stalkers with multiple victims each.

Reporting systems require reform and consolidation. Victims should not be required to submit identical complaints to multiple platforms, police forces, and regulators without coordination. The burden on victims is enormous when this happens, and submitting the complaints becomes a full-time job. When there are multiple stalkers or a group, it can become virtually impossible to do whilst traumatised. A centralised reporting portal for coordinated digital stalking, integrated with law enforcement and regulatory bodies, would reduce retraumatisation and improve pattern recognition. It would also mean that the platforms could be held responsible for ignoring reports, takedown requests and formal complaints.

At present, social media and other online platforms operate as if they all have their own internal police force, that decides their own laws, their own thresholds, their own processes and their own responses, which makes no sense at all when laws already exist in every country in the world which govern what is, and what is not, illegal.

Despite this, social media and online platforms will regularly reject reports and formal complaints from victims, even when there are clear death threats in the posts.

As an example of this, a man had tweeted me several times in 2020. His tweets were clear threats to attack and harm me. One said that if he ever saw me, he would rape me and spit in my face. I reported his account and his posts, and Twitter responded to say there had been no breach of their rules. In anger, I quote tweeted his post and called him a coward. He reported my tweet immediately, I was suspended from Twitter for breaching their terms of service, and they deleted my post.

Similarly, back in 2021, *The Metro* reported when I was banned from Facebook for 24 hours due to calling a man a 'fucking creep' for harassing me with sexual messages and telling me to do porn. Facebook said that his posts were fine and did not breach their terms, but my singular response, which he reported, was enough to get me banned.

Whilst these examples are appalling, represent a total failure to safeguard and govern online spaces, and platforms clearly have a huge problem on their hands, it is not only a problem for them.

Cultural change must accompany regulatory reform. Public education initiatives from the earliest possible ages should address the normalisation of humiliation, abuse, stalking and threats as entertainment. Digital literacy programmes must differentiate critique and 'free speech' from surveillance, stalking and coordinated harassment. The myth that visibility constitutes consent must be actively dismantled.

The past year has demonstrated that institutional inertia is not immovable. It does respond to pressure, evidence, and sustained advocacy. However, momentum remains fragile. Platforms will invoke free expression and will not want the responsibility of dealing with the immense levels of crime and abuse on their websites. Agencies will cite resource constraints and will also not want the responsibility of addressing millions of online crimes. Cultural habits, biases and attitudes are slow to shift.

But having seen the life-changing harm of online stalking, we cannot just let this go. The online world is the real world now. And if we do not bring about urgent systemic change, the only other direction for this will be the normalisation of these behaviours – in a weird, digital, lawless land – where the impact on the victim is real, but the consequences for the perpetrator are not.

We will see the normalisation of reputational mobbing and stalking. The normalisation of children being dissected and harassed on anonymous forums. The normalisation of false mass reports as tactical leverage in everyday life. The normalisation of women being dismantled publicly for entertainment.

We are already here. The future is now, and all of these things are happening every single day online. Victims are left floundering, gaslit and terrified.

This trajectory is not irreversible. The digital world is designed by humans, and design can be altered by humans. Regulation and law can be strengthened. Enforcement can be prioritised.

The task now is not modest adjustment or campaigns about online abuse, but deliberate and significant restructuring.

We all need proactive regulation, complaints processes that work, integrated strategies, accountability and criminal justice processes that recognise online stalking as stalking.

The past year has proven that silence protects perpetrators and exposure destabilises them. It has also demonstrated that institutional change, while slow, is possible when harm is documented rigorously and pursued strategically.

Stalking evolved because technology evolved. Our response must evolve with equal sophistication. We cannot be on the back foot any longer, whether as professionals, as governments, as law enforcement or as victims.

Online stalking is real. It is extremely harmful. It is illegal.

But with so many people enjoying it, watching it, and minimising it, are we prepared to reform the systems and cultures that enable it?

Note from the author: During the final edits of this book, there were three tragic and important events.

In February 2026, Princess Dickson, the 16-year-old daughter of influencer, Sophie May Dickson, committed suicide after being directly targeted, mocked and abused on Tattle Life for years of her life. Sophie May Dickson has given multiple public statements in which she talked about how the abuse and bullying on Tattle Life had contributed to her daughter's mental health. She has spoken of the way her daughter would read the relentless threads about her and her mother and were even being shown the posts by other children at school. Tattle users had also created TikTok accounts to harass the child online, take screenshots, and leave comments about her mother, and had written direct comments addressed to Princess. When Princess died, Tattle users immediately began monitoring and stalking everyone around Princess, Sophie, and their networks, in order to gain information about the death, and the funeral details. One user wrote that they hoped Sophie May Dickson 'was next', referring to wishing for her death.

In April 2026, a Tattle Life user, who was also a police officer, pleaded guilty to stalking offences and was sentenced to 16 months in prison, suspended for 18 months, handed a three-year restraining order, and ordered to pay victim compensation. The stalker had targeted their victims for several years and submitted a guilty plea just before the trial was due to take place.

Again, in April 2026, in an unrelated case in the UK, a second Tattle Life user pleaded guilty to stalking offences which included graphic death threats and rape threats both towards the adult victims and their children. At the time of going to press, the sentencing hearing was expected to be scheduled for June 2026.

CHAPTER 13

Outro

If you made it this far without launching the book at a computer screen, I applaud you.

In fairness, even if you did launch this book at some point, that's totally understandable, too. It is a mind-bending and traumatic topic in all fairness.

We do not judge our trauma responses or coping mechanisms here. But if you broke anything, please do not send me the bill.

In all seriousness though, thank you so much for staying with me on this journey as I have explored the disturbing and tactical world of online stalkers, whilst also telling a little bit about my own experiences of being hounded for years online. I never thought I would write a book about being stalked – hell – I wasn't sure I would ever write a book again after all that. So, thank you for reading.

I know that many of you will have personal experience of being stalked and that you will likely have related to lots of the content, findings and stories contained within these pages. Being stalked in any way – online, offline, or hybrid – is an extremely traumatic, exhausting, frightening and confusing experience for anyone. I just want to validate that as we come to the end of this book.

So, if you are reading this outro and you are currently being stalked, or if you are still trying to process your trauma from being stalked, I have some closing words for you:

1. No matter what anyone tells you, you did not 'go crazy'. You are not mad. You are not paranoid. You do not have a personality disorder. You are not delusional or attention seeking. Many people benefit greatly from pathologising your stalking trauma, but you are not one of those people. One of the most powerful things you can do for yourself is to stop seeing yourself and talking about yourself as if there was something mentally wrong with you during the stalking (or since the stalking). Validate your trauma. It is heavy, and it is real.

2. If you have been left frightened, exhausted and hypervigilant, you are not suffering from paranoia. You are having a natural, purposeful and normal response to a very traumatic experience.

3. The confusion you feel is not because there is anything wrong with you, it is part of the stalking tactics. Stalking thrives on plausible deniability and legal ambiguity. If you feel like you have been constantly second-guessing your own reality, that is not a weakness or deficit of you.

4. You are allowed to be angry after being stalked. Those feelings of rage, of injustice, of frustration and horror are all valid. Stalking takes so much from you, and it is important that you do not repress your feelings. When you have been stalked for long periods of time, you often have to repress and lock away your true feelings in order to cope day-to-day. Bottling up is a necessity in survival mode, but it will come out one way or another. Don't ignore it, okay?

5. If you are currently seeing a therapist or doctor who gaslights you or blames you for being stalked, bin them off today and go and find someone who understands stalking. You will need someone who can validate you and hold you through this.

6. If you, like lots of us, have been blamed for being stalked, or if you have blamed yourself, I just want to be the person to remind you that the only person with responsibility for stalking is the stalker. It is their choice to target and abuse you. They are making active decisions to carry out their behaviour. It is not your fault. Ever.

7. If you have noticed your health deteriorating and cannot get to the bottom of this, it is possible that it is caused by chronically high levels of cortisol and sleep deprivation. It is very common for traumatised victims of stalking and abuse to develop health issues, only for them to be told that they are in their head. So, if you have been through long periods of trauma and now have health issues that don't seem to show up on any tests, it may be the impact of trauma on your body. You are not making this up or going crazy – you may just need a trauma-informed doctor.

8. Being stalked in the ways I have discussed in this book is life-changing. The tactics are designed to control, oppress, traumatise and destroy your sense of self. One of the most important things you can do for yourself is to make sure you have one person or one outlet that grounds you in reality – especially if you are struggling with reputation, career, financial, social or psychological destruction. You don't need a big network to survive this, but you do need someone or something solid.

9. If you are currently being stalked online or in person and no-one knows, please tell someone you trust as soon as you put this book down. Do not try to cope or fight this alone. The safest organisations to talk to are specialists in stalking in your country. If you don't have any stalking specialist organisations where you live, find some online resources or organisations who can signpost you.

10. You can get through this. You can. You will.

Keep going. One foot in front of the other.

And I promise to do the same.

Reference List

Abaido, G. M. (2020). Cyberbullying on social media platforms among university students in the United Arab Emirates. International Journal of Adolescence and Youth, 25(1), 407–420.

Abu-Ulbeh, W., Altalhi, M., Abualigah, L., Almazroi, A. A., Sumari, P., & Gandomi, A. H. (2021). Cyberstalking victimization model using criminological theory: A systematic literature review, taxonomies, applications, tools, and validations. Electronics, 10(14), 1670. https://doi.org/10.3390/electronics10141670

Ahlgrim, B., & Terrance, C. A. (2018). Perceptions of cyberstalking: Impact of perpetrator gender and fear severity. Journal of Interpersonal Violence, 33(24), 3813–3838.

Albrecht, B., Spivak, B., Daffern, M., McEwan, T. (2022). The temporal relationship between mental health service use and stalking perpetration, Australian & New Zealand Journal of Psychiatry 2022, Vol. 56(12) 1642–1652 DOI: 10.1177/00048674211072449

Alhaboby, Z. A., Barnes, J., Evans, H., & Short, E. (2019). Cyber-victimization of people with chronic conditions and disabilities: A systematic review of scope and impact. Trauma, Violence, & Abuse, 20(3), 398–415. https://doi.org/10.1177/1524838017717743

Alimu, Y., Wang, T. Y., Yang, D., & Chen, J. (2025). The invisible catalyst: How belonging collapse and bystander complicity mediate toxic disinhibition's path to cyberbullying. Crime & Delinquency. https://doi.org/10.1177/00111287251384661

Ayerza, J. M., Lee, J. R., O'Malley, R. L., & Lee, C. S. (2026). Cyberstalking and online dating: Examining cyberstalking victimization among dating app users. Asian Journal of Criminology, 21, 5. https://doi.org/10.1007/s11417-025-09480-2

Bailey, B., & Morris, M. C. (2021). Longitudinal associations among negative cognitions and depressive and posttraumatic stress symptoms in women recently exposed to stalking. Journal of Interpersonal Violence, 36(11–12), 5775–5794. https://doi.org/10.1177/0886260518807905

Blaauw, E., Winkel, F. W., Arensman, E., Sheridan, L., & Freeve, A. (2002). The toll of stalking: The relationship between features of stalking and psychopathology of victims. Journal of Interpersonal Violence, 17(1), 50–63.

Beech, A., Elliott, I., Brigden, A. & Findlater, D. (2008) The Internet and Child Sexual Offending: A Criminological Review, Aggression and Violent Behavior 13(3):216-228 DOI: 10.1016/j.avb.2008.03.007

Begotti, T., & Acquadro Maran, D. (2019). Characteristics of cyberstalking behavior, consequences, and coping strategies: A cross-sectional study in a sample of Italian university students. Future Internet, 11(5), 120.

Begotti, T.; Ghigo, M.A.; Acquadro Maran, D. Victims of Known and Unknown Cyberstalkers: A Questionnaire Survey in an Italian Sample. Int. J. Environ. Res. Public Health 2022, 19, 4883. https:// doi.org/10.3390/ijerph19084883

Begotti, T., Bollo, M., & Acquadro Maran, D. (2020). Coping strategies and anxiety and depressive symptoms in young adult victims of cyberstalking: A questionnaire survey in an Italian sample. Future Internet, 12(8), 136.

Binns, A. (2017) Don't feed the trolls! Managing troublemakers in magazines' online communities, Journalism Practice, Volume 6, Issue 4, Routledge

Bonagura, A. G., & Widom, C. S. (2023). Child maltreatment and psychiatric disorders increase risk for stalking victimization. Journal of Interpersonal Violence, 38(1–2), 60–83. https://doi.org/10.1177/08862605221078889

British Psychological Society (2022) Working with individuals who have engaged in stalking

Brooks, S. K. (2021). FANatics: Systematic literature review of factors associated with celebrity worship, and suggested directions for future research. Current Psychology, 40, 864–886. https://doi.org/10.1007/s12144-018-9978-4

Bronwyn McKeon, Troy E. McEwan & Stefan Luebbers (2015) "It's Not Really Stalking If You Know the Person": Measuring Community Attitudes That Normalize, Justify and Minimise Stalking, Psychiatry, Psychology and Law, 22:2, 291-306, DOI: 10.1080/13218719.2014.945637

Brown, A., Gibson, M. and Short, E. (2017) Modes of Cyberstalking and Cyberharassment: Measuring the negative effects in the lives of victims in the UK, Annual Review of Cybertherapy and Telemedicine: A healthy mind in a healthy virtual body: The future of virtual reality in health care, Volume 15, Interactive Media Institute

Brenik, M., Tuluceanu, A.-C., Smillie, E., Carpes Barros Cassal, L., Mead, C., & Mojtahedi, D. (2025). Impact of Perpetrator and Victim Gender on Perceptions of Stalking Severity. Behavioral Sciences, 15(2), 120. https://doi.org/10.3390/bs15020120

Bussu, A., Pulina, M., Ashton, S.-A., Mangiarulo, M., & Molloy, E. (2025). Cyberbullying and cyberstalking victimisation among university students: A narrative systematic review. International Review of Victimology, 31(1), 59–90. https://doi.org/10.1177/02697580241257217

Chan, E., Viñas-Racionero, M. & Scalora, M. (2022) Bridging the Gap: The Predictive Roles of Emotion Dysregulation and Stalking-related Attitudes on Offline and Online Stalking and Intrusive Harassment Journal of Interpersonal Violence 2022, Vol. 37(21-22) NP19331– NP19357

Chen, Jieru et al. (2020). Sexual Violence, Stalking, and Intimate Partner Violence by Sexual Orientation, United States. 10(1).

Christie, N. (1986). The Ideal Victim. In E. A. Fattah (Ed.), From Crime Policy to Victim Policy: Reorienting the Justice System (pp. 17–30). Macmillan

Citron, D. K. (2014). Hate crimes in cyberspace. Harvard University Press.

Cupach, W. R., & Spitzberg, B. H. (2000). Obsessive relational intrusion: incidence, perceived severity, and coping. Violence & Victims, 15(4).

De Fazio, L., Krause, A., & Sgarbi, C. (2020). Italian adolescents' experience of unwanted online attentions: Recognizing and defining behaviours. European journal of criminology, 17(5), 647-660.

Dick, B. (2025) SLAPPs, DARVO, and Weaponised Language in #MeToo-Era Defamation Suits, Feminist Legal Studies, https://doi.org/10.1007/s10691-025-09584-1

Didde Hauch & Ask Elklit (2023) The psychological consequences of stalking: cross-sectional findings in a sample of Danish help-seeking stalking victims, European Journal of Psychotraumatology, 14:2, 1-16, DOI: 10.1080/20008066.2023.2281749

Diette, T. M., Goldsmith, A. H., Hamilton, D., Darity Jr, W. & MacFarland, K. (2013) Stalking: Does it leave a psychological footprint? Social Science Quarterly, Volume 95, Number 2, Southwestern Social Science Association

Dreßing, H., Bailer, J., Anders, A., Wagner, H., & Gallas, C. (2014). Cyberstalking in a large sample of social network users: Prevalence, characteristics, and impact upon victims. Cyberpsychology, Behavior, and Social Networking, 17(2), 61-67.

Dressing H, Kuehner C, Gass P. The epidemiology and characteristics of stalking. Curr Opin Psychiatry. 2014 Jul;19(4):395-9. doi: 10.1097/01.yco.0000228760.95237.f5. PMID: 16721170.

Elliott IA, Beech AR, Mandeville-Norden R, Hayes E. Psychological profiles of internet sexual offenders: comparisons with contact sexual offenders. Sex Abuse. 2009 Mar;21(1):76-92. doi: 10.1177/1079063208326929. PMID: 19218479.

Ertl, M. M., & Ahn, L. H. (2025). Development and initial validation of the measure of internalized misogyny with cisgender U.S. women. Journal of Counseling Psychology. Advance online publication. https://doi.org/10.1037/cou0000829

Every-Palmer, S., Barry-Walsh, J. and Pathe, M. (2015) Harassment, stalking, threats and attacks targeting New Zealand politicians: A mental health issue, Australian & New Zealand Journal of Psychiatry 2015, Vol. 49(7) 634–641 DOI: 10.1177/0004867415583700

Festinger, L. (1954). A Theory of Social Comparison Processes. Human Relations, 7(2), 117-140.

Fernandez-Cruz, V., Agustina, J. & Ngo, F. (2021) An Exploratory Investigation of Traditional Stalking and Cyberstalking Victimization among University Students in Spain and the United States: A Comparative Analysis

Fissel, E. R., Reyns, B. W., Nobles, M. R., Fisher, B. S., & Fox, K. A. (2024). Cyberstalking victims' experiences with fear versus other emotional responses to repeated online pursuit: Revisiting the fear standard among a national sample of young adults. Crime & Delinquency, 70(4), 1116–1147. https://doi.org/10.1177/00111287221096374

Fissel, E. R & Reyns, B. W. (2020) The Aftermath of Cyberstalking: School, Work, Social, and Health Costs of Victimization, American Journal or Criminal Justice, 45:70–87, https://doi.org/10.1007/s12103-019-09489-1

Fox, W., Coupland, S. & Hart, S. (2024) Online stalking of Instagram Influencers, Journal of Threat Assessment and Management, Vol. 11, No. 4, 229-247, American Psychological Association

Hamid, S., & Qazi, K. A. (2023). Cyberthreats, cyberbullying, and cyberstalking: A critical examination of digital harassment in the contemporary era. ShodhKosh: Journal of Visual and Performing Arts, 4(1), 1182–1187. https://doi.org/10.29121/shodhkosh.v4.i1.2023.3132

Harsey, S., & Freyd, J. J. (2020). Deny, attack, and reverse victim and offender (DARVO): What is the influence on perceived perpetrator and victim credibility? Journal of Aggression, Maltreatment & Trauma, 29(8), 897–916. https://doi.org/10.1080/10926771.2020.1774695

Harsey, S. J., & Freyd, J. J. (2022). Defamation and DARVO. Journal of Trauma & Dissociation, 23(5), 481–489. https://doi.org/10.1080/15299732.2022.2111510

Harvey, N. (2020). Every breath you take: An exploration of perceptions of stalking and the consequences of stalking victimization (Professional doctorate thesis, University of Nottingham). University of Nottingham.

Harris, N., Sheridan, L., & Robertson, N. (2023) Prevalence and Psychosocial Impacts of Stalking on Mental Health Professionals: A Systematic Review, TRAUMA, VIOLENCE, & ABUSE 2023, Vol. 24(5) 3265–3279, Sage Publications

Henry, N., Flynn, A. & Powell, A. (2020) Technology-Facilitated Domestic and Sexual Violence: A Review, Violence Against Women 2020, Vol. 26(15-16) 1828– 1854, Sage Publications

Igwe, Ori (2020) A qualitative enquiry into the threshold of acceptable behaviour on the internet: perceptions of police officers and prosecutors on the barriers to successful investigation and prosecution of cyberstalkers. Doctoral thesis, Univeristy of West London.

Ivask, S. (2025) "It is Easier to Leave Death Threats than to Get Them Taken Down!" – Systematising Journalists' Battles with Online Mobs, Digital Journalism, 13:5, 1009-1027, DOI: 10.1080/21670811.2025.2475181

James, D. V., Mullen, P.E., Pathe, M.T., Meloy, J.R., Preston, L.F., Darnley, B. & Farnham, F.R. (2009) Stalkers and harassers of royalty: the role of mental illness and motivation, Psychological Medicine (2009), 39, 1479–1490. f Cambridge University Press, doi:10.1017/S0033291709005443

Janickyj, M., Blom, N., & Tanczer, L. M. (2025) Online and Offline Stalking Victimisation in the Crime Survey for England and Wales: Its Predictors and Victim/Survivors' Views on Criminalisation, The British Journal of Criminology, 1-24, https://doi.org/10.1093/bjc/azaf064

Jin, S. V., & Ryu, E. (2020). 'I'll buy what she's #wearing': The roles of envy toward and parasocial interaction with influencers in Instagram celebrity-based brand endorsement and social commerce. Journal of Retailing and Consumer Services, 55, 102121. https://doi.org/10.1016/j.jretconser.2020.102121

Kaur, P., Dhir, A., Tandon, A., Alzeiby, E. A., & Abohassan, A. A. (2021). A systematic literature review on cyberstalking: An analysis of past achievements and future promises. Technological Forecasting and Social Change, 163, 120426. https://doi.org/10.1016/j.techfore.2020.120426

Kavish, N., & Naidu, B. M. (2022). Cyberstalking: Behavioural patterns, victimisation, and legal implications. Journal of Criminal Psychology, 12(4), 251–267.

Kelley, H. H. (1967). Attribution theory in social psychology. In D. Levine (Ed.), Nebraska Symposium on Motivation (Vol. 15, pp. 192–238). University of Nebraska

Kenneth O. Ugwu & E. Trejos-Castillo (31 Jul 2025): How Cyberstalking Victimization Shapes Academic and Mental Health Outcomes in College Students, Deviant Behavior, DOI: 10.1080/01639625.2025.2537443

Kircaburun, K., Jonason, P. K., & Griffiths, M. D. (2018). The Dark Tetrad traits and problematic social media use: The mediating role of cyberbullying and cyberstalking. Personality and Individual Differences, 135, 264–269. https://doi.org/10.1016/j.paid.2018.07.034

Kuehner, C., Gass, P. and Dressing, H. (2012) Mediating Effects of Stalking Victimization on Gender Differences in Mental Health, Journal of Interpersonal Violence 27(2) 199–221, Sage Publications

Krishna, N., Fischer, B., Miller, M., Register-Brown, K., Patchan, K. & Hackman, A. (2013) The role of social media networks in psychotic disorders: A Case Study, General Hospital Psychiatry, 35 576-576

Lambert, E. G., Smith, B., Geistman, J., CluseTolar, T., & Jiang, S. (2013). Do men and women differ in their perceptions of stalking: an exploratory study among college students. Violence and Victims, 28, 195 209. doi: 10.1891/0886-6708.09-201

Lee, S.-S., & Park, C. S. (2025). Gender differences in cyberstalking: The roles of risk, control, and opportunity factors in social media. Behavioral Sciences, 15(5), 566. https://doi.org/10.3390/bs15050566

Lerner, M. J. (1970). The desire for justice and reactions to victims. In J. Macaulay & L. Berkowitz (Eds.), Altruism and helping behavior (pp. 205–219). Academic Press.

Logan, T.K. (2020) Examining Stalking Experiences and Outcomes for Men and Women Stalked by (Ex)partners and Non-partners, Journal of Family Violence (2020) 35:729–739, https://doi.org/10.1007/s10896-019-00111-w

Lowry, P. B., Zhang, J., Wang, C., & Siponen, M. (2016). Why do adults engage in cyberbullying on social media? An integration of online disinhibition and deindividuation effects with the social structure and social learning model. Information Systems Research, 27(4), 962–986. https://doi.org/10.1287/isre.2016.0671

Loveluck, B. (2020) The many shades of digital vigilantism. A typology of online self-justice, Global Crime, 21:3-4, 213-241, DOI: 10.1080/17440572.2019.1614444

Lumsden, K. & Morgan (2017) Media framing of trolling and online abuse: silencing strategies, symbolic violence, and victim blaming, Feminist Media Studies, 17:6, 926-940, DOI: 10.1080/14680777.2017.1316755

Malecki, W. P., Kowal, M., Dobrowolska, M. & Sorokowski, P. (2021) Defining Online Hating and Online Haters. Front. Psychol. 12:744614. doi: 10.3389/fpsyg.2021.744614

Mandeville-Norden, R., Beech, A. & Hayes, E. (2008) Examining the effectiveness of a UK community-based sexual offender treatment programme for child abusers, Psychology, Crime and Law, Routledge

March, E., Litten, V., Sullivan, D. H., & Ward, L. (2020). Somebody that I (used to) know: Gender and dimensions of dark personality traits as predictors of intimate partner cyberstalking. Personality and Individual Differences, 163, 110084.

Marcum, C. D. & Higgins, G. E. (2021) A Systematic Review of Cyberstalking Victimization and Offending Behaviors, American Journal of Criminal Justice (2021) 46:882–910, https://doi.org/10.1007/s12103-021-09653-6

Mardon, R., Cocker, H. & Daunt, K. (2023) When parasocial relationships turn sour: social media influencers, eroded and exploitative intimacies, and anti-fan communities, Journal of Marketing Management, 39:11-12, 1132-1162, DOI: 10.1080/0267257X.2022.2149609

Martellozzo, E., Bleakley, P., Bradbury, P., Frost, S. and Short, E. (2022) Police responses to cyberstalking during the Covid-19 pandemic in the UK, The Police Journal: Theory, Practice and Principles 2022, Vol. 0(0) 1–17, DOI: 10.1177/0032258X221113452

McCutcheon, L. E., Lange, R., & Houran, J. (2002). Conceptualization and measurement of celebrity worship. British Journal of Psychology, 93(1), 67–87.

McLaughlin C. & Wohn, D.Y. (2021) Predictors of parasocial interaction and relationships in live streaming, Convergence: The International Journal of Research into New Media Technologies, Vol. 27 (6) 1714-1734, Sage Publications

Meloy, J. R., Mohandie, K., & Green, M. (2011). The female stalker. Behavioral Sciences & the Law, 29(2), 240–254. https://doi.org/10.1002/bsl.976

Miller, K. C. (2023). Harassment's toll on democracy: The effects of harassment towards US journalists. Journalism Practice, 17(8), 1607–1626. 10.1080/17512786.2021.2008809

Miller, K. C., & Lewis, S. C. (2022). Journalists, harassment, and emotional labor: The case of women in on-air roles at US local television stations. Journalism, 23(1), 79–97. 10.1177/1464884919899016

Miller, L. (2012). Stalking: Patterns, motives, and intervention strategies. Aggression and violent behavior, 17(6), 495-506.

Monckton Smith J. (2019) Intimate Partner Femicide: Using Foucauldian Analysis to Track an Eight Stage Progression to Homicide. Violence Against Women. 2020 Sep;26(11):1267-1285. doi: 10.1177/1077801219863876. Epub 2019 Aug 5. PMID: 31378158.

Mullen, P. E., Pathé, M., & Purcell, R. (2000). Stalkers and their victims (2nd ed.). Cambridge University Press.

Naguy, A., & Alhumoud, A. (2021). Talking about stalking. Annales Médico-Psychologiques, 179(2), 186–191. https://doi.org/10.1016/j. amp.2020.11.004

NCA/CEOP (2013) Threat Assessment of Child Sexual Exploitation and Abuse (TACSEA)

Nesbitt, S. & Carson, S. (2021) The cost of reporting: Perpetrator retaliation, institutional betrayal, and student survivor pushout, Know Your IX, Advocate for Youth Project

Paullet, K. & Chawdry, A. (2020) Cyberstalking, 'No means no!': An Exploratory study of university students, Issues in Information Systems, Volume 21, Issue 1, pp. 125-130

Piotrowski, C., & Lathrop, P. J. (2011). Cyberstalking and college-age students: A bibliometric analysis across scholarly databases. College Student Journal, 46(2).

Purcell. R., Pathe, M. & Mullen, P. (2001) A study of women who stalk, The American Journal of Psychiatry 158 12 2056-2060

Quinn-Evans, L., Keatley, D., Arntfield, M. & Sheridan, L. (2021) A Behavior Sequence Analysis of Victims' Accounts of Stalking Behaviors, Journal of Interpersonal Violence 2021, Vol. 36(15-16) 6979-6997

Racine, C. and Billick, S. (2014) Classification Systems for Stalking Behavior, Psychiatry and Behavioural Sciences, J Forensic Sci, January 2014, Vol. 59, No. 1 doi: 10.1111/1556-4029.12262

Reyns, B. W., Henson, B., & Fisher, B. S. (2012). Stalking in the twilight zone: Extent of cyberstalking victimization and offending among college students. Deviant Behavior, 33(1), 1–25.

Reyns, B. W., (2010) A situational crime prevention approach to cyberstalking victimization: Preventive tactics for Internet users and online place managers, Crime Prevention and Community Safety (2010) 12, 99 – 118. doi: 10.1057/cpcs.2009.22

Reyns, B. W., Henson, B. & Fisher, B. (2011) Being Pursued Online: Applying Cyberlifestyle-Routine Activities Theory to Cyberstalking Victimization CRIMINAL JUSTICE AND BEHAVIOR, Vol. 38 No. 11, November 2011 1149-1169 DOI: 10.1177/0093854811421448

Rodríguez-Castro, Y.; Martínez-Román, R.; Alonso-Ruido, P.; Adá-Lameiras, A.; Carrera-Fernández, M.V. (2021) Intimate Partner Cyberstalking, Sexism, Pornography, and Sexting in Adolescents: New Challenges for Sex Education. Int. J. Environ. Res. Public Health 2021, 18, 2181. https://doi.org/10.3390/ijerph18042181

Roese, N. J. (1997) Counterfactual Thinking, Psychological Bulletin, 121, 133-148

Ross, L. (1977). The intuitive psychologist and his shortcomings: Distortions in the attribution process. In L. Berkowitz (Ed.), Advances in experimental social psychology (Vol. 10, pp. 173-220). New York: Academic Press

Rotter, J. B. (1966). Generalized expectancies for internal versus external control of reinforcement. Psychological Monographs: General and Applied, 80(1), 1–28

Santos, I. L. S., Lima, D. C. N., Pimentel, C. E., & Mariano, T. E. (2024). Attitudes toward violence and cyberstalking: Gender's moderating role. Deviant Behavior, 45(12), 1698–1710. https://doi.org/10.1080/01639625.2024.2321481

Scott, G. G., Brodie, Z. P., Wilson, M. J., Ivory, L., Hand, C. J., & Sereno, S. C. (2020). Celebrity abuse on Twitter: The impact of tweet valence, volume of abuse, and dark triad personality factors on victim blaming and perceptions of severity. Computers in Human Behavior, 103, 109–119. https://doi.org/10.1016/j.chb.2019.09.020

Scott, G. G., Wiencierz, S. & Hand, C. J. (2019) The volume and source of cyberabuse influences victim blame and perceptions of attractiveness, Computers in Human Behaviour, 92, 119-127, Elsevier

Shaikh, A. (2015) Perceived dangerousness of cyberstalkers whom victims have known before versus cyberstalkers who are strangers, Doctoral Dissertation, Alliant International University, Los Angeles

Shaver, K. G. (1970). Defensive attribution: Effects of severity and relevance on the responsibility assigned for an accident. Journal of Personality and Social Psychology, 14(2), 101–113.

Sheridan, L., James, D. V., & Roth, J. (2020). The phenomenology of group stalking ('gang-stalking'): A content analysis of subjective experiences. International Journal of Environmental Research and Public Health, 17(7), 2506. https://doi.org/10.3390/ijerph17072506

Sheridan, L., North, A. C., & Scott, A. J. (2019). Stalking in the workplace. Journal of Threat Assessment and Management, 6(2), 61–75. https://doi.org/10.1037/tam0000124

Sheridan, L. P. & Grant, T. (2007) Is cyberstalking different?, Psychology, Crime & Law, 13:6, 627-640, DOI: 10.1080/10683160701340528

Sheridan, L., Scott, A. & Campbell, A. (2019) Perceptions and Experiences of Intrusive Behavior and Stalking: Comparing LGBTIQ and Heterosexual Groups, Journal of Interpersonal Violence 2019, Vol. 34(7) 1388–1409

Smoker, M., & March, E. (2017). Predicting perpetration of intimate partner cyberstalking: Gender and the Dark Tetrad. Comput. Hum. Behav., 72, 390-396.

Spitzberg, B. H., & Hoobler, G. (2010). Cyberstalking and the technologies of interpersonal terrorism. New Media & Society, 12(1), 71–92.

Stark, E. (2019) Coercive Control: Update and Review, Violence Against Women, Sage Journals

Storey, J., Pina, A. & Williams, C. (2023) The Impact of Stalking and Its Predictors: Characterizing the Needs of Stalking Victims, Journal of Interpersonal Violence 2023, Vol. 38(21-22) 11569–11594, Sage Publications

Suler, J. (2005). The online disinhibition effect. International Journal of Applied Psychoanalytic Studies, 2(2), 184–188.

Tajfel, H., & Turner, J. C. (1979). An integrative theory of intergroup conflict. In W. G. Austin, & S. Worchel (Eds.), The social psychology of intergroup relations (pp. 33-37). Monterey, CA: Brooks/Cole.

Taylor, J. (2020) Why Women Are Blamed For Everything: Exploring the victim blaming of women subjected to violence and trauma, Little Brown, Hachette

Taylor, J. (2022) Sexy But Psycho: Uncovering the psychiatric labelling of women and girls, Little Brown, Hachette

Taylor, J. (2025) Stalking, Harassment, and Doxxing on Tattle.Life Online Forums, Victim Impact and Experience Report. Prepared for Government July 2025, VictimFocus

Taylor, J. & Shrive, J. (2023) Indicative Trauma Impact Manual, VictimFocus, London

Thelwall, M., Stuart, E., Mas-Bleda, A., Makita, M., & Abdoli, M. (2022). I'm nervous about sharing this secret with you: YouTube influencers generate strong parasocial interactions by discussing personal issues. Journal of Data and Information Science, 7(2), 31–56. https://doi.org/10.2478/jdis-2022-0011

Trottier, D. (2020). Denunciation and doxing: Towards a conceptual model of digital vigilantism. Global Crime, 21(3–4), 196–212. https://doi.org/10.1080/17440572.2019.1591952

Ubelacker, S. (2011) Trauma from cyberstalking even more intense than in-person harassment: expert: Cyberstalking can cause intense trauma, The Canadian Press; Toronto

Van Geel, M., Goemans, A., Toprack, F. & Vedder, P. (2017) Which personality traits are related to traditional bullying and cyberbullying? A study with the Big Five, Dark Triad and sadism, Personality and Individual Differences, Volume 106, pp 231-235

Vlad Demsar, Jan Brace-Govan, Gavin Jack & Sean Sands (2021) The social phenomenon of trolling: understanding the discourse and social practices of online provocation, Journal of Marketing Management, 37:11-12, 1058-1090, DOI: 10.1080/0267257X.2021.1900335

Waisbord, S. (2020). Mob Censorship: Online Harassment of US Journalists in Times of Digital Hate and Populism. Digital Journalism, 8(8), 1030–1046. https://doi.org/10.1080/21670811.2020.1818111

Weekes, C. J., Storey, J. E. & Pina, A. (2025) Cyberstalking Perpetrators and Their Methods: A Systematic Literature Review, TRAUMA, VIOLENCE, & ABUSE, 1-17, DOI: 10.1177/15248380251333411

Worsley, J. D., Wheatcroft, J. M., Short, E., & Corcoran, R. (2017). Victims' voices: Understanding the emotional impact of cyberstalking and individuals' coping responses. Sage open, 7(2), 2158244017710292.